W9-CXE-225

GUIDE TO FINANCIAL SUCCESS
WHAT TO KNOW BEFORE YOU START YOUR OWN BUSINESS

- The Success Ingredients of the Small Business Personality
- Taking the First Steps: How to Prepare
- Choosing your Base of Operation
- Financing your Business from Start-Up through Success
- To Franchise or Not?
- Your Going Concern: Taxes, Accounting, Advertising, Management
- Special Opportunities for Special People
- How the Private Sector Watches Out for your Interests
- Postscript: Business People Speak for Themselves
- Glossary of Common Business Terms
- References
- Counseling Notes on 45 Popular Businesses

making it on your own

by
Dr. S. Norman Feingold
and
Dr. Leonard G. Perlman

PREFACE by
Edwin L. Herr
Professor and Head, Division of Counseling
and Educational Psychology
The Pennsylvania State University
Past President, National Vocational Guidance Association

FOREWORD by
Kenneth M. Callaway
Chairman of the Board
Capitol Publications, Inc.

ACROPOLIS BOOKS LTD.
Washington, D.C. 20009

Copyright © 1981 by Acropolis Books Ltd.

All rights reserved. Except for the inclusion of brief quotations in a review, no part of this book may be reproduced or utilized in any form or by any means, electronic or mechanical, including photocopying, recording or by an information storage and retrieval system, without permission in writing from the publisher.

ACROPOLIS BOOKS LTD.
Colortone Building, 2400 17th St., N.W.
Washington, D.C. 20009

Printed in the United States of America by
COLORTONE PRESS, Creative Graphics Inc.
Washington, D.C. 20009

Library of Congress Cataloging in Publication Data

Feingold, S. Norman,
    Making it on your own.

    Bibliography: p.
    Includes index.
    1. Small business—Management—Handbooks, manuals, etc.
    2. Small business—Finance—Handbooks, manuals, etc.
    I. Perlman, Leonard G.   II. Title.
HD62.7.F44   658'.022   81-12909
ISBN 0-87491-287-3   AACR2
ISBN 0-87491-288-1 (pbk.)

Contents

5

ACKNOWLEDGEMENTS

Our deep appreciation is expressed to all of those busy entrepreneurs who gave so freely of their time and talents in being interviewed for this book. Their words within this text will stand as a tribute to their ideas and ideals.

Thanks are also due to Margaret Hickey, Librarian at the U.S. Small Business Administration in Washington, .D.C. for keeping us informed as to the latest development in small business, Ms. Gerry Perlman for her research, editorial assistance and constant encouragement, Mr. Al Hackl, Kathleen Hughes and Deborah Salem for their stewardship and invaluable assistance throughout the development of MAKING IT ON YOUR OWN. And finally warm thanks to the thousands of small business owners who provide millions of jobs to make our economy a much stronger one.

S.N.F.   L.G.P.

BUSINESS:
We are all manufacturers -
some make good,
others make trouble
and still others make excuses.
— Anonymous

PREFACE

The phrase "Making it on your own" is a part of the American credo. It reflects the continuing promise of this nation as a land of opportunity for those who are challenged by and grasp that opportunity. But, a promise of opportunity is not an assurance of opportunity. Most opportunities lay dormant until individuals recognize their potential and do something to convert them into a vital, dynamic reality.

Not everyone wants to make it on his or her own. Doing so involves accepting a risk of failure, the possibility of being alone in the face of pressures, willingness to be a learner and to chart areas for which formulas and blueprints are sometimes unavailable, and confidence that one can lead as well as follow. Such traits are not shared by all people. Many of us prefer to have others tell us what to do and to let them take the risks. We prefer the anonymity and security which sometimes comes from following rather than stepping out on our own.

On the other hand, many persons would really like to make it on their own. They admire those who have done so and wish

9

they could be like them. Their problem is not fear or lack of interest but rather a lack of information. They are not sure what step to take, what business they would like to enter, what specific things other people have done to make it on their own.

The book you are about to read, MAKING IT ON YOUR OWN, is for the people described in the previous paragraph: the people who want to "go for it." It is intended to supply the insights, information, and inspiration to help you convert your dreams into actualities. In it you will find recognition that there are many ways of making it on your own; America is a 'smorgasbord' of possibilities. You will have to choose which opportunity will be yours. The book's contents will help you to weigh and sort such alternatives.

In the final analysis, MAKING IT ON YOUR OWN is reinforcement of the fact that life is a personal journey. We can drift along and be buffeted by chance. Or, we can create our own realities by the planning we do and the actions we take. This book is about the latter. I commend it to you.

Edwin L. Herr

Professor and Head, Division of Counseling
  and Educational Psychology
The Pennsylvania State University
Past President, National Vocational Guidance Association

FOREWORD

Ever since I can remember I always wanted to make a lot of money and have the free time to enjoy it. That is the reason I went into business for myself. I must confess that I was encouraged, albeit unintentionally, by the employers I had after leaving college and before starting on my own. I held five different jobs in that length of time and all of them were for small companies started by entrepreneurs. I always held positions high enough in the small hierarchy so that I knew the owners well and called them by their first names. To a man they were making lots of money and taking the time to enjoy it! And yet, as I came to know them closely, they did not seem to be any smarter than I was. If they could do it so could I.

So I tried. The first time I failed. The second time I succeeded. What I learned from the first experience helped me during the second. If I had to state just a few cardinal rules they would be:

1.   Recognize your own abilities and also your own weaknesses. Concentrate on what you do well and find

someone else to do the things you do not do well. For example, I cannot balance a checkbook. But from the beginning I had a junior in business administration from a local college as my part-time business manager.

2.   You don't have to go first class at the beginning. I kept a full time job for two years after starting my present business. It was run during the day by other part-time college students and I would show up at night. Those students, incidentally, didn't go first class either since I paid them $1 per hour and all the beer they could drink.

3. Do not over extend yourself financially. One of the luckiest things that ever happened to me was that I could not talk anyone into lending my business money in the early stages. As a result, we had to generate our own growth capital. It took a long time, but now we are doing $5.5 million in sales, we have money in the bank and do not owe anyone anything. In fact, we are now buying out our competitors that grew on borrowed money.

4.   Don't be in too big of a hurry to start making lots of money and enjoying it. Those bosses I talked about in the first paragraph had each put in about 15 years of hard work before I saw them taking it easy. It has taken me about that long, too.

But now I've arrived. My business is successful, I make good money and since I have built a solid management team I can take the leisure time to enjoy the income. In actual fact, going into business for myself is one of the few things I have ever done in my life that worked the way I hoped it would. It might work that way for you, too. Good luck!

Kenneth M. Callaway
Chairman of the Board
Capitol Publications, Inc.

INTRODUCTION

If you go into any bookstore, you will find a host of books designed to tell you how to start and operate your own business. We have not written MAKING IT ON YOUR OWN as an addition to that list. Instead, we have drawn upon our extensive experience in career vocational counseling to create a resource guide that you will be able to use to make other decisions not only about your business, but about yourself as well. For, you see, the most important factor in running a successful business, it turns out, is not talent, or hard work, good business advice or luck. It's not even having the right idea at the right time (although the merchandisers of the light bulb, Pet Rock or natural foods might disagree). The most important factor is the personality of the small businessperson himself, or herself. All those other factors are important, certainly, to turning an on-paper possibility into a profit-making enterprise, but after interviewing dozens of successful people we have learned that certain specific personal qualities were shared by all of them. No one is born with a shortage of personal qualities, but determining whether you are the type of person most likely to succeed in small business may be the most important determination you make. After reading MAKING IT ON YOUR OWN, you will probably know yourself much better and know that, whatever decision you make, it has a greater chance of being the right one for you.

If you are like the successful people we interviewed, you already know why you want to give up the security of a nine-to-five job or to venture, perhaps for the first time, into the business world. "I needed more freedom," said one; "I wanted to use my creative talents and couldn't on my regular job," said another; "I wanted the satisfaction of knowing I could succeed on my own," said a third; "I wanted to get rich," laughed a fourth who is, five years later, laughing all the way to his bank — he did make his million!

These people aren't alone. In 1979, over half a million new businesses were started, an increase of 60% from only five years earlier. Despite high rates of inflation and gloomy economic forecasts, more people every year decide that the security that comes with a "steady" job is not *real* security at all, that they would rather trust their own ingenuity, skill and hard work to see them through. Just ten years ago, only 4% of the teenagers questioned in one study (by the authors) stated an interest in starting their own businesses, although 27% of their parents were self-employed. Today, more than 25% of the young adults polled want their own businesses. The increased freedom and expression of individuality found in small business attracts full-time, traditionally employed workers. Those who have been left out of American business, housewives, handicapped, retired or minority workers, have found they can create satisfying work for themselves. Disenchanted bureaucrats, executives and administrators in secure, but unsatisfying jobs long for the day when they can take an early retirement and start all over again in a business they build themselves, from the ground up. There is an appeal for almost every segment of society; at that rate, it would seem that traditional workplaces would be deserted — fast — and there would be no room for your newborn business. Not so. A high percentage of new businesses fail, and others must spring up to take their places. With good advice and careful planning you will be able to avoid the pitfalls that befall so many others; a second goal of this book is to give you a variety of places where you can go to find that advice. The bibliographies at the end of each chapter should give you an idea of the kinds of resources available to you, depending upon your individual needs, tastes and specific interests.

There is one aspect of small business that doesn't vary from individual situation to individual situation — the satisfaction successful entrepreneurs feel every day they are operating their own concerns.

"I have something I can call my own. I don't have to worry about being jobless when inflation takes over. I always have something to fall back on. It means security to survive these times," states Jerry Grissett, owner of a combination delicatessen and record store.

"Gathering together a group of employees and seeing an efficient and viable organization which runs well with or without me — that's gratifying," said Kenneth Rosen, owner of the American Candy and Tobacco Wholesalers, a business he started after a few years in a wholesale tobacco company.

"Being your own decision maker, that's what I like best, that and having a sense of creativity and being able to reap the benefits of your own work in the form of profits. You can create a feeling of camaraderie and enthusiasm in a small company — you develop the attitude that it can and will be done," observed Edie Fraser, president of her own burgeoning public relations firm.

"Freedom, flexibility, growth — going on instinct and by the seat of my pants," agreed Sue Garland, a former teacher who founded Traveling Tutors, a service begun on $1,000 in 1974, with five students.

For successful people, the satisfactions are many, more than they expected when they started out, and worth the hard work, uncertainty and sacrifice of the early years. They really tell the story of success in their own words, and we will invite them to speak for themselves throughout the book.

Some day, we may call you and ask for your experiences as a successful small marketer. If we do, we hope you will say that MAKING IT ON YOUR OWN gave you a start towards your new life and a better feeling about yourself. That will be *our* greatest satisfaction.

CHAPTER ONE

The Small Business Personality Profile

"**I** went into business to get rich. I had always worked for a small company — small enough to call employees by their first names. I saw them making money and, since they were no smarter than I was, I decided to try it myself," laughed Ken Callaway, chairman of the board of Capitol Publications and publisher of management newsletters.

"I was tired of making money for other people who were getting rich on my talent," Nancy Block, a busy portrait photographer in the Washington, D.C. area.

"My father and grandfather were in the food business — I didn't know anything else. I wanted to try my own ideas, but my father never thought I did anything well enough, so I left his business and went out on my own," Samuel Zuckerman, in the wholesale food business for over fifty years.

"I didn't like having to stay in one location all the time and I wanted to be my own boss. But the real reason is that I love the thrill of making things grow!" Lois Ornstein, owner of Plants, Etc., a busy office and house plant maintenance service.

You probably have your own reasons for wanting to go into business for yourself. Although the specific circumstances change — some people "fall into" their businesses or buy into existing concerns while others purposely strike out on their own uncharted territory — there are common threads throughout the stories of most of the entrepreneurs we interviewed. Whenever or wherever they found themselves at a crossroads in their lives, they faced one of the following realizations, as you may have:

- I can't find a job I like.

- I want to be my own boss more than anything else.

- I need more money than I can make at a fixed wage for necessities (or luxuries).

- I've helped someone else make money for years — now it's my turn.

- I want to avoid being laid off or fired or passed over for promotion because of office politics.

- No one will give me a chance to prove myself because of my background so I'll have to do it on my own.

- I come from a family of small businessmen — it's in my genes!

- My idea can't miss and I want to put it together myself before someone else thinks of it.

Naturally, almost everyone, at some time in his life, yearns to be free of the boss or remembers that time when a good idea of his own was appropriated or, even worse, ignored, but almost everyone doesn't respond by going out and setting up shop on his own. Only certain kinds of people make that decision and only certain of *them* succeed at the businesses they start.

No reason is any more valid than any other for starting a business for yourself. Whether you are a widow or divorcee forced into the labor market due to a change in family situation, a disenchanted bureaucrat escaping the gamemanship of the rat race, a retired, handicapped, disabled or minority person who has found traditional business closed to you or a successful executive itching to start a new venture on your own makes no difference to your chances for success. Although life circumstances may play the major role in your decision to start a business, they play a minor role in determining whether you will be able to make a go of it. What will make the difference is the personal qualities you bring to the challenge of planning and operating a business. It's as simple as that.

Although talent, luck, a unique idea and good business advice are all important, strength of character is the one factor all successful business people seem to have in common. Our interviews with dozens of these people prove that no matter what kinds of business they pursue, they possessed, to a startling degree, similar personal traits. As you might suspect, leadership was high on the list, but we learned that leadership by itself is not enough; simply wanting to be your own boss will not make you an entrepreneur. A general in the military, for example, has no shortage of leadership capability or desire for achievement, but he may be quite happy to spend his entire career in the structured environment of the army. It takes leadership plus —

Plus, what? What qualities will make you a success in business?

Take this test for yourself. Answer each question honestly; consider what kind of person you are, not what kind of person you would like to be. This is the time to identify your present strengths and weaknesses and evaluate them, *before* you decide whether owning a business is for you.

1. Are you a self-starter?

i I do things on my own. Nobody has to tell me to get going.

ii If someone gets me started, I keep going all right.

iii Easy does it. I don't put myself out until I have to.

2. How do you feel about other people?

i   I like people, I can get along with just about anybody.   _____

ii   I have plenty of friends — I don't need anyone else.   _____

iii   Most people irritate me.   _____

3. Can you lead others?

i   I can get most people to go along when I start something.   _____

ii   I can give the orders if someone tells me what we should do.   _____

iii   I let someone else get things moving. Then I go along if I feel like it.   _____

4. Can you take responsibility?

i   I like to take charge of things and see them through.   _____

ii   I'll take over if I have to, but I'd rather let someone else be responsible.   _____

iii   There's always some eager beaver around wanting to show us how smart he/she is. I say let him.   _____

5. How good an organizer are you?

i   I like to have a plan before I start. I'm usually the one to get things lined up when the group wants to do something.   _____

ii   I do all right unless things get too confused. Then I quit.   _____

iii   You get all set and them something comes along and presents too many problems. So I just take things as they come.   _____

6. How good a worker are you?

i   I can keep going as long as I need to. I don't mind working hard for something I want.

ii   I'll work hard for a while, but when I've had enough; that's it.

iii   I can't see that hard work gets you anywhere.

7. Can you stick with it?

i   If I make up my mind to do something, I don't let anything stop me.

ii   I usually finish what I start — if it goes well.

iii   If it doesn't go well right away, I quit. Why beat your brains out?

8. Can you make decisions?

i   I can make up my mind in a hurry if I have to. It usually turns out okay, too.

ii   I can if I have plenty of time. If I have to make up my mind fast, I think later I should have decided the other way.

iii   I don't like to be the one who has to decide things.

9. Can people trust what you say?

i   You bet they can. I don't say things I don't mean.

ii   I try to be on the level most of the time, but sometimes I just say what's easiest.

iii   Why bother if the other person doesn't know the difference?

10. How good is your health?

i   I never run down!   ———X———

ii I have enough energy for most things I
want to do.   —————————

iii I run out of energy sooner than most of
my friends seem to.   —————————

Now Count the Checks You Made

1. How many checks are there beside the
first answer to each question?   —————————

2. How many checks are there beside the
second answer to each question?   —————————

3. How many checks are there beside the
third answer to each question?   —————————

If most of your checks are beside the *first answers*, you
probably *have what it takes* to run a business. If most are by
the second answer to each question, you're likely to have more
trouble than you can handle by yourself; you might want to
find a partner who is strong on the points you are weak on. If
most checks are beside the *third answer*, you should
reconsider your plans very carefully since you will probably
have an uphill battle ahead of you.

Why? Because initiative, positive attitudes towards others,
leadership, a sense of responsibility, organization, a strong
commitment to work, industriousness and adaptability are
the keys to success for the independent person.

Are you a self-starter, **do you have the initiative** to do
more than asked to do? Are you resourceful — willing and
able to seize opportunity when it appears and turn it to your
advantage?

Do you have a positive and friendly interest in
others? If so, it is a tremendous asset in most business
ventures — especially in those where face-to-face contact

with customers is a must. If you seem to end every discussion with a quarrel or go through life with a chip on your shoulder, you may have a tough time coping with customers you depend on day in and day out. Unless you hire others to do your selling or handle your public relations, you could face an uphill battle in making your business profitable.

Good interpersonal skills are also essential if you are to inspire employees to put forth a sincere effort in making the business flourish. "An organization can survive and grow if it meets the needs of its employees," said one of our interviewees. How true, how true!

Are you a leader? Do people listen to you? Do you inspire confidence and loyalty? An ability to lead is an important skill — one that is bound to enhance your chances for success. Even if you have only an employee or two, you will have to maintain discipline, check their work and productivity, train them to do the job the way *you* want it done and arbitrate among them if they disagree with each other. Even companies with full-time personnel officers sometimes find it difficult to hire the best people for a job; training and retaining people can be a time-consuming and costly process. A leader who can motivate and reward employees will get his or her business off to the best start.

You may decide that you don't have a great deal in common with General Patton, after all; if personnel management is important to your business you may want to consider taking courses in leadership and supervision offered by business schools and colleges. You can develop leadership qualities on the job, through trial and error, but outside assistance can speed up the process and avoid costly misjudgments.

Can you handle responsibility and do you enjoy taking charge? Are you the one who volunteers for tasks or responsibilities at meetings or do you sit quietly while others raise their hands? If you usually avoid responsibility when a situation calls for it, starting your own business could be a difficult chore. Being your own boss is one thing, but being responsible for the livelihood of others on your payroll and for the well-being of those people during their workday — as well as for customers' needs — may be too much for you to handle.

Are you a good organizer? Are you capable of recognizing and arranging items, ideas or concepts into logical and meaningful action? Do you usually make plans carefully before trying something? Are you on time? Do you remember to pay bills, file your tax form, keep your appointments? Running a business, whether you have one employee or one hundred, requires pre-planning, purchasing merchandise, maintaining financial records, documenting sales and marketing your product or service. To keep up with the thousands of small details that are sure to be part of your business, you will either have to start out with good organizational abilities, develop them or hire someone to assist you with them. They won't get done on their own!

Are you prepared to put in the long hours it might take to get your business running successfully? People often think that when they work for themselves they will be working less than they were before and make their own hours.

One of our interviewees stated, "I work between 48 and 72 hours per week, but we spend hours discussing the business even when we are not there ... We are not under a structured time schedule, if we want to take time off we can, but we don't do it as much as we should ... We have been building new stores."

Especially during the first months of being in business, owners find themselves working harder and longer than they ever did as paid employees. As the owner, you will have more to gain, of course, since it is your investment, but you also have more to lose if your business does not make a profit. Plan on "eating, sleeping and breathing" your new venture for the foreseeable future, and be pleasantly surprised if it doesn't turn out to be necessary.

Do you make up your mind quickly or do you drag your feet rather than come to a decision? Are you hesitant — even fearful — about a decision you must make? Are your decisions quick but accurate or quick but unsound? The ability to sum up a situation quickly and make a realistic choice for action will stand you in good stead a thousand times during your business life. Making decisions doesn't have to be an isolated activity — you can and should consult experts, colleagues, even employees, before coming to your conclusions, but the final decision will be yours to live with.

Can people rely on you? Can they trust what you say? If your word is your bond, you will find yourself reaping rewards since a good reputation brings in new business and, unlike advertising, is free of charge. You may be someone whose good intentions outstrip his ability to following through. Face that now.

If you are the kind of person who can run all day and night, you'll be far ahead of the competition as you start your business life. Long hours can be hard on people who do not have the physical stamina to keep a shop open or finish up that last order on time. If you have a physical disability, consider a business that allows you some flexibility on deadlines or performance, or consider taking a partner who can handle some of the most exhausting activities, like deliveries. While a high energy level is important, it's not *essential* to running a successful enterprise. Will you stay with the work until it's completed or will be give up after a moderate six-to-eight hour period?

Can you withstand business reversals without quitting? If you discover the source of a problem with your business and it appears to be something you can see through to the end, will you have the strength to do it? Can you analyze a problem and take steps to correct it or will you panic and throw in the towel at the first opportunity?

Can you adapt to changing situations? To be able to recognize and react to changes in your market, the likes and dislikes of your customers, the changes in a neighborhood, etc., will be invaluable over the long run. No matter what type of business you run, you will face changing times.

Rare (maybe non-existent) is the person who has an abundance of all these traits or who doesn't need to improve one or more in order to be a better businessman. There are ways to help yourself, improve things both before and after you begin your business.

• Observe the actions and responses of others in similar situations. The guy who owns the corner restaurant is famous for keeping his waiters and waitresses forever; and your front desk seems to have a new face behind it every week; why not ask him how he keeps — and treats — his staff? If your own plumber always gives service with a smile, take a minute to watch how he handles himself when he is faced with a complaint. On the job observation seems to come more easily with time; you may find yourself analyzing how someone answers his phone, handles dinner reservations or keeps track of overdue accounts, without even realizing it.

• Attend conferences or lectures on aspects of your business with which you are unfamiliar. Experts on business management often have tips garnered through years of experience with other businesses like yours. Accounting systems, identification of good credit risks, inventory control are sciences that don't change from business to business. You may find that a problem you have been wrestling with has been solved by someone else n an unrelated field twenty years ago. Such information can be worth its weight in revenue — and peace of mind.

• Read books and articles. This doesn't mean you have to subscribe to THE WALL STREET JOURNAL right away, just spend some time reading what has already been written about your field. There is no law that says you must use what you read, but you might consider seriously any advice that seems to have worked for others in your circumstances.

• Seek professional counseling to back-up your weak points. Professional counseling could include advice from a lawyer, bookkeeper, accountant, tax specialist, marketing expert, trade association staff or other business professionals. Local colleges usually offer courses in many aspects of business. Check these opportunities.

This is not the time to kid yourself that you are the most organized person in six counties if you haven't found, much less paid, last month's phone bill; nor should you "promise" to do better once you open shop.

In some cases, you may compensate for your weaknesses by taking in a partner, someone who has these strengths, or by hiring employees to handle specific tasks. If you are great at planning but lack patience to be a salesperson, find a partner or employee who has these skills.

Often, a business will be a composite of talents and strengths designed to produce a successful business. If your check list total was unsatisfactory, don't just give up; try to understand which areas need improvement and start improving. You may also want to see a career counselor or vocational or counseling psychologist to work with you in developing more favorable habits — those needed to get you closer to your career goals.

CHAPTER TWO

Taking
the
First Steps

What Business Should You Enter?

"Well, the first thing you need in starting a business is the concept. You have to have a reason why you should have a business. What makes you unique? Why will customers come to you? Why should people deal with your product? What kind of a need are you filling that others are not satisfying? You must be knowledgeable about your business; if you want to be a buyer, you must know something about the industry first. If you want to enter a retail establishment and all you know is that you like pretty clothes and like to pick them out, and you think everyone in the world will come to you, you will find that it just doesn't happen that way. "You have to cater to your customers and not to yourself," stated one of our interviewees.

"One goes into a business when one is turned on to a particular image or style of life that can create an end product that gives a romantic vision of oneself in the business. Some people want to be in the book business because they perceive this as a kind of bookstore selling

books to one's friends. That is not reality. Know
yourself. Know what you like to do and do not like to do
before starting a business. Analyze what the impact of
opening a business is on you and your personal life."
                    WILLIAM KRAMER, an owner of Sidney Kramer Books.

"Choosing a business? Talent, that's what it takes. If you
have the talent for what you do, you'll do all right. If
you don't have the talent, you had better go and get a
job with someone else."   NANCY BLOCK, photographer.

"I came to catering naturally; my parents owned a
restaurant and that is where I learned about food
preparation. I would like to own my own restaurant
some day."   STEPHANIE WILLIAMS, Williams Caterers.

"Before you go into business, you should know your
field. Roger had 25 years of experience in the direct
mail business; his contacts were of major importance.
Direct mail is a highly specialized field and, while we
do have some fancy equipment, we need to be good at
all aspects of the business. Although there was no
conscious effort to go into direct mail as a full-time
effort, his experience and contacts made it a natural
choice for us."
                    JOAN HENEBRY, partner, Performance Marketing.

Everyone has a different reason for choosing the business
he or she starts and thus everyone has different advice on how
to do it. For some, the continuation of a family tradition (and
the ability to tap the family's wellspring of experience) tips
the scales in favor of a specific line of work; for others, years of
working in a field have given them the knowledge and
contacts to make them almost immediately successful. A
smaller number of people are so downright talented that
their choice of business is a foregone conclusion, but for them,
being terrific at what they do gives them a big jump on their
less gifted competition. Another group of successful entrepreneurs had a unique idea (an endangered, but not yet

extinct species) or a way of packaging an old idea that made people think it was unique.

Almost no one just picked something out of the blue when he decided to start a business; the idea had been simmering for some time, waiting for the right combination of timing, talent and capital to pull things all together.

Your choice of business may already be found in your previous background and experience, but you may not have asked the right questions, so far, to make your choice clear to yourself. Do you have traits that make you ideal for detailed, organized kinds of work? An attractive phone voice that could sell products? A way with people that might make you a sales person on a one-to-one basis? Do you have a way with tools, or plants, or children? Even if you have never been paid for your activities, you may have skills that you can turn into employment. So long as you like what you intend to do for a living, you have a much greater chance to succeed at it. Chaining yourself to something you hate, no matter how profitable it may seem on paper, is one thing no one recommends. Life is too short and the days in the shop too long.

Once you have a business in mind, carefully research as many aspects of the business as you can before you commit yourself to your new venture. It may be a poor time to start a construction business in certain locations due to economic conditions, or the rage for a "fad" business may be about over, leaving you to ride the ripples of the craze rather than the wave. The SBA has a good deal of information in most of its business profiles, or in counseling notes that appear at the end of this book. In these, the SBA attempts to answer as many nuts-and-bolts questions about each business as it can.

Private counseling centers, school and college guidance offices and local libraries may also be of help as well so be sure to check any and all sources.

You might want to talk to people already in the business you want to enter. While businesspeople are usually forthcoming when it comes to talking about their business experiences (remember, they probably like their work), you would be better off not approaching a direct competitor one block over and asking specific questions on the state of her business. If you have not yet left your present employer, direct inquiries to suppliers and competitors might be out of the question and might not remain confidential. Word can "get out" very quickly and, unless you are prepared to move quickly, your questions might be misinterpreted. If you are not employed or are changing careers, obviously, you have more options available to you; ask away!

What kinds of questions should be ask? Some may be obvious, others not so. Here is a list of common questions that should provide a good starting place for discussion:

1. What kind of skills, training or experience are needed?

2. How much money (capital) is needed to start?

3. How long did it take you to break even or begin to make a profit?

4. How much help (in terms of full or part-time employees) is needed to run the business adequately?

5. Where do you get your materials, products, or items for sale?

6. How much advertising do you do; is it necessary; where do you advertise?

7. What is the short range (2-3 years) outlook for your business? Is it expected to increase?

8. Are licenses needed to operate the business? If yes, what kinds?

9. How many hours do you need to put in to keep the business running effectively?

10. Is your location a good one?

11. What are the most frequently encountered problems in this business?

12. Is the business supporting you now?

As we have mentioned, formal training in a field is not always necessary before starting a business. Say you wanted to open a bakery: home "practice" or an apprenticeship might be enough to get you underway.

"Originally I started a small grocery store, but I left that business when I realized I should go into a small business I knew something about. As a refugee from Europe, I worked for free in order to get experience, pressing and cleaning my own suit for practice. That's when we went into the drycleaning business — my brother is a tailor. My advice: learn all about the business you are going into."
HENRY GREENBAUM, Windsor Cleaners.

Reviewing Your Decision

Can you describe in a few sentences why your business will be different — or better — than the ones already established in your neighborhood or field? Do you just feel in your heart that people would flock to a Western-style restaurant in a downtown location or can you point to specific events or trends that back up your hunch? Everyone wants to have confidence in his ability to read a market, but realistic assessment of your business's chances for success, at this stage, is vital. Remember, you will still have time to change or modify your dream to enhance its possibilities for success if you consider every option now. It will be much more difficult to change direction in mid-stream, after supplies are bought, space leased, staff hired. Don't waste this opportunity to look at everything connected with your business or industry.

Here is a worksheet, adapted from one put out for you by the SBA, to help you look at your business before you make a final choice.

All about you: *(The most important person!)*

	Yes	No
• Are you the kind of person who can get a business started and make it go?	X	___
• Have you worked in a business like the one you want to start?	?	___
• Have you ever worked for someone else as a foreman or manager?	X	___
• Have you had any business training in school?	X	___
• Have you saved any money?	___	X

All about money: *(Usually a real necessity — not a luxury)*

	Yes	No
• Do you know how much money you will need to get your business started?	?	___
• Do you know how much money of your own you can put into the business?	___	___
• Do you know how much credit you can get from suppliers — the people you will buy from?	___	___
• Do you know where you can borrow the rest of the money you will need to start your business?	___	___
• Have you figured out what *net* income per year you expect to get from your business? (Be sure to count your salary and your profit on the money you put into the business!)	___	___
• Have you talked to a banker or lending institution about your plans and money needs?	___	___

If you need a partner: *(Don't pick just anyone)*

	Yes	No
• If you need a partner with money or "know how" that you don't have, do you know someone who will fit in with your plans and can you get along with that person?	____	____
• Are you familiar with the good as well as bad points about starting on your own, having a partner, or incorporating your business?	____	____
• Have you discussed the above points with a lawyer?	____	____

What about customers? *(This is not a luxury item)*

	Yes	No
• Do most businesses in your community seem to be doing well?	____	____
• Are there businesses like the one you want to start in your community or nearby areas? Are they doing well?	____	____
• Do you know what kind of people will want to buy your kind of products or services?	____	____
• Is a business like yours needed?	____	____
• If a business like yours is not needed in the area where you live, have you thought of a different location or opening a different kind of business?	____	____

Your building or where you will locate: *(An area too often overlooked)*

	Yes	No
• Do you need and have you found a suitable building or site for your business?	____	____

Yes   No

• Will you have enough room for
expansion if your business should grow?   ____   ____

• Can you fix the building the way you
want without spending too much money?   ____   ____

• Can people get to it easily; are there
parking spaces, bus stops? (Will it be
accessible to people with handicaps or
older folks with problems walking
flights of stairs?)   ____   ____

Equipment and supplies: *(Don't forget to shop
around)*

• Do you know what kind of equipment
and supplies you will need and how much
they will cost?   ____   ____

• Can you save money buying second-hand
equipment?   ____   ____

Your products: *(Make sure you get this right)*

• Have you decided what things you will
sell or services you will provide?   ____   ____

• Do you know how much or how many of
each item you will need to open your
business?   ____   ____

• Have you found suppliers who will sell
you what you need and at a good price
(have you gotten estimates)?   ____   ____

• Can you get credit terms from
suppliers?   ____   ____

Your recordkeeping: *(Start out with good plans)*

• Have you planned a recordkeeping
system to keep track of your income and
expenses; what you will owe and what
others owe you?   ____   ____

Yes   No

• Have you worked out a way to keep
track of your inventory (of stock or other
items for sale) so that you will have
enough on hand to sell, but not more than
you can sell?)   ___   ___

• Do you have a system on how to keep
your payroll records and take care of tax
payments and reports?   ___   ___

• Do you know of or have an accountant
to assist you with bookkeeping, taxes
and other financial matters?   ___   ___

Your business and the law: *(Keep it legal)*

• Do you know what licenses and permits
you need?   ___   ___

• Do you know what business laws you have
to obey?   ___   ___

• Do you have or know oɪ a lawyer who
can assist you with legal advice and legal
papers?   ___   ___

Protecting your business: *(This could make or break you)*

• Have you made plans for protecting
your store or other business against thefts
of all kinds — shoplifting, robbery,
burglary, employee stealing?   ___   ___

• Do you know what your insurance needs
are and have you talked to an insurance
agent?   ___   ___

Advertising: *(Customers must know you are there)*

• Have you decided how you will
advertise? (Newspapers, posters, handbills,
radio, mail, TV?)   ___   ___

Yes   No

- Do you know where to get help with your ads?   ___   ___

- Have you observed what other businesses do to get customers?   ___   ___

The prices you charge: *(Can be crucial to being a success)*

- Do you know how to figure what you should charge for your services or the items you will sell?   ___   ___

- Do you know what others in a similar business charge for their services or products?   ___   ___

- Are your prices competitive with the current market?   ___   ___

Plans for buying: *(Be ready to serve your customers)*

- Do you have a plan to find out what your customers want?   ___   ___

- Do you plan to buy most of your stock from a few suppliers rather than a little from many, so that those you buy from will want to help you succeed?   ___   ___

Selling: *(Know your market and customer needs)*

- Will you have sales clerks or self-service?   ___   ___

- Do you know good sales techniques?   ___   ___

- Have you thought about why you like to buy from salespeople, while others turn you off?   ___   ___

Your employees: *(A key to survival)*

- If you need to hire help, do you know where to look?   ___   ___

	Yes	No
• Do you know what kind of person you need?	——	——
• Do you know how much to pay?	——	——
• Do you have a plan for training your employees?	——	——

Credit for your customers: *(Caution: dangerous territory)*

• Have you decided whether to let your customers buy on credit?	——	——
• Do you know the good and bad points of joining a credit card plan?	——	——
• Can you tell a good credit risk from a bad one?	——	——

Some additional questions: *(Burning questions — be sure to answer them)*

• Have you figured out whether you could make more money working for someone else? (Does it matter?)	——	——
• Does your family go along with your plan to start your own business?	——	——
• Do you know where to find out about new ideas and new products that pertain to your business?	——	——
• Do you have a work plan for yourself and your partner or employees?	——	——

We realize that no one person, and no one book, will be able to help you answer all of these questions. It may take you weeks or months to find satisfactory answers to all of them. You should keep the worksheet questions in your mind, almost as a "final exam," to be passed before your sign goes out on the front door. Some of the answers may be ridiculously easy; you may know that you and your Uncle Joe will sell lemonade from your home at 10¢ a glass with virtually no risk to anyone, but if your business is *any* more complicated than that, you'll want to pass the exam with flying colors.

Some of the answers will come from the upcoming chapters of MAKING IT ON YOUR OWN, and some of the questions will be asked, again, in light of the information in those chapters. Now that you are making your first choices, is the time to begin to think about them.

"I had worked in various government jobs and I realized that there was a need for a different kind of public relations firm that recognized the need for public policy communication from a managerial point of view to be made available to business constituencies to build support for programs. I thought it over a year before I opened my agency. It was a big decision, but it turned out to be a good one."

EDIE FRASER, Fraser and Associates, public relations

She obviously answered a number of these questions well in advance of plunging ahead in her business.

How Should You Organize Your Business?

A pizza parlor can be a corporation. A machine shop can be a partnership. "Jones and Sons" can be a proprietorship. Whatever your business, it will have to assume a "shape" of its own, a form of organization to whose laws it must conform. Depending upon how you want to structure your business, how you want it to live or die, how you want its financial business to be carried out, you will choose to be a single proprietorship, a partnership or a corporation. Your lawyer or tax consultant will be best able to help you decide which structure will be most advantageous to you, but a bit of information now may get you thinking.

Most businesses are single proprietorships, the simplest form of business. The individual owns and operates his own concern by himself. The advantages are several: start-up costs are minimal; the business is under direct control of the owner; there is the greatest freedom from government regulation; a minimum of working capital may be needed; all profits are held by the owner, and tax advantages may be had as well. The disadvantages are that the owner is personally responsible for all of the business's debts (his car or home could be sold to satisfy the company's creditors); banks may be reluctant to give money to a sole proprietor; and the company's lifespan is limited — when the owner dies, the company dies with him.

In a partnership, two or more persons share in the profits and losses of a particular enterprise. All owners are equally responsible for the firm's debts and the partnership must dissolve upon the death or withdrawal of any member. However, sharing your business with someone else can bring needed money into the effort — and needed talent. If you lack technical skills to run your business, you might want to choose a partner who can bring them with him. No matter what your reason for taking on a partner, be sure to select someone with whom you are compatible, personally, professionally and philosophically. Any of the partners can withdraw company money, sign for company commitments or act on its behalf so communication and compatability are crucial. No matter how informal your arrangement, have the terms of the partnership drawn up — in writing — in advance, to avoid any misunderstandings.

The corporation is the most complicated form a business can take. An association of owners or stockholders becomes a single legal entity under the law, with officers elected, by-laws established and longevity assured. A corporation remains in existence despite the death of a principle or the transfer of stock. It protects its members through limited liability; each stockholder is liable for company debts only up to the extent of his individual investment in the concern.

As anyone who reads the newspaper financial section can testify, corporations are closely regulated and require extensive recordkeeping to satisfy the IRS and other government bodies. Corporation profits are taxable when they come to the corporation and again when owners declare the income ("double taxation"), but for most small businesses, this is less of a problem than it is for General

Motors. There are hundreds of books on corporate law and finance — but this is not one of them. We suggest that you apply the same diligence in researching corporate structure and its cousin, the Small Business Corporation (through which lucky folk can avoid double taxation) that you used in deciding what kind of business to enter before either accepting or rejecting corporate status for your business.

Choosing your business may be simplified by the fact that you want to buy an existing concern for yourself. Although it is your first step into the business world, many of the problems of start-up will not be yours, so long as the business is sound. You may be attracted to the property because you have always wanted to sell foreign auto parts. You will need your own separate check-list for review before the purchase:

	Yes	No
• Do you know the real reason why the owner wants to sell?	___	___
• Have you compared the cost of buying this business with the cost of starting a new business (taking into account that the present business is, or will be, making money sooner)?	___	___
• Is the stock up-to-date, in good condition and useful?	___	___
• Is the building or present location of the business in good condition?	___	___
• Will the owner of the building transfer the lease to you?	___	___
• Have you talked to other business people in the area to hear their views on the business?	___	___
• Have you talked to the business's suppliers?	___	___
• Have you talked with a lawyer about any possible problems with the purchase?	___	___

There are many good reasons why a business is for sale — the age or health of the owner, the lack of family interest in running the business, a change in interests — but there are many other reasons that are not so good. You may want to give serious thought to whether you want to buy someone else's mistakes in location, stock or staff. An established business must be explored at least as carefully as a new business for profit-making potential.

If, by this time, you know what kind of business you will undertake and what form it will take, you are well on your way. The final step to completing the visual picture is to plant your new business some place and watch it grow.

Resources: Selected Bibliography in the Area of Incorporating Your Small Business

How to Form Your Own Corporation Without a Lawyer for Under $50. Nicholas T. Enterprise Publishing Co., 1000 Oakfield Lane, Wilmington, Delaware 19810.

Management Aids for Small Manufacturers, #231, *Selecting the Legal Structure for Your Firm.* Available free from the Small Business Administration. Write SBA, P.O. Box 15434, Ft. Worth, TX 76119.

Management Aid No. 223, *Incorporating a Small Business.* Available free from the Small Business Administration. See address above.

Subchapter S Taxation, Grant, I. 1974. McGraw-Hill Book Company, Shepard's Citations, Inc., P.O. Box 1235, Colorado Springs, CO 80901.

The Family-Owned Business *(or What To Do When Brother-in-Law Needs a Job)*

Family-owned businesses are a popular type of venture and for good reasons. It's very often a natural thing to do. You have a spouse and three children. They can go immediately to work for mom or pop and maybe even become partners and eventually owners of the business. However, before we make it sound all too easy, you should be aware of the pitfalls of this kind of arrangement. As Levinson (1978) stated, "Management problems in a family-owned business are somewhat different from the same problems in a non-family business. When close relatives work together emotions often interfere with business decisions." This information is not intended to discourage you, but merely to make you aware of the potential booby-traps that may go along with this type of business approach.

It's All Relative

There can be conflict and personality clashes even in a non-family-owned business, and when you add to this mix, uncles, aunts, second cousins, in-laws, etc. — look out! Anything can happen and often does. We have now added the dimensions of ego, personality, and emotions that often get in the way of rational and sound business decisions, decisions that have as a focus the best interest of the company at heart. In addition, various family members have different views of business and styles of operation. Some relatives are the so-called "silent partners" — they put up the money and are interested only in the dollars that come into or flow out of the business. Other relatives work on the day-to-day operations and their interest is in the sales or services aspects (as well as in the profit-making angle). These two orientations can and often do erupt into family squabbles.

Another set of common problems often emerge when nontalented or poor business persons are thrust into a position of power (or maybe just a job) in the business, and are ineffective and at times a nuisance. For example, the wife or husband, daughter or son of the founder of the company, who may have no business sense often becomes part of the firm despite a lack of ability.

Many are the family feuds that have been fired by the family-owned business. Let's face it, family problems arise over many issues even without being on the job together. You could expect the very same personality factors and characteristics to extent into the family venture. Except, now we are talking profit and loss — money!

Family fights or power struggles in a firm are not only demoralizing, but the effects can be disastrous on the business as well as on other non-family workers. Soon the unrelated worker may take sides and this could end in increased tensions and even lead to employee turnover.

Another common problem is that the non-family employee will often base their behavior and decisions on their knowledge of the family's internal problems and struggles. The employee can manipulate the situation to his or her own advantage knowing who he or she must please rather than making a decision as to what is best for the company.

Hiring a relative can be a double threat if the relative is not suited for the job. He may need one badly, but getting a job through relatives under this condition can be costly. Not only must you pay the person, but if he is a poor worker, who loafs on the job, and avoids difficulty or "dirty" tasks, the morale of others in the firm becomes undermined.

How do you get rid of the family member who is a menace to your company? The relationship of the person in question to the "boss" will often dictate the answer. Whatever you decide, someone will be unhappy with your decision. Firing any relative is a difficult chore, to say the least. It may be an impossibility in some cases depending on the emotional currents in the family and would defy even a high level diplomat to solve the problem.

Solving the Unsolvable — Some Helpful Tips to Ponder

As in many other aspects of life, correct answers for each instance are not always obvious or at times not available. If you are planning a family-owned business here are a few suggestions to think about as you make plans to start your business. Take a moment now — before you open your doors, to discuss the potential issues and trouble spots that are out there if you and your spouse (and children) are going to work together. This could save a lot of grief later on when the business is really taking off.

— If you are going to manage a family-owned business and you feel uncomfortable directing your relatives, consider hiring an outsider to manage the company. This takes the heat off of you and will allow for a more objective and less emotional day-to-day operation of your business.

— Be certain to set up realistic lines of authority. Is Aunt Bertha in charge when Uncle Louis is on vacation? This should be clearly understood from the very beginning of the venture. It should not have to be debated when Uncle Louis takes off two weeks in the summer. Everyone in the business should know their roles. This alone will cut down on disagreements and disputes brought about by lack of defined duties and authority.

— If you *Must* hire an incompetent nephew or other relative in dire need of work, try to keep him out of the way of other workers trying to do their jobs. Be creative and develop some definite duties for that relative. Give him minimal contact with others and also keep him away from critical decisions. You should also, wherever possible, try to tap his potential in any form that you can find. It would be worth your while since his job is costing you money — make the most of it.

— Still another way to deal with the troublesome relative "who can't be fired" is to help this person start their own business in an area that doesn't compete with your line. This is assuming he or she has the ability to manage the new business. You can even try to get them a job in another company, one where their abilities can be put to good use and away from the cozy nest of the relatives.

While statistics on how many businesses are family-owned are not easy to find, experience tells us that the numbers of family-owned businesses are large. A good example, and one that all of us are familiar with is the husband-and-wife team that operates a business. These have always been popular and there is good reason to believe that this trend is now on the upswing. Again, everything that we talked about earlier is just as important when considering opening a business with your spouse. Each of you has talents and skills. Examine them and fit them into your plans as to how to best use these abilities in your business. It is also essential that you assign roles and duties and lines of authority if you expect to have other relatives (sons, daughters, in-laws, etc.) involved in the business. Don't be afraid to put these operating procedures in writing. *What about trust,* you might say? Trust is important, but you should treat your business venture seriously and as if it were business and not just a family picnic. This is also one way to bring some objectivity into your business plans. There will be enough emotional factors to deal with as far as family relationships are concerned. Go to it, but be prepared!

Resources: Selected Bibliography in Family-Owned Businesses

Management Check List for a Family Business, Management Aids No. 225, Small Business Administration, Becker, B. M. and Fred Tillman. Available free from SBA, Washington, D.C. 20416.

The Family-Owned Business, Becker, B. M. and Fred Tillman, 1975, Commerce Clearing House, Inc., Chicago, Illinois.

How To Start and Manage Your Own Business. Greene, G. G., 1975, McGraw-Hill Book Company, New York, N.Y.

Winning the Money Game. Dible, D. M. Editor, 1975. The Entrepreneur Press, Mission Station, California.

Problems in Managing a Family-Owned Business, Management Aids No. 208, Levinson, Robert E. 1978, Available free from SBA, Washington, D.C. 20416.

CHAPTER THREE

Choosing Your Location: Will You Work at Home Or Away?

Depending upon the kind of business you plan to operate, choosing your location may be the most important decision you will make. There are two options: working out of your house or apartment, or renting space somewhere else. Each has its positive aspects and, naturally, its drawbacks.

There's No Place Like Home

"After working as a hardware store employee, auto body and appliance repairman, I knew I could fix anything, and I was tired of working 9 to 5 as a TV repairman in a job with no future. I started my business, called 'The Fix It,' with the tools I had accumulated over several years and placed ads in the local papers as 'the repair shop on wheels.' I took some jobs — home remodeling, carpentry, plumbing, electrical work — at night after work and, pretty soon, I was making more money with my part-time business than I was during the day. By then, I proved to myself

that a 'handyman' could support a family and, in fact, make the 'fix it' business as lucrative as I wanted it to be — while working out of my own home."
GENE SPREHN, owner of "The Fix It."

Some people are able to use their homes as their primary places of employment. Construction contracting, secretarial services, freelance writing, editing and consulting, mail order sales, babysitting all can be part-time or full-time occupations you undertake from your house. The advantages are many: your overhead is lower — no renting space, or paying utilities — and your flexibility greater. You can begin part-time, evenings, weekends or while the baby naps, without a major up-front investment and allow your business to expand naturally without the pressure of meeting added operating expenses such as rent or utilities. If you outgrow your home you can always find an outside location later on.

There are also substantial tax advantages to working at home, but the IRS has very stringent requirements for office-in-home deductions. Federal law requires that the portion of your home used for your business must be used *exclusively* and *regularly* for its activities. No bedroom/warehouse combinations are allowed! The IRS also prefers that the office look like an office — desk, telephone, typewriter, filing cabinets. (There have been reports of unscrupulous tax-payers hiring contractors to build bogus offices in spare rooms about tax time and dismantling them after the audit!)

For all of us honest folks, working at home can have other real pluses:

"I've operated my house plant business out of my home for seven years. I now have five employees, full and part-time, who help me grow, sell and maintain house-plants in homes and offices. I went into business because I love to make things grow, but I also appreciate the great freedom of movement I have at home. I didn't like being tied to one location. Although it has been hectic taking phone calls from customers and dealing with employees, I have solved the problem by

setting aside a room with desks, phones and records —
all the business's needs — in one area and by setting
standard business hours for answering the phone. It
takes a lot of patience, understanding and cooperation
from other family members to make the business a
success. I can always rely on my husband or children to
help move the heavier plants onto the van."

LOIS ORNSTEIN, owner, Plants Etc.

Businesses that require large space for inventory or
customer ambience don't work out of a home so well. A
business with heavy customer traffic could be disruptive to
your family life and might be prohibited by local zoning laws
governing commercial business in residential areas. If you
live in a rural or suburban location, a business needing
customers might be too isolated from its source to get off the
ground, even if you wanted customers to come to you.

If your business can take a home setting, consider these
other advantages:

- You can work at your own pace and convenience.

- You can start up for very little money.

- You needn't worry about babysitters or that family
obligations are met on time.

- You will keep your overhead costs (space, utilities,
equipment) to a minimum.

- You will save time and money on commuting to a
place of business.

- You could realize tax savings on operating a business
out of your home (check with your tax accountant for
particulars).

- You will save money on wardrobe and incidental
expenses (lunch, coffee machine).

- Your earnings will, generally, be greater than those
from piece-rate or fixed income wages.

The major disadvantages of working out of your home are:

• You might have limited space in which to conduct or expand your business.

• You may find family obligations slow down productivity by "getting in the way."

• Your family life itself may be disrupted by phone calls, deliveries, customers, etc.

• You may dislike isolation from lack of social business environment.

• You may find the temptations of home — easy chair, television — get in the way of a full day's work.

• Residential zoning restrictions may make it difficult to conduct your kind of business in your location.

This last point is an important one. Local licensing and/or zoning departments may have requirements you must meet in order to operate your business out of your home legally. A hair salon, for example, must be run only by a licensed operator in some jurisdictions due to the chemicals used in dyes and permanent waves and may be prohibited from rental buildings where increased customer traffic and utility use (hot water and electricity) would not be allowed by a landlord. Check your telephone directory white pages for listings of the proper licensing body in your town or county.

Your own skills, experience, hobbies and interests will help you determine what kind of business you will want to start. Remember, you and your family will be literally living with your business night and day, so more than a passing interest in the field is a good idea.

Here is a list, by no means complete, of some of the businesses that can, under appropriate circumstances, be conducted from your house or apartment on either a part-time or full-time basis. Review this list to see how many of these areas you could handle. Do your hobbies or interests match any of those on the list?

Advertising
Addressing letters, addressograph or mailing service
Antiques
Appliance repair
Arts and crafts sales
Animal care and grooming

Bakery/supply of baked goods wholesale
Bookkeeping/accounting
Boarding house operation
Babysitting

Camera repair
Consulting
Catering
Commercial art *(sign painting)*

Doll repair and doll making
Day care
Dog training

Earthworm growing and sales
Enveloping, addressing/stuffing
Exercise class instruction

Free-lance writing/editing
Furniture refinishing/repair

Gold-plating
Gunsmithing
Graphic art

House and plantsitting
Herb farming and sales
Home handcrafting *(aprons,
    pocketbooks, etc.)*
Hairdressing

Jewelry repair/sales

Invisible mending

Locksmithing
Lawnmower and small engine repair
Leather goods repair

Mail order fulfillment *(notions, stamps)*
Music instructing
Manicuring

Newspaper clipping service

Odd jobs/repair *(lawnmower repair, painting, stone masonry)*

Photography
Picture framing
Party planning and novelty supply
Printing
Pet hotel/grooming
Pet training
Proofreading

Raising pets *(such as guinea pigs, hamsters, gold fish, etc.)*

Stamp and coin dealing
Sewing and tailoring
Speakers bureau operation
Sign/letter painting

Tax return preparation
Tax preparation service
Telephone answering service
Telephone sales
Toy maker
Typing *(clerical services)*
Translating
Tutoring

Typewriter/business machine repair
Travel agency/planning

Upholstery and furniture repair

Watch and jewelry repair

Beware of Deals That Are
Too Good To Be True

Have you ever seen ads that look like these?

"Earn $400 to $800 IN YOUR HOME.
CHOOSE YOUR OWN HOURS
NO EXPERIENCE NECESSARY"

"YOU CAN EARN $1,000 A MONTH
WITHOUT LEAVING YOUR HOME.
NO INVESTMENT NECESSARY!"

If the deal sounds too good to be true, it usually is. Magazines, matchbook covers, etc. are used to advertise get-rich-quick, or easy-money schemes and each year thousands are victims; those who can afford it the least. These promotions are aimed at those who are home-bound and include the elderly, shut-ins, unemployed persons and housewives looking to supplement their incomes.

The most common types of ads are for "envelope stuffing," addressing letters, lacing baby booties, and mailing circulars. There are of course a number of other items, but it is up to you to be careful and beware of these kinds of swindles.

You should know that WORK-AT-HOME deals, no matter how good they may sound, will not guarantee you regular employment or a steady amount of income. In addition, you will probably be required to invest your money before you are told how their plan really works. In other words, you may have to lay out ten or more dollars just to find out what you are going to do. If you decide not to go through with the deal you will have already lost some money.

Investigate carefully before you invest!

For your own protection you should do the following when tempted to answer the get-rich-quick at home ad:

• Exercise extreme caution.

• Don't send any money in advance, not even $1.00.

• Read any information about the "deal" as carefully as you can.

• Any doubts, check with your local Better Business Bureau.

• Report any possible mail fraud schemes to your local Postmaster.

• If you do answer an ad, save as evidence any material received or sent through the mails.

Whatever you do, Please Be Careful.

Out In the Real World

"When I was going to start my own shoe shop, the most important decision I had to make was where I was going to locate. I had worked in my father's shoe shop for years and I had called on rubber suppliers and seen the difference between successful shoe shops and those that just hung on. But I needed to know what location would be best: should I open in downtown Washington, around already established businesses with plenty of customer traffic, or should I open in the suburbs? I talked to a successful businessman who said, 'Go to the suburbs and grow with the community.' I did! I opened a shoe store and repair store in Bethesda. That was 36 years ago, and I've never regretted my decision."

JOSEPH FORTUNA, proprietor of Fortuna, Inc.,
shoe and luggage store.

"I located 'The Gingham Goose' in a shopping mall in suburban Washington about six years ago, along with three other women who took turns with me minding the store. We kept our costs down by using used furniture and shelving. We even used old fish crates for displaying our stock — hand-made dolls, toys, baby gifts, handbags and novelties — and it worked out very well. We broke even financially within three months because rent and utilities were our only expenses; we sold everything on consignment."

MAUREEN SULLIVAN, owner of The Gingham Goose.

Most retailers say that choosing their exact location was the most important decision they had to make when they started out. Large companies select their locations in a very systematic way; they assign people to do nothing but chart traffic flow, parking availability, population growth patterns and "demographics," the study of the exact make-up of a community and its pool of potential customers. If you decide you want to rent a store-front, warehouse or other property, you can make use of many of the same techniques that big companies use to find the perfect location. You must narrow down your choice by *town* or *city*, *area* within the city and *specific site*. Most people starting out in business choose the city in which they live — it is the one they know most about and the easiest about which to find good information. Contact wholesalers that service your city with your product; discuss with manufacturers who supply equipment or merchandise whether there is a need for more businesses like yours; contact your local Chamber of Commerce and owners of similar businesses to see if they can help to give you a feeling for the overall growth of your city. Your Chamber of Commerce should be able to provide you with U.S. Census Bureau statistics. They can give an indication of the economic health of your city, composition of potential customers, their ages, occupations, educational backgrounds, all of which may not only influence where you set up shop but what kinds of merchandise or services you choose to offer. Your town's environmental, cultural and economic situation can all have impact on your enterprise — find out as much as you can about all aspects.

When the time comes to commit yourself to a specific store-front, assess the most important factors for success: if walk-in traffic is crucial (for impulse purchases such as magazines, snacks, gifts) you might want to consider a busy shopping mall or downtown corner location; if railroad access or ware-house space is more important, you would be better off in a more industrialized part of town. If referral business will make up your clientele, you could do well with a less expensive, less conveniently located space and still find that serious customers will find their way to you.

The SBA publishes an excellent check-list of factors that could help you make your decisions.

Score each factor with an A for excellent, B for good, C for fair and D for poor. (Not all factors may be important in your own case, and you may even want to add an item or two).

Factors to consider

Score

1. Centrally located to reach my market _____

2. Merchandise or raw materials available readily _____

3. Nearby competition situation _____

4. Transportation availability and rates _____

5. Quantity of available employees _____

6. Prevailing rates of employee pay _____

7. Parking facilities _____

8. Adequacy of utilities (sewer, water, power, gas) _____

9. Traffic flow _____

10. Taxation burden _____

11. Quality of police and fire protection   _____

12. Housing availability for employees   _____

13. Environmental factors (schools, cultural, community activities, enterprise of businessmen)   _____

14. Physical suitability of building   _____

15. Type and cost of lease   _____

16. Provision for future expansion   _____

17. Overall estimate of quality of site in ten years   _____

Now, where do the potential problems exist? If parking facilities are poor and your trade depends upon people coming to your store, you had better look for another site. We know of one bookstore that went bankrupt partially because the town took the two parking spaces in front of the store for an additional traffic lane. Other parking was so limited or inconvenient that customers gave up in disgust and business just disappeared.

When you find a good spot, check to see whether it meets all local licensing and health code regulations. You don't want to sign a lease only to discover that you are liable to improvements in lighting or plumbing that should have been taken care of before you moved in. You might want to "snoop" around to discover why the store is vacant — have three businesses tried to make a go of it and failed in the past year? Are adjacent businesses thriving — filled with customers who could also stop in your shop? Better locations may sport higher rents, but they may be worth it to you.

All we are saying is, take your time finding floor space that is going to house your hopes and dreams for an independent life. Then move yourself in, open your door and put up your sign.

Resources: Selected Bibliography on Home Businesses

How to Make Money With Your Crafts. Clark, Leta, W. New York: William Morrow.

The Family Circle Book of Careers at Home. Gibson, Mary Bass, New York, New York, Cowles.

The Complete Handbook of How to Start and Run a Money-Making Business in Your Home. Hammer, Marian Behan, Englewood Cliffs, N.J. Prentice-Hall.

The following are some of the many "how to" books for opening specific home businesses:

Animals and pets

Dogs: Modern Grooming Techniques, Harmer, Hillary. 1970, Arco Publishing Company, Inc., 219 Park Ave. South, New York, NY 10003.

Understanding Your Cat. Fox, Michael W., 1977, Bantam Books, Inc., 666 Fifth Ave., New York, NY 10019.

Parakeet Breeding for Profit and Other Aviary Birds. Glick A. Borden Publishing Co., 1855 West Main Street, Alhambra, California 91801.

Antiques

Basic Book of Antiques. Michael, George. Arco Publishing Co., 219 Park Ave. South, New York, NY 10003.

Book of Pottery and Porcelain. Cox, Warren E. 2 Volume, Revised Edition, 1970. Crown Publishers, Inc., 419 Fourth Ave., New York, NY 10016.

Antiques: How to Identify, Buy, Sell, Refinish and Care for Them. Cole, Ann K. 1970, McKay, David Company, Inc., 119 West 40th Street, New York, NY 10018.

For additional information on antiques contact the Art and Antique Dealers League of America, 136 East 55th Street, New York, NY.

Babysitting

The Basics of Babysitting. Branson, Mary Kinny, 1976, Paperback, Broadman Press, 127 Ninth Ave. North, Nashville, TN 37203.

The Babysitter's Guide, Moore, Mary F. Paperback, Barnes & Noble, c/o Harper and Rowe Publishers, Keystone Industrial Park, Scranton, Pa. 18512.

Bookkeeping

Bookkeeping for Beginners. Hooper, W. E. 1970, Beekman Publishers, Inc., 30 Hicks Street, Brooklyn Heights, NY 11201.

Publications available free from the Small Business Administration (write to nearest SBA Field Office for copies).

Data Processing for Small Businesses, SBB No. 80, 1977 (Free).

Keeping Records in Small Business, SMA No. 155, 1976. (Free).

Recordkeeping Systems — Small Store and Service Trade, SBB No. 15, 1977. (Free).

Accounting Services for Small Service Firms, SMA No. 126, 1979. (Free).

Catering

Buffet Catering, Finance, Charles, Ahrens Publishing Company, Inc., 116 West 14th Street, New York, NY 10011 ($13.50).

Catering Handbook, Weiss, Hal and E. Weiss. 1971, Ahrens Publishing Co. ($12.50). See above citation for address.

Successful Catering, Splaver, Bernard R. 1975, ($14.95), Canners Books, 89 Franklin Street, Boston, Mass. 02110. ($5.95).

The Waiter and Waitress Training Manual, Dahmer, Sondra J. and Kurt W. Kahl, 1975, ($5.95). Canners Books. See above citation for address.

Clocks and watches

The Watch Repairer's Manual, 3rd Edition, Fried, Henry B. 1974, Chilton Book Company, Radnor, Pa. 19139.

Clock Guide: Identification with Prices. Miller, Robert W. 2nd Edition, 1975, Wallace-Homestead Book Company, 1912 Grand Avenue, Des Moines, Iowa 50305.

Electric appliances

Home Appliance Servicing, Anderson, Edwin P. 1974, $7.95) Audel, Theodore & Company 4331 West 62nd Street, Indianapolis, Indiana 46268.

Furniture and woodworking

Woodworking and Furniture Making. Endicott, G. W. 1976, Drake Publishers, Inc., 801 Second Avenue, New York NY 10017.

The Build-It Yourself Furniture Catalogue. Peterson, Franklyn N., 1976. Prentice-Hall, Inc., Englewood Cliffs, N.J. 07632.

The Furniture Maker's Handbook. Scharf, Robert, 1977, Scribner's Charles, Sons. 597 Fifth Avenue, New York, NY 10017.

Home improvement and repairs

Remodelers Handbook. Williams, Benjamin, 1976 (paperback), Craftsman Book Co., 542 Stevens Avenue, Solana Beach, Calif. 92075.

The Nothing Left Out Home Improvement Book. Philbin, Tom and Fritz Koelbel, 1976, Prentice Hall, Englewood Cliffs, N.J. 07632.

Jewelry

Jewelry Craft Made Easy. French, Bernada. 1976 Gembooks, P.O. Box 808, Mentone, Calif. 92359.

The Jewelry Engraver's Manual, Hardy, Allen R. 1976, (paperback) Van Nostrand Reinhold Company, 451 West 33rd Street, New York, NY 10001.

Mail Order

How to Start and Run a Successful Mail Order Business. Martyn, Sean. McKay, David Company, Inc., 119 West 49th Street, New York, NY 10018.

How to Start a Money-Making Business at Home. Robertson, Laura Fell, Fredrick, Inc., New York, NY.

How to Start and Operate a Mail Order Business, Simon, Julian, McGraw-Hill, Inc., New York, NY.

Free Small Business Administration booklets:

Selling by Mail Order. SBB No. 3, 1977.

National Mailing List Houses. SBB No. 29, 1979.

Write for the above SBA booklets: P.O. Box 15445, Fort Worth, Texas 76119.

Picture Framing

The Frame Book, Newman, Thelma. 1974, Crown Publishing, Inc., 419 Fourth Avenue, New York, NY 10016.

A Complete Do-It-Yourself Guide to Picture Framing. Duren, Lista, 1976. Houghton Mifflin Company, 2 Park Street, Boston, Mass. 02107.

Plants

The ABC of Potted Plants. Nightingale, Gay. 1973. Arco Publishing Company, 219 Park Avenue, South, New York, NY 10003.

Grow Your Own Plants. Kramer, Jack, 1973, Charles Scribner's Sons, 597 Fifth Avenue, New York, NY 10017.

Stamps and coins

Appraising and Selling Your Coins, 5th Edition Edited by Friedberg, Robert and Jack Friedberg. Coin and Currency Institute, Inc., 393 Seventh Avenue, New York, NY 10001

Fell's Official Stamp Guide. Burns, Franklin R., Fell, Frederick, Inc., 389 Park Avenue, South, New York, NY 10016.

American Numismatic Association (regarding coins), 818 Cascade, Colorado Springs, Colorado 80903.

American Philatelic Society (regarding stamps and stamp collecting), P.O. Box 800, State College, Pa. 16801.

American Stamp Dealers Association, 147 West 42nd Street, New York, NY 10036.

Society of Philatelic Americans (regarding stamps), P.O. Box 9086, Cincinnati, Ohio 45209.

Toys

Creative Soft Toy Making. Pegke, Pamela, 1974, Bobs-Merrill Company, 62nd Street, Indianapolis, Indiana.

American Folk Toys: How to Make Them. Schnacke, Dick, 1974, Penguin Books, Inc., 625 Madison Avenue, New York, NY 10022.

Soft Toys for Fun and Profit. Bertrand, Mary, 1974. Reed, A. H. and A. W. Books, Rutland, Vermont 05701.

Price Guide to Dolls, and *Price Guide to Toys.* Both books are by Miller, Robert W., 1976, Wallace-Homestead Book Company, 1912 Grand Avenue, Des Moines, Iowa 50305.

Typing

How to Earn $25,000 a Year or More Typing at Home. Drouillard, Ann, and William Keefe, 1973, Fell, Frederick, Inc., 386 Park Avenue, South, New York, NY 10016.

Writing for a profit

How to Make Money in Your Spare Time. Edited by Polking, Kirk, Writer's Digest, Cincinnati, Ohio 45242.

Writing Juvenile Stories and Novels, Whitney, Phyllis A., 1976, Writer's Inc., 8 Arlington Street, Boston, Mass. 02116.

CHAPTER FOUR

Financing Your Business From Start-Up To Success

How Much Money Will You Need To Start?

"How did I get started in business? I had no money at all. Luckily, I started out in a small way — I was acting as the agent for a matzoh business — you know, Kosher food — and the supplier furnished me with a half-ton truck and gave me some stuff on credit. That was in 1928. I've been in the same business ever since."

SAMUEL ZUCKERMAN, wholesaler of specialty foods.

"My brother, who was a tailor, and I bought our dry-cleaning business for $18,000 in 1953, with a deposit of $7,000 from our savings."

HENRY GREENBAUM, partner in Windsor Cleaners.

"I borrowed $6,000 from a bank on my father's signature."   DAVID ADLER, publisher of *Dossier* Magazine.

We cannot tell you how much money you will need to start your business or the one best way to go about finding the money once you know. We talked to people who started with, literally, nothing and others who had to come up with $100,000 (for an exclusive leather goods business) before they opened their doors. The most frequently mentioned amount was between $1,000 and $5,000, spent on inventory, supplies, equipment (an expensive camera for a photographer, kitchen appliances for a caterer), rental of retail space and utilities. Businesses that require extensive inventories of retail goods will cost more to launch than service-related businesses you can begin in your home with only a modest investment in utilities and advertising. Although you probably will want to start out small, don't make the mistake of starting out under-capitalized (too little money to keep you going) — down that road lies almost certain failure.

To estimate exactly how much start-up cash you need will involve some careful planning. The kinds of merchandise you will sell, the type of equipment you will need, the luxurious-ness of your selling space, the number of employees you will hire, will all be important to your calculations. Make precise estimates as best you can — don't overlook anything. Estimating a bit on the high side (some experts estimate adding 25% to every item) will give you an important "safety net" when the time comes to purchase, rent and hire.

The Small Business Administration provides two work-sheets for prospective business owners that will be helpful to your deliberations. Worksheet No. 1 lets you figure your estimated monthly expenses; Worksheet No. 2 is for one-time expenses. One item that these worksheets doesn't include is a "reserve" amount. Experts differ, but many believe that you should have a cash reserve that will cover all overhead, or set, expenses during three straight months of no profit. Why? An unexpected shortage of customers, unfore-seen purchase or breakdown of equipment, spell of bad weather or industry slow-down could turn into the big wave that swamps your small boat and sinks it. Another thing: many analysts recommend that you not plan on drawing a salary for the first six months of business; assume that you will have to live on savings or other income. Any profits (and they may be considerable, if you are lucky) should be put back into your business for its long-term well being.

How will you come up with your figures? Go shopping, just as you would for a new car or other major purchase. Get several quotes from competitive suppliers; they should be happy to have the chance to bid on your business even if it doesn't exist — yet. Check with real estate agents who specialize in retail space, contact your local City Hall or County Building for information on the minimum wage or licensing costs. Make a dry run through the whole process now and you will know what you will need later. This plan will reap other benefits as well; when the time comes to raise money, you will have detailed listings of expenses that will reassure any potential lender.

Where Will You Find The Money?

Without the money to start, your plans for going into business for yourself will never get off the drawing board. The traditional list of possible sources of money is short, unfortunately, and no one seems to have added to it in years:

- Personal savings
- Funds (gifts or loans) from relatives or friends
- Contributions by potential partners
- Loans from commercial banks or credit unions
- Loans from special sources (the SBA and other government agencies)

You will, very likely, find yourself using several of these sources for "seed money." If you accept a loan, even from friends or Uncle Harry, make sure a lawyer reviews any documents before you sign them. If you receive a loan from anyone unknown to you (say, a "friendly" loan company), make sure you are dealing with a reputable firm and have legal counsel review the terms of the loan agreement.

WORKSHEET NO. 2
LIST OF FURNITURE, FIXTURES, AND EQUIPMENT

Leave out or add items to suit your business. Use separate sheets to list exactly what you need for each of the items below.	If you plan to pay cash in full, enter the full amount below and in the last column.	If you are going to pay by installments, fill out the columns below. Enter in the last column your downpayment plus at least one installment.			Estimate of the cash you need for furniture, fixtures, and equipment
		Price	Down-payment	Amount of each installment	
Counters	$	$	$	$	$
Storage shelves, cabinets					
Display stands, shelves, tables					
Cash register					
Safe					
Window display fixtures					
Special lighting					
Outside sign					
Delivery equipment if needed					
TOTAL FURNITURE, FIXTURES, AND EQUIPMENT Enter this figure also in worksheet 1 under "Starting Costs You Only Have To Pay Once"					$

Alone With Your Loan....

If you end up going outside your circle of personal friends and acquaintances for money, plan to shop for a bank just as you shopped for cost estimates. Unfortunately many banks are reluctant to advance money to small businesspersons these days, particularly to those who want to start, rather than expand, a business. A going, and presumably thriving, concern with a proven performance record is much more reassuring to a lender, for obvious reasons. Don't be surprised if even your personal banker, the one who financed your car, house or other major purchase is less than enthusiastic about your plans. Go to your own bank first, but consider as well those banks that promote their progressive, adventuresome approaches to lending. Lending officers are people first, and the individual personality of the banker who hears your proposal may have a great deal to do with whether you will get the money you want or not. A smaller, newly established bank may be more eager for your business than an older, conservative institution but try several, in any case. Banks generally limit their loans, when they do grant them, to 50% of the starting capital you will need, so you will need some money of your own even then. They must be convinced that your business has real potential for success, that you are the kind of person who will make the business go and that, of course, you will be able to pay them back in a reasonable and timely fashion.

A bank will expect detailed, business-like answers to the following:

• What is the purpose of the loan (specifically) — to buy equipment or supplies, to enlarge or improve your location, to move to a better location (in terms of the business).

• How much money do you need (this is where those worksheets come in).

• How do you plan to repay the loan and over what period of time?

• What collateral or assurance can you provide that the bank will get its money back (more about this later).

• What is the present financial condition of the business (advance orders or contracts from potential clients would help a new business here).

• How will your business grow over the next two or three years?

• What kind of financial shape are you in personally (a personal financial statement describing assets in the form of real estate, insurance, cash income plus all debts, including a mortgage will help here).

• Are your plans realistic?

Under some circumstances, your bank will give you money based on your signature; more often, it will require more assurance that their money isn't going down a rat hole. You may be required to produce an endorser, co-maker or guarantor, anyone willing to guarantee that the loan will be repaid whether the business succeeds or not. An endorser would be required to pledge assets (real estate or other property) in support of the loan; a co-maker would borrow the money jointly with you and would be equally liable for its repayment. A guarantor guarantees the payment of the loan by signing a personal commitment (this is similar to a co-signer). Private or public lenders often require collateral in the form of property. You might want to bone up on the whole subject of loans before you go in to the bank. "The ABCs of Borrowing," a pamphlet that outlines the kinds of loans and credit practices you may run up against, is available from the SBA (P.O. Box 15434, Fort Worth, Texas 76119).

If The First National Turns Me Down . . . .

"Yes, we went to the SBA for a loan to expand our franchise operation. The paperwork was a nightmare! It took us two months to get the loan, and that's considered fast! I had a background in finance and management. I hired a loan packager that specializes in SBA-guaranteed loans to take care of the details, otherwise it

Making I

• *Th*
may ʒ
Oppoɪ
which
the cø
terms
credit,

Consti
contracte
contract
months]
obtain t
guaranty

There ɛ
if you qu̟

Some
managen
Administ
we have ɗ
you may ·

• *The*
Assist
and act
training
problen
Busines
graduat
counseli
Progran
assistan∈
consultiʁ
also issu
marketi̟
informai
various ɗ

• *Speci*
businesse

would have taken even longer. It was worth it in the
end, though, we got all the money we asked for and ten
years to pay it back. We had to put up all of our stores
as collateral and come up with a personal guarantee
from a friend as well before we got our money. At least,
this time we *got* the money — two years ago we gave a
loan packager $2,000 to help us get a loan from SBA
and they went bankrupt — no loan, no $2,000. This time
we learned to choose a reliable packager. Check with
the SBA, with your bank or other lenders in your area
before you give your money to one of those outfits."

LEN AND GAIL BRISKMAN, franchise operator of candy
and nut stores.

Talk to a dozen small businesspersons who have done business with the SBA and you may hear a dozen different
experiences, some good some not so good. The fact remains
that in the face of scarce money in the private sector, the SBA
may be the only way for you to obtain the money you need. As
private banks have become less and less sympathetic to small
businessmen (during the recent tight money crunch) a
crucial source of growth and expansion has dried up. In the
last few years, Congress and the federal government have
tried to ease the lot of the small businessman who is, after all,
vital to the country's economic growth. This is where the SBA
comes in. In the past few years, the government has
mandated a major expansion of the SBA's loan guarantee
activity: SBA loans rose from 26,000 in 1976 to 30,000 in 1979.
The dollar value of these loans increased from $1.8 billion to
$3.1 billion, or a 72% increase over the same period.

Congress also:

• Reduced the maximum tax on long-term capital gains
from 49% to 28%.

• Replaced the three-step corporate tax income
structure with a five-step rate, lowering the tax on the
first $100,000 of corporate income by $7,750.

• Amended federal rules defining the fiduciary responsibility of the nation's pension fund managers to

and obtain prime contracts and subcontracts, direct them to government agencies that buy the products or services they supply, help them get their names placed on bidders' lists, and assist in obtaining drawings and specifications for proposed purchases. These specialists also supply leads on research and development projects as well as new technology and assistance in the latest advances in the transfer of technology.

The SBA offers representation to the small business community at national, state and local government levels and to business, professional and trade organizations and associations. The SBA Advocacy Office wants to find out what problems small businesses are having and to alert other agencies to deal with those problems.

The Franchise — Another Way To Go

Many small business owners have started their venture by investing in a franchise, an individually-owned business operated as if it were part of a large chain. All services or products are standard and uniform trademarks and equipment are used. The franchisor (or supplier) gives the individual dealer (the franchisee) the right to sell, distribute or market the franchisor's product or service using the *franchised name* and selling techniques in a certain territory. You know many franchised businesses: McDonalds (known for its golden arches), H and R Block, Ponderosa restaurants, AAMCO Transmissions, Evelyn Wood Reading Dynamics, Radio Shack and Econo-Lodge motels and hotels.

Although there is nothing really new about the concept of franchising, over the past 30 years it has become a popular form of small business. Franchises in today's marketplace are recognized as opportunities for a person to own his or her own business even if inexperienced and lacking in adequate capital. In the period from 1978 to 1980, franchised businesses accounted for $312 billion in annual sales; in 1979 alone, this was equal to 32 percent of all retail sales in the United States.

There are over 1,200 different companies that offer franchises, including over 700,000 small business persons.

You can buy a franchise in auto and trailer rentals; beauty salons and supplies; campgrounds; children's stores; construction and remodeling services; educational products; cosmetics and toiletries; food and donuts; groceries; pet shops; hotels and motels; printing; security systems; real estate; etc. There are even franchises for hot tubs, parking garages, insect and pest exterminators, fireworks and artificial fingernail salons (where over 50 percent of the customers are nail-biters referred by a physician)!

An excellent way to review the hundreds of franchises available is to locate a copy of the *Franchise Opportunity Handbook*, published by the U.S. Department of Commerce (July, 1980 edition). This book lists each franchise by type of product or service, a description of the operation, number of franchises they have in operation, length of time in business, financial assistance available, type and length of training provided to franchisees, and type of managerial assistance available.

The International Franchise Association, the main trade association in this field defines franchising as "a continuing relationship in which the franchisor provides a licensed privilege to do business, plus assistance in organizing, training, merchandising, and management in return for a consideration from the Franchise."

Franchises have advantages and disadvantages. You can view a franchise as an easy method for gaining independence (as an owner of a business) with a minimum amount of risk and a greater chance for success by using the experiences, products and marketing techniques of a proven product or service. That certainly sounds good, doesn't it? There are however, drawbacks; the franchisee, for example, must give up some freedom of action in business decisions that are made by the franchisor. In some aspects of the arrangement the franchisee is not really his own boss since he or she will always need to reflect a certain degree of uniformity and standardization about the products to be sold and the way he or she goes about doing business.

Some of the advantages of owning a franchise are:

• A recognizable trade name.

• A wide range of assistance and support from the franchisor including:

   — A thorough analysis of the best location.

   — Building construction planning.

   — Legal assistance.

   — Financial assistance.

   — Management training.

   — Centralized purchase power (quantity buying means that you can get products at cheaper rates).

   — Systemized advertising (often in the form of national or regional media campaigns such as television, radio or newspapers).

   — Good profit margins.

The disadvantages are:

• You must adhere to the rules of the franchisor.

• You may lose your sense of personal identity. You may not really be *your own boss.*

• You need total understanding of all the fine details of the franchise contract. (Get a lawyer to help you with this one!)

• The contract may be unduly slanted in favor of the franchisor; look out for unreasonably high sales quotas, or overlapping territories that could seriously hurt one franchise or another.

• You may have to prepare time-consuming reports to satisfy the franchisor.

Before you invest in a franchise, the SBA advises that you check out the franchisor completely; his product or service; the franchise contract; the market and the potential affect on you, the franchisee.

For another look at franchises and additional details look at *Starting and Managing a Small Business of Your Own,* 3rd Edition, U.S. SBA, Washington, D.C.

The Franchise Checklist:

1. Has your lawyer approved the franchise contract?

2. Does the franchise ask you to take any steps which, according to your lawyer, are either illegal in your area (city, state or county) or simply unwise from a business or legal standpoint?

3. Does the franchise give you an exclusive territory for the length of the franchise or can the franchise sell a second or third franchise in your territory?

4. Is the franchisor connected in any way with any other franchise firm that handles a similar product or service? If the answer is yes, do you have any protection against this second franchisor organization?

5. Under what conditions can you terminate the franchise contract and what would the costs be to you should you want to terminate the contract?

6. If you sell your franchise, will you receive any compensation or payment for your "good will" (developing a good name and establishment of customers and a following) or will all of this be lost with the termination of the franchise contract?

The Franchisor Checklist:

1. Has the firm offering the franchise been in business long enough to be reliable and stable?

2. Does the franchisor have a good reputation for honesty and fairness among the local firms holding its franchise? (It pays to ask around, make a few visits and phone calls. It will be worth your time and effort.)

3. Has the franchisor shown you *certified* figures showing exact profits of one or more of the firms which you personally have seen?

4. Will the franchisor help you with a management training program; an employee training program; a public relations program; acquiring capital; acquiring credit, and merchandising ideas and methods?

5. Will the franchisor help you find a suitable location for your franchise?

6. Is the franchisor adequately financed to carry out its plans for financial assistance or expansion?

7. Is the franchisor a one-person company or is it a corporation with an experienced management team?

8. Has the franchisor checked you out to assure that you can successfully operate the franchise to profit both you and the franchisor?

9. Does your state have laws regulating the sale of franchises and has the franchisor complied with the law?

Questions For You — As The Buyer Of A Franchise:

1. Do you have the equity capital needed to purchase the franchise and run it until your income equals your expenses?

2. Where will you get the capital?

3. Do you have what it takes in terms of ability training or experience to work effectively with the franchisor, any employees (if you should need them in your business) and your customers?

4. Are you prepared to give up some independence in order to gain the advantages of the franchise?

Your Potential Market For The Franchise:

1. Have you checked out carefully whether there is a market for the product or service in the territory that you have chosen to open the franchise?

2. Have you checked on population trends for the territory in which your business will be located? Does it look like the population will increase or decrease over the next five years? (Check with your local Chamber of Commerce for information on trends.)

3. Will your product or service be in greater demand in the next five years?

4. Is there competition in the territory for the same products or services you plan to sell? If so, will there be enough business to go around?

As a final note, we might mention that even the field of career counseling has been franchised. In 1981, the Career Counseling Corporation, offering two-year career counseling sessions and computer access to an exclusive occupational information system, opened its doors. A national urban network of career counseling centers was planned, so that people all over the country could receive advice on a career shift or advancement. The Career Counseling Corporation, 4626 East Fort Lowell, Suite J, Tucson, Arizona 85712, can give you the location of the center closest to you.

Where To Find Additional Assistance

Better Business Bureaus: These offices, located in most cities, can give you free information on various franchises, their records and reputations. Find the bureau nearest you by checking the white or yellow pages of your telephone book. You can also write directly to the Council of Better Business Bureaus, Inc., 1150-17th Street, N.W., Washington, D.C. 20036. They will either fill your request or refer you to the appropriate address for information. (Be sure to include the name of the franchise you are interested in with your request.)

International Franchise Association: This non-profit trade association represents more than 370 franchising firms here and abroad. They speak on behalf of member franchise companies, set standards for business practices and provide assistance in the form of education and training for franchise managers. IFA has supported full disclosure of all important information to potential franchisees. They publish *Investigate Before Investing*, available for $2.50, and a directory of their member franchises, available from them free of charge. (If the franchise you are interested in is a member, you will probably be able to learn more about the company than if it is not.)

National Franchise Association Coalition: This organization, made up of 18 associations and a number of individual franchises, provides franchisors with the opportunity to act together in areas that interest them and are beneficial to their collective interests. Their legal committee assists with problems involving franchises and the law. Contact the National Franchise Association Coalition, P.O. Box 366, Fox Lake, Illinois 60020.

Other sources of information on franchises

A Franchise Contract. Van Cise, Jerrold C. International Franchise Association, 1025 Connecticut Ave., Suite 1005, Washington, D.C. 20036 ($4.00). A legal examination of the necessary elements of a contract that will protect both franchisor and franchisee.

A Franchising Guide for Blacks. Jones, Thomas E., Pilot Books, 347 Fifth Avenue, New York, NY 10016 ($2.00). Addressed to black people who are interested in owning a franchise, this book describes financing, legal advice, evaluation of a franchise opportunity and other aspects of purchasing a franchise.

A Woman's Guide to Her Own Franchised Business. Small, Anne and Robert K. Levy, Pilot Industries, Inc., address directly above, ($2.50). A chronicle of opportunities created for women and how to take advantage of them, this paperback includes a list of over 150 franchise opportunities.

Business Building Ideas for Franchises and Small Business. Serif, Ned, Pilot Industries, address above, ($2.50). Filled with useful tips and suggestions on the promotional aspects of establishing your new business.

Directory of Franchising Organizations (revised annually), Pilot Industries, Inc., address above ($3.50). A comprehensive listing of the top moneymaking franchises in the United States, including a brief description and amount needed for an investment.

The Franchise Game. Nedell, Harold. Olempco, Dept. C. P.O. Box 27963, Houston, Texas 77027 ($8.00). This text deals with the emotional, physical and mental traumas experienced by franchisees. It includes insights from the point of view of the franchisor as well as the franchisee.

Investigate Before Investing: Guidelines for Prospective Franchisees. Fels, Jerome L. and Luis G. Rudnick, International Franchise Association, 1025 Connecticut Avenue, N.W., Suite 1005, Washington, D.C. 20036, 1974, ($2.50). A step-by-step approach to, how to investigate and evaluate a franchise before investing in one.

Your Fortune in Franchises. Finn, Richard P. Contemporary Books, Inc., Chicago, 1979. Brief descriptions of signing a contract, the franchisor's rights, promoting a franchise, recording-keeping, franchises for minority group members and women and the best franchising opportunities.

Franchise Opportunities Handbook. U.S. Department of Commerce, July 1980, ($8.50). Stock #003-009-00325-1 U.S. Government Printing Office, Washington, D.C. 20402. A massive handbook containing a comprehensive listing of franchises in the U.S. Included are a brief description of the franchise, the number of franchisees, the amount of money needed to invest, whether financial assistance is available through or with the help of the franchisor, etc.

CHAPTER FIVE

Your Going Concern: Accounting, Taxes, Advertising, Management

Imagine your business as a going concern: you have decided what kind of business you want to be in, what form it is going to take, how to find funding where you are going to locate.

How will you operate on a daily basis? Presumably, customers will come in or call in their business, stock will be purchased or services rendered, bills will arrive and customers billed. You will become known in your community and known well enough to need someone else to help you answer your phone or fill the orders that arrive on your doorstep. At the end of the week, there will have to be enough left after everyone and everything has been paid to pay for *your* groceries.

No matter what kind of business you dream up, it will have to be run as a business if you are going to succeed. Since 55% of all businesses in the U.S. fail (go bankrupt or are discontinued) within the first five years of operation, many of your friends out there are not running their businesses like businesses — they can't make them pay the rent. You will want to avoid that calamity at all costs and you can, by learning how a business, whatever its nature, must be run.

Keeping the Books

"How long did it take us to break even financially? Actually, that's an interesting question. With Selby Productions, we just worked real hard and just kept shoveling all the receipts and answers and papers and envelopes in boxes and finally got it to an accountant and got him to work on things. We found out that we had broken even and gone into a very, very substantial profit margin at the end of our first year of full-time effort. The problem we ran into was that we ended up in a pretty poor tax situation liability-wise. I recommend that you don't throw everything into a shoe box, but get yourselves properly set up. At least, take care of the basics so you know you have a good idea where you are so that you can take advantage of the various tax advantages that become available to the small businessman instead of paying too much in taxes."

ED HELVEY, partner, Selby Productions.

"In our previous attempts in business, we went through a lot of accountants and they were costing us a fortune. Poor accounting put us out of business; without monthly projections and quarterly reports, we had no idea how we were doing from month to month. Now we know: we have a tax consultant, an accountant, a bookkeeping service and a marketing consultant."

CYNTHIA HELVEY, partner, Selby Productions.

"Accountants can be the most important people if they know their job well. They can tell you trends in your business, perhaps more objectively than you can see for yourself. It is important to have an excellent accountant or CPA."

Who are these wonder workers and how do they fit into your business? Certified Public Accountants (CPAs) receive formal training in accounting; they have college degrees and must pass a tough certification exam in their state. In many states, CPAs must continue their professional education after certification in order to maintain their status after they pass the exam, a process that makes sure they stay up-to-date on the latest accounting methods and information available. A non-CPA accountant is not necessarily college trained and does not have to take the certification examination in order to conduct his/her business. A bookkeeper is, simply, a recorder of entries in the books kept by a business. He/she keeps track of all receipts, all bills, all money going out or coming in to the business. A tax consultant is one of two individuals, the one you see at the end of the year to prepare your business's tax returns or someone who can assist you or your CPA in restructuring your business's tax status to avoid any potential problems.

To answer the second question — where do they fit into your business — you need to know a bit about accounting yourself.

As anyone who has ever filed a personal tax form knows, you need to keep track of your earnings for Uncle Sam. It's the law. If you have been employed, your employer has been required to keep track of what he paid you and withhold part of your earnings for taxes. When you are the employer, even if you only employ yourself, you will have to keep track of what you make and how much you spend to keep your business operating in order to satisfy the IRS (Internal Revenue Service) tax laws.

But an even more important reason for keeping precise records of all money transactions, no matter how small, is that it is the only way you can make decisions on how your business should be run. How seasonal is your business? Can you afford to add a part-time person to your payroll? Are your prices to customers too high or too low compared to what it costs you to buy and process your product? Does it pay you to carry customers' unpaid bills from month to month? Are you doing land-office business, but still going broke?

These are crucial questions. You had better have the answers to them, starting on the day you open shop. You can try to keep your records yourself (and learn basic accounting procedures through college or night school courses) or you can hire an accountant or CPA on a monthly basis, to do this for you. Although the last thing you need is an unnecessary expense when you begin your business, hiring an accountant can be a wise move.

Joel O. Wasserman, a Philadelphia accountant, explains, "You should see a CPA *before* you go into business, not after. Small businesses fail for two basic reasons, lack of management skills and lack of money. A CPA can provide you with guidelines on operating expenses, find out how many of your product you must sell before you break even, figure what your gross (before expenses) profit percentage will be, even help you gain credit so you can properly finance your business. Find a CPA who is familiar with, and handles, the kind of business you plan to operate. We have often seen people who are planning to open a business who we find are not really in a position to open due to a lack of capital. We can save this kind of person a lot of time, money and grief, before he makes a mistake."

Your accountant will show you how to set up a business bank account, separate from your personal account, and, if you choose to keep your own books, how to enter all deposits, withdrawals (including "cash" withdrawals for your personal use) and balance the account at the end of each month. He will suggest how long to keep all cancelled checks and statements, how to apportion expenses that are partially business, partially personal, and other things. He may advise whether your business is suited to single-entry bookkeeping, where only one entry is made for each transaction; or double-entry bookkeeping, where every action is entered twice, as a debit and a credit. Although much more complicated than the single-entry system, double-entry is a good system for many businesses. It almost always requires the use of a "real" bookkeeper (who might, by the way, be another small businessperson like yourself).

What will an accountant cost you? As with everything, costs vary depending upon the size of your business and the size of the accounting firm. Some CPAs do not charge for the initial consultation in which you set up your business. Some small businesses require special work on payroll and tax problems over and above the routine kinds of service.

Whether you need monthly profit and loss statements, quarterly tax payments and audits also influence the total cost. A modest beauty shop might cost you $50 to $100 per month; two or three small shops or a small manufacturing firm would require more time — and cost more.

"Don't be afraid of the cost of a reliable CPA. Look for quality, not just cost. How you start and manage your finances can make or break you. Spend the time and money, but get a good CPA before you launch your business venture," counsels Joel O. Wasserman. We couldn't agree more!

The Tax Tangle — and How To Stay Out Of It

We all know how popular the topic of taxes is, so we won't dwell on how unappealing but unavoidable their presence is in our lives. It is definitely a chore to fill out the forms, keep track of the deadlines and stay on top of tax items, but the fact remains that it is a necessary part of your business, even if your business is a modest one.

No matter who handles your taxes, you as the owner are responsible for your federal, state and local tax payments. A good accountant should advise you on the way to meet your tax obligations; failure to pay amounts due the government on time will only lead to problems and penalties.

The Small Business Administration counsels that the owner-manager of a small business plays two roles in the management and collection of taxes, debtor and agent. As a debtor, you are liable for various taxes and pay them as part of your business obligation. As an agent, you collect various state and local taxes and pass them on to the appropriate government agency. For example, if you have employees, every pay day, you deduct social security and income taxes from their wages. In addition, in some areas, you may have to collect local or state taxes from your customers for products or services they purchase from you.

Here are some of the characters in the great tax drama:

Federal taxes: the amount owed to Uncle Sam depending on the earnings of the company and its business organization. If you are the sole proprietor, you pay taxes as would any other individual; the difference is that your income is from the earnings of the business instead of from a set wage or salary. You would file the same form as does an individual taxpayer, plus an additional form which identifies all your business expenses as well as income from your business.

If you are part of a partnership, you would file the income and expenses of the business, but report only your share of the profits on your own income tax form.

If you are an individual owner or a partner, you are required by a law to "pay-as-you-go" as far as income and self-employment (social security) taxes are concerned. To do this, you must file with the Internal Revenue Service on or before April 15th of each year.

If you are a new owner of a business, you may be required to file a Declaration of Estimated Taxes on a date other than April 15th. (For further information on any changes that occur in your status — such as a change in income or number of dependents — contact your accountant or tax specialist or the IRS directly.)

Excise taxes: federal taxes imposed on the sale or use of certain products and occupations, for example, the occupational tax on retail dealers in adulterated butter, retail and wholesale beer and liquor dealers. Certain motor and diesel fuel and tires have an excise tax to be collected by the retailer. There are other occupations and products that have excise taxes; check with the IRS for details.

Unemployment taxes: federal taxes that must be paid if you paid wages of $1,500 or more in any quarter of the year. The tax laws and forms are subject to change from one year to the next so get up-to-date information before you file.

Another good idea is to obtain a copy of the *Tax Guide for Small Business* (IRS publication #334) from any office of the IRS. It is an excellent book and has sample forms and due dates for when various taxes must be paid.

State taxes and local taxes: taxes which vary from locale to locale. The three most important taxes are the *unemployment* tax, *state income* and *sales* tax. To find out which taxes must be paid in your state, contact a state taxation office or, again, ask your accountant. Counties, cities and boroughs impose a wide variety of taxes all their own, including personal property taxes, taxes on the gross income of your business, real estate taxes — there are even taxes on the size of your sign, if you have one. Some cities have their own income tax.

Try to manage your taxes the way you handle any other part of your business; pay them when due and save yourself a lot of heartache.

It really can pay to advertise — really. It may seem so obvious to you that your business is needed in your town that you have overlooked your need to advertise in your enthusiasm. While advertising can be a real expense, it is an important investment in your business. Don't be spooked off by the lavish campaigns for national products that bombard you every day — your advertising budget can be as modest as the money it takes to buy a sign for your front door. In those instances your reputation may be all you need to sell your services and products. You may already be so well-known for your cooking or decorating that your friends are just waiting to pounce on your new enterprise and give you all the business you can handle.

If, however, your business needs image-making, increased sales or expansion, or if you face a lot of competition from other businesses in the neighborhood, advertising should be part of your plans.

What does advertising do? First, it lets people know you exist, that you are located on Joy Street and are open from 8:30 to 6:00 (closed Sundays). It also informs people about the kinds of services you offer (saddle repair, Volkswagen parts, etc.). Finally, it builds an image of your business and the clientele you hope to attract.

Between the hand-painted sign and the national TV campaign is a wide range of advertising media. Handbills passed out in neighborhoods, direct mail ads that come into people's homes, contests, newspaper and magazine ads, exhibits at malls, trade shows or county flea markets all qualify.

> "I started with an advertisement of a one-dollar-off coupon in a neighborhood paper. This brought in business and I knew I was on my way."
> NANCY BLOCK, photographer.

As you examine the kinds of advertising that may work best for you, consider:

• What is the nature of your business? Will you be selling a product, service, or both?

• What kind of image do you want to project — are you trying to attract an exclusive clientele from all over town or are you aiming at ordinary neighborhood trade? If you specialize in discount sportwear your campaign may be different from someone selling designer fashions.

• Who will your customers be? Teenagers, tourists, neighborhood drop-ins? Each group would be reached through different means: teenagers through a local rock radio station, perhaps; tourists through local guidebooks or the Yellow Pages; neighbors through giveaway fliers offering a free introductory service.

• How do you stack up compared to your competitors; do they run full-page ads once a week or use direct mail?

• Can you handle the business your advertising will generate? You should be able to accommodate customers with enough stock and sales personnel; it could be disastrous if you advertised a product, got a great response, but ran out of stock and had to turn away hundreds of people. This kind of problem could ruin your image for future advertising campaigns.

• Is your location accessible? If no one can find your store or it is hard to get to it, your advertising dollars may be wasted. (This is one thing you won't have to worry about if you run a small order business or deliver products ordered by mail or phone.) In this type of business you can locate almost anywhere, including your home.

"When I started my business, I wasn't familiar with advertising and marketing, but I learned quickly. A friend said, 'Here's a copy of a book on the subject,' and I read it. How I wish I hadn't waited so long to learn about the importance of advertising. I could have made a lot more money much earlier. My advice is to build an image of quality for yourself through your stationary, business cards, everything."

> JUDY DIAMOND, owner, Insurance Research, Inc. and ERISA benefit Funds, supplier of financial information to insurance companies.

"We have a marketing consultant who helps us with promotional ideas. For example, we plan to set up a series of seminars for people who want to tackle plumbing problems themselves. We will run these seminars on Saturdays, from 20-25 people at a time, and charge $20.00 per person, including coffee and doughnuts. We figure that each attendee will save at least one service call and that will pay for their seminar. We try to encourage people to do the small jobs themselves and, of course, call *us* to remodel their kitchen or bathroom. We also give our customers a complimentary newsletter, called *The Pipeline,* we print ourselves, with tips on how to do things themselves. We send them postcards periodically to remind them of things they can do themselves to save money; their names are kept on a computer. The type of services we provide are different from most plumbers; we're unique, we believe. The newsletter was also the marketing consultant's idea — we get together and brainstorm twice a year."

> DENISE AND RICHARD McMAHON, owners, McMahon Plumbing Company.

You may not be in a position to offer your customers a free newsletter, but you may come up with other ideas, equally individual, that will set you apart from your competitors, create goodwill among your customers and reap real benefits for your business.

Only you will be able to discover whether a particular medium is effective for your business; advertising is not a science. Ask your customers how they heard about you or keep track of the number of introductory coupons from the local paper that are actually returned. If you are not brave enough, right off the bat, to try a newsletter like *The Pipeline*, consider some of these basic kinds of advertising (pricing based on 1981 estimates):

1,000 sheets of 8½ × 11 stationery and 1,000 #10 envelopes, printed with store name and address	$ 71
1,000 two-color business cards	25
⅛-page ad in large metropolitan Yellow Pages	144/ month
1,000 match books printed with store name and address	74
⅛-page ad in local weekly "giveaway" paper (circulation 50,000), 3 × 3½	$33-$47 /month depending on frequency of ad

Remember, everything connected with your business has the potential to make a good, repeated impression on your customers. A sign painted on the side of your car or van; professionally designed menus with "Tell Your Friends" information printed prominently on the front or back; catalogues with your merchandise information all can be vehicles for your store's message.

Other tips on advertising come from the SBA's *Advertising Guidelines for Small Retail Firms:*

1. Inquire about the cooperative advertising policies of your suppliers. Consult your vendors for the requirements you must meet in order to qualify, apply for and receive payments.

2. Goodwill advertising is an excellent method of advertising your business and enhancing good public

relations. Every retailer receives requests and solici-
tations for ads by all kinds of social organizations such
as church groups, schools, etc. Do not charge these
donations to advertising but to publicity or "contributions" so that you don't distort your true advertising
budget.

3. The only purpose of an ad is to sell: avoid
unnecessary words, keep your sentences short, use terms
your readers will understand and get to the point of
your message.

4. Advertising should be viewed as a sales building
investment and not just a business expense. It *will* bring
you business.

You may want to contact these organizations or a
professional agency for more information:

> American Advertising Federation
> 1225 Connecticut Avenue, N.W.
> Washington, D.C. 20036
>
> American Marketing Association
> 222 Riverside Plaza, Suite 606
> Chicago, IL 60606
>
> Association of National Advertisers
> 155 East 44th Street
> New York, NY 10017
>
> National Retail Merchants Association
> 100 West 31st Street
> New York, NY 10001

A Word On Management

Really, this whole book has to do with management of one
kind or another. Many of our interviewees summed up their
experiences so concisely that we will let publisher David
Adler speak for them:

"The reality of the situation is awfully important. Always
be aware that if you fluff off, you can lose the business. It can
go down the drain very quickly. Be on top of everything. It is
very important to keep good business records and good
monitoring of the system. Keep charts. Know where

everything is in various departments of your business in terms of inventory and financial records. Hire good people. Sometimes it is worthwhile to pay people more than you are getting out of the business in order to build the business. It is always the little things that become the big things. It is the bookkeeping department that can screw up a business. If someone in small business is not pulling his weight, you know it right away, not like a bureaucracy. You also have to know how to inspire people. You have to not waste time. Run your own small business and stay on top of it as much as possible. You can say that you don't have to come to work if you don't want to, but you really have to in a small business, more so than in a big company. You can't take vacations, at least not in the beginning. You have to get on the phone and ask people for money. You have to watch your accounts receivable and accounts payable. You have to be a sort of clergy for the employees and at the same time take the low-key approach and not be a bastard tough guy. At all times you have to be yourself. The hardest thing for people to learn is that in order to be an 'executive' they don't have to be tough. If it's not your style, it won't work. Always keep your object in front of you. Pitch in and be willing to do anything, whether it is turning out the lights or anything else. Try as hard as you can and, whether you fail or succeed, you grow."

Selected Bibliography In Accounting And Financial Management

Accounting, Finance and Taxation, Baker, Richard F. A basic guide for small business. Boston, CBI Publications, 1980. Detailed examples, illustrations, tables and charts do a good job on clarifying difficult material.

Taxation for Small Business, Lane, Marc J., New York, Wiley, 1980. A first rate guide to every tax aspect of setting up and running a business with checklists for performing all the vital steps that can lead to tax success.

Finance and Accounting for Non-Financial Managers, Droms, William G. 1979. Addison-Wesley Publishing Company, Massachusetts. A text designed for managers and executives who are untrained in finance and accounting and want to develop basic skills. It includes accounting, taxes, financial statement analysis, budgeting and capital budgeting.

Self-Correcting Problems in Finance, Robinson, Roland I. and Robert W. Johnson, 1976. Allyn and Bacon, Inc., Boston, Massachusetts. This paperback is designed to accompany any fundamental business finance text; its self-teaching format will help you understand the ins and outs of financial computation.

Introduction to Financial Management, Mathur, I. 1979. Macmillan Publishing Company, New York, New York. This is an approach to financial management written from the "trenches". Real situations make the text lively.

Fundamentals of Financial Management, VanHorne, James C. 2nd ed., This is a basic finance text on financial management theory for decision-makers. The author stresses the concept of risk versus return.

Techniques of Financial Analysis, Helfert, Erich A. 1977. Richard D. Irwin, Homewood, Illinois. Written to give a student or business person or analyst a precise reference collection of the more important tools and techniques of financial analysis.

U. S. Government Publications

Small Business Bibliography: (these are 4 to 12 page-pamphlets). Each title in this series deals with a specific type of business or business function, giving reference sources. These are free from SBA, P.O. Box 15434, Ft. Worth, Texas 76119.

Recordkeeping Systems — Small Store and Service Trade (SBB 15)

Retail Credit and Collections — (SBB 31)

Inventory Management (SBB 75)

Management Aids for Small Manufacturers

Financial Audits: A Tool For Better Management (MA 176)

Basic Budgets for Profit Planning (MA 220)

A Venture Capital Primer for Small Business (MA 235)

Small Marketers Aids:

Controlling Cash in Small Retail and Service Firms (SMA 110)

Steps in Meeting Your Tax Obligations (SMA 142)

Getting the Facts for Income Tax Reporting (SMA 144)

Budgeting in the Small Service Firm (SMA 146)

Sound Cash Management and Borrowing (SMA 147)

Simple Breakeven Analysis for Small Stores (SMA 166)

Small Business Management Series: Each book in this series discusses in depth the application of a specific

management technique. Prices vary and these may be ordered from the Superintendent of Documents, Government Printing Office, Washington, D.C. 20402.

Cost Accounting for Small Manufacturers — Assists managers of small manufacturing firms, producing a broad range of products, establish accounting procedures that will help to document and control production and business costs. Order #045-000-00020-6 (Price $1.10).

Handbook of Small Business Finance — For the small business owner who wants to improve financial management skills. Order #045-000-00139-3 (Price $3.00).

Financial Recordkeeping for Small Stores — Written for the small store owner or prospective owner whose business doesn't justify hiring a full-time bookkeeper. Order #045-000-00142-3 (Price $4.00)

Employers Tax Guide, IRS Publication 15, Dept. of Treasury, Internal Revenue Service, Washington, D.C. 20224. Containing withholding rates and calendar of employer's reporting dates and responsibilities. This guide is updated annually to include changes in tax laws and rates. Free.

Tax Guide for Small Business, (IRS Publication 334) Edited specifically to help small business owners prepare their federal tax returns for the preceding year. This guide is usually useful during the current year for federal tax problems including individuals, partnerships, corporations, income, excise and employment taxes. Available annually in December, and can be obtained from the Government Printing Office or local District Director of Internal Revenue.

Associations

There are a number of professional and trade associations that offer a variety of services to members and others interested in their specialties. Feel free to write directly for information or services offered.

American Management Association
135 West 50th Street
New York, NY 10020

American Bankers Association
1120 Connecticut Ave., N.W.
Washington, D.C. 20036

The Institute of Management Sciences
146 Westminister Street
Providence, Rhode Island 02930

American Finance Association
Graduate School of Business
New York University
100 Trinity Place
New York, NY 10006

National Association of Accountants
919 Third Avenue
New York, NY 10022

Selected Bibliography in Advertising

Successful Direct Marketing Methods. Stone, Bob, 1975. Grain Books, Chicago, Illinois. The book covers the entire scope of creating and applying marketing techniques. 100 examples of effective advertisements, direct marketing procedures, and numerous case histories of large businesses.

Advertising — Its Role in Modern Marketing. Dunn S. Watson and Arnold M. Barban. Undated, Dryden Press, Hinsdale, Illinois. This is a blend of theory and practice explaining the many phases of advertising — research, copy, campaign creation and an explanation of the use of media.

Advertising for Modern Retailers. Milton, Prof. Shirley, (undated) Fairchild Publications, New York City. Here is good coverage of copy, art, media and budget and an emphasis on easy to understand promotion strategies.

Making TV Pay Off. Abarahams, Howard P. (undated) Fairchild Publications, Inc., New York City. A how-to-do-it book for retailers, it explains how to use TV to move merchandise and increase store traffic on small budgets.

Modern Display Techniques. Mauger, Emily M. (undated) Fairchild Publications, New York City. It provides the how and the why of effective display, from the mechanical aspects of the area size and lighting to the use of lighting to create effects.

Advertising, Kirkpatrick, Charles A. Houghton Mifflin Company, Boston (undated). Covers all phases of advertising with a chapter devoted to retail advertising. There are also sections on point-of purchase, brand names, and trademarks.

Businessman's Guide to Advertising and Sales Promotion. Lewis, H. G. 1974, McGraw-Hill Book Company, Inc., New York City. Takes the reader through the maze of theory, terminology and procedures.

Retailing Principles and Practices. Richert, G. H. 1974, McGraw-Hill Book Company, New York City. Covers just about every kind of retailing — merchandising, store operations, credit, personnel and sales promotion.

Government publications

Small Business Bibliography: (these are 4 to 12 page pamphlets). Free for the asking. Write to SBA, Washington, D.C. 20416, for publications list or request directly for the item of your choice.

Selling by Mail Order, (SBB 3).

Retailing, (SBB 10)

National Mailing List Houses (SBB 29)

Advertising — Retail Store (SBB 20)

Selecting Advertising Media — A Guide for Small Business (SBMS 33)

Knowing Your Image, Blackwell, Roger D. (SMA 124)

Advertising Guidelines for Small Retail Firms, Riso, Ovid (SMA 160)

Do You Know the Results of Your Advertising? Sorbet, Elizabeth M. (SMA 169)

Effective Industrial Advertising for Small Plants, Marshall, Harold. SBA Management Aids #178. Reprinted April 1979.

Business and trade publications

Because trade publications in the field of advertising are usually rather broad, retailers often rely on these trade papers in their own line of business in order to obtain ideas on advertising and selling. Listed below are various advertising related associations that publish useful material to meet the tastes of various businesses. Write directly to these for information:

The Advertising Council
825 Third Ave., New York, NY 10022

Advertising Research Foundation
3 East 54th Street, New York, NY 10022

American Advertising Federation
1225 Connecticut Ave., N.W.
Washington, D.C. 20036

Direct Mail/Marketing Association
230 Park Ave., New York, NY 10017

Newspaper Advertising Bureau
485 Lexington Ave., New York, NY 10017

Television Bureau of Advertising
1 Rockefeller Plaza, New York, NY 10022

CHAPTER SIX

Special Opportunities For Special People

"**I**'ve been in the construction business for about a year. As a woman in construction, I am discriminated against because there are so few women in it; I have had trouble being taken seriously since no one thinks I know what I'm talking about. But I've applied for my AA minority status, a special consideration given people who have been deprived from getting ahead and receiving government contracts. If I'm granted AA status, I'll be the first woman to receive it in a male-dominated field and I will never have to bid on a government contract again; they will negotiate directly with me. I'll expand to thousands of employees then. I am a firm believer that you can do anything you want to — men, women, whoever, this is the time to go into small business. Take up the challenge, that's what I say!"

LINDA DONATO, President, Lindy Contractors and Associates

By this time, almost everyone must realize that women, handicapped people, disabled veterans and members of minority groups have, in the past, faced almost insurmountable difficulties in becoming financially independent. Traditional lenders have found it hard to take seriously the credit worthiness, goals and needs of anyone who didn't fit their model of the typical businessman. Times are changing — and government attitudes towards non-white-male members of society are changing as well. Opportunities now exist for virtually anyone who wants to start a business.

Success, Thy Name Is Woman

Women of all backgrounds are flocking to small business — according to the U.S. Department of Commerce, women in this country own 702,000 enterprises with annual receipts totaling $41.5 billion. Although women own only 7.1% of all businesses in the United States, that figure is up 30% from five years ago. Traditionally discouraged from doing battle in the economic wars, women were believed to be woefully inadequate to the task of balancing their checkbooks, much less managing a business. Not so any longer.

"Women are the next great group of entrepreneurs," predicts Beatrice Fitzpatrick, Chief Executive of the Manhattan-based American Women's Economic Development Corporation (AWED), a federally funded pilot program that trains and counsels business people. Only two of the 322 businesses run by AWED-trained women have failed. Many of these successful graduates are widows, almost all of whom had been advised by their husband's lawyers to sell the businesses. Many others are single, or divorced, young or middle-aged. Despite their diversity, all are part of the growing movement of women toward financial independence.

AWED conducts seminars on personnel and overall management techniques, financing and marketing. It provides help for women with specific problems through its team of business consultants as well. Its services are free and available to any woman in business. The AWED address is 1270 Avenue of the Americas, New York, NY 10020 (telephone number 212-397-0880).

The federal government has attempted to assist women in small business — trying to make up for lost time, we suppose. In 1979, President Carter issued an Executive Order creating a national women's business enterprise policy of affirmative action to aid women-owned businesses. Simply put, that means arrangements for the development, coordination and implementation (a favorite government word) of a national program for women's business enterprise. (A women-owned business was defined as one that is at least 51% owned by a woman or women who also control and operate it.)

Any number of federal agencies have been brought into the act — the SBA, of course, first and foremost. It agreed to establish a goal of $50 million in fiscal 1980 for direct loans to women business owners and initiate a new mini-loan program for women needing less than $20,000 to start or expand their businesses. It also agreed to encourage full participation by women in procurement activities by instructing SBA's Procurement Center Representatives to locate and assist women-owned businesses and to add 15,000 women-owned firms to SBA's new Procurement Automated Source System (PASS) by the end of fiscal 1980.

The Office of Federal Procurement Policy, responsible for the awarding of lucrative government contracts to private firms, set goals for the offering of federal prime contracts approximately doubling the dollar amount of those contracts to women-owned firms in fiscal 1980, to at least $150 million, redoubling this amount in fiscal 1981; and revising government-wide procurement regulations to assure that federal prime contractors increase their use of women-owned firms as subcontractors, from everything from defense to social service research and development projects.

The Farmer's Home Administration launched a major effort to assist women interested in owning their own business and set aside special assistance funds for business women in rural areas. It initiated women's affirmative action outreach program as well, to encourage women business owners to participate in its program.

If you want more information on any of these new programs, including how you can qualify for assistance, write to the Executive Director of the Inter-agency Committee on Women's Business Enterprise, at 1441 L Street, N.W., Room 501, Washington, D.C. 20416.

The SBA has, traditionally, *not* discriminated on the basis of sex, race, color, religion or national origin. All of its services are available to anyone who qualifies, but there are four major areas of assistance that should be of particular interest to anyone not familiar with SBA.

Most important, to most ways of thinking, is *financial* assistance. We have seen some of the loan programs available through SBA; the regular business loan program, known in the trade as 7(a), is the largest and is the one that supply the start-up funds described in this chapter.

Under another program, a business damaged as a result of a natural disaster can borrow up to $500,000 to rebuild or replace its facilities and inventories. (But we still don't recommend building your shop in Tornado Alley!)

Economic Opportunity loans of up to $50,000 can be approved for socially or economically disadvantaged business people. If you think you are eligible for consideration apply through your regional SBA office. Find out for sure.

Non-physical disaster loans help small business owners squeezed by federal air and water pollution and occupational safety and health regulations or offset problems caused by government activities such as highway construction or closing of military bases (if 90% of your customers, for example, are from old Ft. Smith down the street) or to relieve economic injuries resulting from energy or material shortages (did you try to hold a Grand Opening during New York City's great blackout?)

Small contractors can obtain Surety Bond Guarantees to enable them to bid on government and non-government contracts. This program assists small contractors by giving up to 90% of losses of private surety (bonding and loan agencies) companies on a particular contract which SBA has agreed to guarantee.

Small Business Investment Companies (SBICs) are an extra added attraction from SBA for companies needing equity capital or long-term financing. The privately owned SBIC (licensed, regulated and sometimes in part financed by SBA) makes equity investments in long-term loans to small firms for the sound financing of their operations, expansion and modernization. The SBIC may also provide management assistance. The initial minimum private investment required in a SBIC is $150,000 and can go as high as $1 million, depending on the location and proposed operations of the business. The SBA will loan or guarantee loans to SBICs amounting generally to twice the *paid-in capital* (capital paid in by the businessperson).

Regional SBA offices make available all kinds of *management assistance* through training courses, workshops, seminars, films and publications. Much of the formal training offered is co-sponsored with educational institutions, professional associations, local civic and business organizations, so it is up-to-date, practical information.

SBA has a management assistance staff that is augmented by experienced volunteer business people from SCORE (Service Corps of Retired Executives) and ACE (Active Corps of Executives). It provides in-depth counseling on an individual basis; many of our interviewees said that their SCORE or ACE volunteers really made a difference in pulling their businesses out of trouble.

The SBA also has a Small Business Institute program which includes over 20,000 business administration students from all over the country who take on small business client problems as part of their college curriculums. A must for any prospective small business owner is the SBA pre-business workshop, a one-day session to help you determine whether you are ready to set up shop. When you emerge into the light of day after your session, you will have a workable business plan in your hands, and potentially more help later.

And, finally, each SBA office has a library of over 300 books on specific businesses that can be used by anyone, a kind of master's degree in business, offered free of charge.

Although *procurement* sound risque, it, simply stated, is the term for government purchase, by contract, of goods and services from private companies. To keep small companies from being overlooked when the money is being handed out, SBA works with government departments to see that they set aside prime contracts for small businesses and encourages the big contractors to subcontract to smaller companies. When a small firm is the low bidder on a contract but the Feds question whether the little guy can deliver the goods, SBA will provide a certificate of competency that attests to the company's credit strength and production capacity. (Actually delivering the 10,000 widgets or gadgets will be up to you, however.)

If you are a small business person who happens to be a woman or a minority person, you may be eligible for inclusion under the SBA's B (a) procurement program, as was Linda Donato. Prime contracts from government agencies are contracted, purposely, to "socially or economically disadvantaged" firms; these can be sources of big money, as more and more women in the government's channeling of supplies of surplus property and resources into the small business community.

If all of these attempts, provisions, negotiations and bids sound distant from your day-to-day struggle to earn a living, remember that they translate into one word — money — for qualified businesses. Your craft shop may not be geared up to supply the infantry with hand-knitted mittens, but if your business is one that has business with the government, you will want to know about attempts to put you on a competitive fotting with the big guys.

The word advocacy means to speak for, and the SBA's *advocacy* program speaks for the small business community, all of it. Naturally, SBA wants to keep the views and interests of the small business community in general, before the Congress and other government bodies but it wants to represent segments of the community as well. A "Women in Business" coordinating committee at the national level is one attempt; an outreach program to inform women's groups of the kinds of assistance SBA offers is another; and the

National Federation of Business and Professional Women's Clubs, Inc. has agreed to counsel business women in conjunction with SBA. SBA has a first rate guide for women called *A Directory of Federal Government Business Assistance Programs for Women Business Owners.* It may not sound like a best seller, but it should be. Get a copy from your SBA regional office if you are interested.

A Credit To Your Sex

Since the passage of the Equal Credit Opportunity Act in 1977, women have found it much easier to receive credit in their own names. It is not necessary to recount all of the difficulties women faced gaining credit prior to the Act. Let's just say, if you ever wondered how a "non-person" might be treated by lenders, you should have tried to convince them that you deserved a loan as a divorced or widowed woman or were single without a loan history, trying to obtain credit under you maiden name or a fully employed young woman who might some day start a family. Fortunately, that is all changed. Although no one has a God-given right to credit, a lender now must apply the same standards of credit worthiness to all applicants, whether they are named Dennis or Denise.

Creditors use a number of criteria to rate you as a credit risk: how much you earn, what kinds of savings and investments you have, what other sources of income you have, how you earn your living, how long you have been employed or have lived at the same address, whether you own or rent your home. They may also examine your credit record — how much you owe, how often you have borrowed money and how reliably you have paid it back.

Basically, the lender wants to be sure you *can* repay him his money and — equally important — that you *want* to pay him back.

In brief, the Equal Credit Opportunity Law guarantees:

• You can't be refused credit just because you are a woman or because of your marital status.

• You can't be refused credit if the creditor decides to discount your income because you are of child-bearing age and may leave the workforce.

• You can't be refused credit because the creditor won't consider regular alimony or child support payments as part of your income.

• You have credit in your own name — maiden or married, — if you are credit worthy in all other regards.

• When you apply for credit on your own, relying on your own income, information about your spouse or his co-signature can be required only under limited circumstances.

• You can keep your own accounts and your own credit history even if you change your marital status.

• You can build up your personal credit record even if married because new accounts must be carried in the names of both husband and wife if both use the account or both are liable for its balance.

• You can't be denied credit without being told why.

• A creditor may not purposely delay your loan and, if action is taken on your loan, you must be notified within 30 days of the decision. If credit has been denied, you must be notified in writing and either given an explanation or told that you are entitled to one. You have these same rights if a credit account is closed.

If you are denied credit, try to find out why. You may be able to solve the problem just by letting the lender know your rights. If you think you have been discriminated against, you can sue for damages. As you can see, times have changed since the days when lenders could lump women, children and mentally-handicapped individuals in the same "useless" pile and ignore them. In today's society, credit is virtually a necessity of life for many people. It can open a lot of doors for the small businessperson — don't give up your opportunity to establish a good credit rating just because one lender tries to give you the cold shoulder.

If You Are A Minority Of One....

The Minority Business Development Agency (MBDA), part of the office of Minority Business Enterprise, is supposed to promote and expand minority small businesses. These days, almost everyone believes he qualifies as "economically disadvantaged" but Black, Hispanic, Native American and Asian people are considered victims of chronically disadvantaged circumstances and so are eligible for special assistance. (Although women as a group are not considered a disadvantaged minority, if you are an Hispanic or other minority woman, you, obviously, qualify.)

The MBDA conducts research that identifies private sector opportunities in marketing, gaining capital, purchasing, retailing, wholesaling and manufacturing. Your contact with these programs will probably occur in the field, where the local offices (known as business development organizations) provide you with management and technical assistance. Identifying, attracting and advising qualified candidates for MBDA programs; supplying the local minority business community with information about future business opportunities, helping minority businesses prepare their business plans, assisting with loan applications and helping firms establish contacts with the financial community all are part of this agency's job.

If you have the urge to go into the construction industry, specialized assistance is available through another MBDA local agency and the construction contractor assistance center. This agency focuses on construction contractors, a highly specialized and technical industry traditionally impervious to penetration by outsiders.

The SBA has also developed a system called the Minority Vendors Program (MVP) to identify minority firms which can furnish products and services to major corporations and government agencies. A large corporation notifies SBA's offices that it is interested in buying from a minority firm and specifies where it wants the product or service delivered. The SBA then makes a computer search to match the request with minority firms that can provide the requested services, kind of like a computer dating service for business. For more information on this program, contact the Associate Administrator for Minority Small Business, SBA, Minority Vendors Program, 1441 L Street, N.W., Room 317, Washington, D.C. 20416.

Being Part Of A Franchise

Many franchisers have developed special programs for minority business people on their own. One requires a two percent down payment which is matched by the franchisor with a 98% financing arrangement and a year of training; another involves a joint venture between a minority business and the established franchisor; each company contributes funds equally, but all responsibility for the daily operation belongs to the minority-owned company.

Remember SBICs? There are some that specialize in providing equity funds, long-term loans and management assistance to minority firms. The SBA may guarantee up to 90% of a loan made by a lending institution to certain SBICs and provide other assistance as well, in a program that should not be viewed as charity or giveaways, but a business-like solution to a national economic challenge.

The Disabled Businessperson: A Remedy For Success

"I wanted to be independent, to make it on my own, despite the cerebral palsy, and I did it. I went into the antique business because I enjoyed meeting the public, reading and reviewing books, newspapers, stereo cards and other communication materials that are my specialty. I travel all over, from city to city, taking part in antique shows or doing my own buying but the hard work is worth it. If you have a disability, don't be afraid to go into business for yourself. Despite all the new laws designed to help handicapped people, many of us still have trouble finding a good job. Being your own boss eliminates many of these problems — you can decide what you can do and how you will do it. I often see people in wheel chairs, and with other disabilities, running their exhibits at antique shows. Physical limitations don't have to be barriers — not in this business. People with disabilities shouldn't live down to others' expectations, but live up to their own abilities and goals."   WALTER GROSSMAN, antiquarian bookseller.

Thousands of disabled people have discovered on their own, just as Walter Grossman did, the realities of being your own boss despite a handicap. If you are among them, you may have based your decision to go into business for yourself on the skills, abilities and interests you have rather than those you lack. Every state has an Office (or Bureau) of Vocational Rehabilitation that offers counseling, testing and training to handicapped persons. These offices are ready and able to help you determine whether a business on your own is feasible. They can also provide information of real value to you as you plan a business career. A list of these offices appears at the end of this book in the Appendix.

The Small Business Administration will make loans to non-profit organizations that hire handicapped workers and to small concerns owned by handicapped persons. To be eligible for a *Handicapped Assistance loan,* a non-profit company must operate the interest of handicapped persons who contribute at least 75% of the man-hours required for the direct production of goods or services generated by the organization. Loan funds may be used for working capital or for construction or conversion of facilities, but may not be used for training, education, housing or other supportive services for handicapped employees.

Loans are also made to profit-oriented small business concerns which are owned 100% by handicapped persons. The handicap must be such that it limits the person's ability to engage in "normal" competitive business practices without the assistance of the SBA.

Veteran's Preferences ....

If you are a veteran, the SBA offers you a wide range of assistance programs designed to help you start a business or expand one you already own. Every district and branch office of the SBA has a veteran affairs officer who concentrates on veterans' concerns. The SBA is under special mandate to give particular consideration to veterans of the Armed Forces and their survivors and dependents; many people who are eligible for this assistance are not aware of it — and you one of them?

Of the millions of veterans in the U.S., few seem to know of the opportunities small business offers them. The resources are there — consider taking advantage of them. You have earned the right! Contact the SBA nearest you for details.

CHAPTER SEVEN

How The Private Sector Watches Out For Your Interests

Throughout MAKING IT ON YOUR OWN, we have been talking about small business on a personal, individual basis. You may want to think about exactly how you, as a small business person, fit into the economy and the community. What kind of impact can you have? Plenty. Of all the non-farm businesses in this country, 97% are considered "small" according to the SBA definitions. Small business accounts for nearly $7 out of every $10 in sales made by retailers and wholesalers annually. Nearly 80% of all U.S. businesses (excluding farms) employ fewer than ten people. The small business part of the economy creates more jobs than any other; it provides, directly or indirectly, the livelihood of over 100 million Americans — that's almost half of every one now living in the United States.

Small business is big business — according to the impact it has on our way of life. Although you may be a single person in a tiny shop in a small town, you are part of an enormous contingent of people who have many of the same problems, needs and goals.

Many studies have shown that small businesses are providing the lion's share of individual innovation and gains in production with the most employment growth. That means that small business is important to both the government and the private sector. We have seen how helpful the SBA can be in its influence and assistance to the small business person although some may resent the government's intervention. "Learn how to become aware of your responsibilities to the community and become more involved in making sure that government does not over-regulate small business," warns Cynthia Helvey. Most people accept some government involvement as a part of modern life in a complex society.

That doesn't mean that private business has let the government rule the roost; many top corporate executives have gone to bat for small business, since many of them started that way. Listen to what a few of them have to say about *you:*

"Small business has been the economic backbone of American life since the earliest colonial days. Traders, craftsmen and merchants spurred the economy and played a vital role in the nation's westward movement and growth. They helped create the multitude of opportunities which have become the hallmark of our free enterprise system — a system which has made American progress the envy of the world.

"In my opinion, the future of small business in our country is going to have a great deal to do with helping the United States economy remain strong as we come down after 25 years of absolutely cornucopian growth to a rather slower-growing economy.

". . . . we are going to have to look to small business to pick up some of the slack to provide note only more jobs, but jobs for which, over the next decade, absorb all the energy and talents of the biggest, best-educated and

potentially the most capable labor force in United
States history."

CARTER HENDERSON, co-director of the Princeton Center
for Alternative Futures at the House of Representatives
Hearings on The Future of Small Business in America.
(Nov. 1978)

"Frankly, I am concerned about the future of small
business. Our economy relies on the vitality and
innovation that small business generates. Keeping small
business healthy ought to be an important social issue in
the country.

"Jobs depend on this. Our ability to contain inflation
depends on this because competition and productivity
are inflation's greatest enemies. There are other areas
where we must rely on the initiative and energy of
individuals and individual business.

"A free and healthy society depends, for its existence,
upon a competitive economy. The kind of over-
regulation we are suffering today is destroying
competition. We must do something about it.

"Small business is too important a factor in the
economic and social fabric of American life to permit it
to wane. Our society was built on imagination and on
daring. If we ever lose this in our society, we will have
lost those very qualities that, for generations, made
American business the economic wonder of the world.
Unless small business thrives, nothing else will.

"Every day, over and over, the American dream finds
reaffirmation in its small businesses. We've had the
dream since we began this country. It's part of our
heritage. If you start small, and you work hard, and you
have a good idea, you can make good. Built into the
dream is a kind of stubborn insistence that a really free
society lets a man take risks, his own risks, if he wants
to take them.

"We all have a stake in the future of small business.
Let's all join in the fight to preserve it."

RALPH LAZARUS, chairman, Federated Department Stores
of Ohio, presented at The Center for Small Business,
Chamber of Commerce of the United States, Washington,
D.C., 1980.

These are powerful words, words that are being backed
up by deeds. Particularly in the area of vocational education,
steps have been taken to get the attention of educators and to
encourage them to focus on earlier training and preparation
for business. J. S. Russell (1980) in his article, "Let's Get
Bullish About Small Business," has said, "The federal
government has a support and assistance role to play in small
business development but the mover, the real agent for
change, is the educational community, particularly vocational education." The major findings of the Task Force
report, completed in 1974, hold true today:

• The primary cause of business failure is lack of
management and business skills.

• There is a chronic shortage of trained talent to meet
present and future needs for owners and managers.

• Small business education and training must become
an integral part of a national education strategy.

• Entrepreneurship as a career opportunity is ignored
by the educational system.

• There are a wide range of resources available now at
the national, state and local levels.

The government cannot ensure the success of your
business, only you can do that. But here are some organizations that can help you do it better:

• Chamber of Commerce of the United States
1615 H Street, N.W.
Washington, D.C. 20062
(For state industrial directories and information on business in all of
the states, as well as foreign countries.)

- The American Association of Minority Enterprise
  Small Business Investment Companies (SBIC)
  1413 K Street, N.W.
  Washington, D.C. 20005
  (Assists with management training seminars and technical
  assistance.)
- Resources for Women, Inc.
  104 Walnut Avenue, Suite 212
  Santa Cruz, CA 95060
  (Publications to assist women in business, as well as seminars and a
  wide range of services.)
- Small Business Reporter
  c/o Bank of America
  Department 3120, P. O. Box 37000
  San Francisco, CA 94137
  (Issues in small business, including profiles on a variety of
  businesses.)
- National Association of Accountants
  919 3rd Avenue
  New York, NY 10022
  (Offers free assistance to those starting a business. They have
  chapters in every state.)
- Dun and Bradstreet Marketing Services
  99 Church Street
  New York, NY 10007
  (For information on business management.)
- National Association of Women Business Owners
  2000 P Street, N.W.
  Washington, D.C. 20036
  (A membership organization providing a wide range of services,
  including seminars.)
- International Council for Small Business
  UW — Extension
  929 N. Sixth Street
  Milwaukee, WI 53203
  (Publications, seminars, etc. dealing with international aspects of
  small business.)
- National Small Business Association
  1604 K Street, N.W.
  Washington, D.C. 20006
  (Membership organization provides conferences, seminars and
  legislative functions.)
- The Small Business Foundation of America, Inc.
  69 Hickory Drive
  Waltham, MA 02154
  (Gives and receives grants in the area of small business research,
  conducts seminars and awareness programs for the public.)
- National Federation of Independent Business
  150 West 20th Avenue
  San Mateo, CA 94403
  (Provides legislative leadership in behalf of small business.)

- Center for Women Policy Studies
  2000 P Street, N.W.
  Washington, D.C. 20036
  (For information on women and business.)
- American Women's Economic Development Corporation
  1270 Avenue of the Americas
  New York, NY 10019
  (Provides a counseling service to assist women in or starting a business.)
- National Retail Merchants Association
  100 West 31st Street
  New York, NY 10001
  (Provides films, books and materials for training and educational purposes.)
- American Crafts Council
  National Headquarters
  22 West 55th Street
  New York, NY 10019
  (Provides members with a wide range of seminars, including when and where craft shows are held in the United States.)
- Urban Business Assistance Corporation
  Graduate School of Business Administration
  New York University
  90 Trinity Place
  New York, NY 10006
  (Provides courses and assistance to small business persons. Priority given to minorities and women.)

CHAPTER EIGHT

Postscript — Business People Speaking for Themselves

We thought it would be appropriate if we let some of the people we interviewed have the final word on their success in small business. They are, after all, the experts on the ups and downs, the satisfactions and disappointments of Making It On Their Own.

"Confidence in my own work was the key factor in my business success."

"I needed the opportunity of expressing myself without having people constantly looking over my shoulders."

"I wanted to be independent — to make it on my own and I proved to myself that I could."

"Bill enjoys being his own boss and also gets satisfaction knowing that the tasks we perform are important to other people."

"My business grew out of a marriage of opportunity and personal objectives."

"I like being in my own small business because I'm the boss."

"The product you sell is basically yourself."

The above are a sampling of some of the quotes made by people in their own businesses. There are, of course, many more quotes and ideas expressed by those interviewed for this book. You will find many similarities, but also many differences in the interviews that follow.

It is one thing to develop checklists about how to be successful in business and "how to do it" manuals for those interested in starting a business, but the *most enjoyable* and *informative* part of writing this book was our interviews with real people who "made it" in their own business.

We developed a list of names of successful small business people in a variety of businesses and from different walks of life, educational backgrounds and ages. Representation included women and men, one person with cerebral palsy (but not handicapped when it came to operating his own business) and those from varying ethnic and racial groups.

While those interviewed came from within a thirty mile radius of Washington, D.C., which includes Maryland and Virginia, the types of business represented in the interviews have national and, in many cases, international applicability. Some of the businesses included direct mail advertising, retail book stores, printing, photographic studio, house remodeling, retail shoes, retail candy, food catering and others. The type of business may not have been the most important feature of these interviews, although we wanted to talk with people in a broad range of activities. What we hope you will notice most are the attitudes and ideas expressed by these entrepreneurs. Some were fairly new to the world of business, while others were thinking of retiring or already have done so.

The interviews were fascinating and revealed much about the motivation and desire to succeed by those involved. Their insights, advice and willingness to share ideas with others aspiring to start a business on their own was both informative and commendable. While all of those interviewed were extremely busy people, they stopped what they were doing and gave freely of themselves with the notion that someone just might be able to use their advice or that someone might be encouraged *to try it on their own.* Incidentally, some even gave us interviews late in the evenings after having put in long hours in their business.

Everyone interviewed was asked the questions from a *Structured Interview Format Sheet* shown at the end of this chapter. The questions included such areas as:

- Why did you go into small business?

- How many dollars did you need to get started?

- What gives you the greatest satisfaction having your own small business?

- Does your family help make a difference in your business success?

- Is this a good time to enter a small business?

The above are a sampling of some of the questions asked of each interviewee.

As you read the excerpts of these interviews, you will notice one thing in common. All were enthusiastic about their businesses and themselves. As the interviewers of the people who made up the heart of this book, we are deeply appreciative. We know that you will find these brief excerpts interesting and informative.

David Adler of Washington, D.C.

David Adler is the owner of a corporation called Adler International, Ltd. David grew up in the advertising business and didn't like expending all his effort on someone else's project. He came up with the concept of a magazine and called it *Dossier Magazine.* He has been in business five years and has 12 full-time employees and 25 free-lance people on a part-time basis. He works about 60 hours each week.

In order to get started, David borrowed $6,000 from a bank on his father's signature. It took David about three and a half years to break even financially.

What David likes most about being in business for himself is "the total creative flow, not being involved in committees, and not having to work for other people. You live and abide by your own mistakes and successes."

David's father was his greatest help in starting his business. He feels that his business is "a family oriented business. There is a family loyalty. The hours we put in are done for the business and not for personal success."

The greatest satisfaction David receives in his business "is to see the product *(Dossier Magazine)* come out at the end of the month. That is seeing the end result and the financial statements when they are profitable."

David's future goals are to make the business a "self-perpetuating enterprise and to be able to expand into other publishing ventures. I want to get into other products in the magazine field and in other cities other than Washington, D.C."

David tries to be active in the publishing community. He reads journals, attends seminars on various subjects and frequently talks to people in the business. He says, "People love to talk about what they are doing."

If David had it to do all over again, he would probably do it differently. He says, "some things we started to do were practically impossible. Our system has changed about a dozen times. It changes at every change in growth. We are now at a point where we are trying to set up what we need for the future."

David tells men and women considering a career in small business, "If you don't have the stomach for it, don't get involved. Reality hits you in the face every day because if you can't pay a bill, you have to collect money to pay it." He also says, "You have to watch your accounts receivable and your accounts payable. I believe more in hard work than in marketing techniques. Pitch in and be willing to do anything whether it is turning lights off to anything else."

One of the most important suggestions that David made was to keep good business records and good monitoring of the system. He says, "keep charts and know where everything is in various departments of your business in terms of inventory and financial records." He also says, "Hire good people. Sometimes it is worthwhile to pay people more than you're getting out of the business in order to build the business."

David believes that business will be better this coming year because "it gets better every day."

David thinks that now is probably the best time to enter a small business. He feels the only way you can go is up. David says, "A good salesman can go into almost anything and make good if he is a sales manager type. If you want security, go into the government and get your month's vacation each year."

David's philosophy about small business is that "small business should be a passion. Don't go into business to sell something you don't care about. Have a passion for the entire operation. Try as hard as you can. Whether you fail or succeed, you grow."

Nancy Block of Silver Spring, Maryland

Nancy is the sole proprietor of a photography studio where she specializes in portraits, family group pictures and special occasions. She especially enjoys "capturing family love" in the pictures she takes. A look at the examples of her photography around her studio (which is in her home) is a real tribute to her work and the pride she takes in it.

Nancy went into business for herself about two years ago. She was convinced that was the way to go after a bad experience with a partnership in a photography studio. She stated that she was "tired of making money for other people and that it seems others were getting rich on my talents." Nancy exudes a lot of self-confidence and knows she has a real talent when it comes to taking pictures of people. "I love people and it is a challenge to get their total personality on film. Sometimes it takes a while, but I usually capture the right pose — this is exciting to me."

Nancy opened her own studio with an initial cost of around $2,000. Her main piece of equipment was a good quality camera. She pointed out that she is selling her talent as a photographer. "I create a product based on my own feelings and that of my subject and this can't be manufactured." Nancy stated that it took about six months to break even financially on her investment.

Nancy notes that her greatest help in starting on her own was herself. Knowing her talents and limitations were most important. "Confidence in my own work was the key factor."

While Nancy does not have any employees, she will use a back-up photographer at a special occasion such as a wedding, in case of emergency. Currently, she would rather take care of her business with the special care she can give to each customer. By not supervising others, she has more time and flexibility to do the job the way she wants it done. She enjoys this type of responsibility and this arrangement allows her to work about twenty hours in a typical week. This schedule also gives her freedom to pursue her other interests.

Nancy's greatest satisfactions come from pleasing her customers. "They appreciate the work I did for them and so far I have not had one complaint." She is quick to add that, "I don't know how much longer that record can go on." She relishes the fact that she is creating beautiful memories for people and "they (her customers) will remember me long after I'm gone, as they look at the albums or portraits I've done."

Nancy's goals are to try to make some money now and also establish a good reputation for her photography.

Nancy noted that for twenty years, she was a housewife and spent a lot of time doing volunteer work for charity. As the children grew up and she had more time for outside activities, she decided that "charity begins at home." She initially went to work setting up a photography studio, since she had worked at this business when she was in her late teens. She is basically self-taught and has strong artistic interests and abilities.

To keep up with events and changes in her field, Nancy reads photography books, but she notes that most of her knowledge still comes from "listening and observing others." She is a keen student of human nature and uses this sense in capturing the feelings of her subjects.

Nancy cautions others not to go into a partnership. "Try to do it alone, if at all possible. You may have those low moments, but if you have the talent and self-confidence to use it, you'll do all right. If you don't have the talent, you had better go get a job with someone else. I started with an advertisement of a one-dollar-off coupon in a neighborhood paper. This brought in business and I knew I was on my way."

Nancy's advice to those starting a photography business is simple, but very sound. "Be sure of yourself and your talent. No one can take that away from you. Be frank with your customers and don't be a penny-pincher. If there is a problem or issue to be solved, find out the best solution in order to avoid making this error again. Try to take positive action and quickly. Indecision can be the worst trait in the world."

Throughout the interview, Nancy stressed the pride in her talents and work produced by her. One trait that exemplified her was a deep feeling of responsibility to her customer — she always produced. Whether she was working for someone else or as her own boss, satisfying the customer was and is her main objective. Pride in her work and talent came through this interview loud and clear!

Gail and Len Briskman of Potomac, Maryland

Gail and Len are the owners of a corporation with retail stores in six major regional malls. Candy and nuts are their business and their stores go by the names, "Jo Ann's Nut House" or "Chez Chocolat."

Both Gail and Len had experience in the retail sales business before this latest venture. It has been over two years since Gail has been totally involved in the day-to-day managing of the stores. Len handles the financial aspects of the stores since his background is business and finance. He also had extensive experience in the financial part of major corporations.

Gail explained that she carefully thought about the reasons retail candy sales would be a good business to develop. "I realized that the majority of shoppers are women and if the price were low enough, she would buy on impulse. This is mainly a cash purchase and there is little thinking or planning for the purchase of these items. Candy is a widely appreciated food and it is enjoyed by all ages."

In getting started, they had to get some loans due to the relatively large capital outlay needed for equipment such as showcases to display the candy and nuts, lighting fixtures, scales and cash registers. The amount of money needed to start will vary, depending on the type of equipment and location of the business.

Gail now supervises about 55 employees and notes that she enjoys training people to work in her stores. "This business has opened up a whole new area of my life and potential that I never knew I had. It forced me into a total re-evaluation of my lifestyle. I went from housewife and mother to a full-time business person." Gail enjoys seeing the business she created running smoothly and also likes seeing those she trained doing a fine job.

Gail felt that a store in a good location could break even financially in about one year. Presently, Gail works six days per week and spends five hours each day at one or more of the locations. She is also on the phone for about an hour in the evenings when she is home to handle questions from her employees. When she first started in business, Gail was putting in about 12 hour days. It also took about three weeks to train new staff.

Her family plays a very important role in her life. Gail's 14 year old is learning to work at the business and "the older he gets, the more I can count on him to help in the business. If anything unexpected happened, I have confidence that he could really fill in very well in helping to run things."

Future goals of the business center around financial security and making sure the stores are secure. "I don't expect to open any more stores and would like to regulate things to the point where I can work less hours and, therefore, have more freedom."

Gail attends twice-yearly candy shows, as well as gift shows, in order to keep up with the latest items and ideas in the candy business.

When asked if she would have done anything differently, Gail responded she would have done it essentially the same. She added, "I did have only a little knowledge of how much I was capable of doing."

Her advice to others thinking of starting their own business was to do plenty of research. "Don't fall in love with a product just because you like it — make sure there is a market for it and then check out the location." Expect to spend a lot of time starting and running a business. Don't expect to run a business from a telephone booth. This is especially true for persons that have young children in the home."

Gail is anxious to help other women who have not been in the labor market for a number of years and will hire women whenever she gets the chance. She feels that they know much about management, inventory control and personal relations, having maintained a household, which is no easy or simple task. Gail has found the women she has hired to be most loyal and responsible employees.

Her final piece of advice was, "Make sure you take yourself and your capabilities seriously. This will really help you in the business world."

Judy Diamond of Washington, D.C.

Judy Diamond is the sole owner of a corporation which trades under the names of Insurance Research, Inc. and ERISA Benefit Funds. This very ambitious person began her first venture in June of 1960. She started Insurance Research, Inc. capitalizing on her experience with a life insurance company in New York City. She was aware of a tax ruling which meant that insurance companies had to provide certain financial details and her company performs the research needed to find that information. For example, Judy is responsible for the 1980-81 Financial Directory of Pension Funds and it is available in 84 separate directories. This specialized research service helps firms specializing in the retrieval of information filed by corporations, associations, unions and political subdivisions. All this information is put on tape. Judy has been in business a total of 20 years and employs 17 people.

In order to start her business, Judy borrowed about $13,000. She noted that this was a rough time in her life since she was in the midst of a divorce, owed a number of debts and cared for four small children. She overcame all of these hurdles and once her business began to flourish, it took about three months for Judy to break even and see a profit.

Mrs. Diamond stated that she was not really familiar with advertising and marketing, but learned quickly. "A friend said, here's a copy of a book on the subject and I read it. This same friend acted as my mentor and was very helpful." Judy noted that you never know where good ideas will come from and has learned much about business methods from the various salespeople that she meets.

Judy currently works about fifty hours per week and really loves her work. She stated, "I can't wait to go to the office, even on Saturday." Her family has also made a difference in her business since her children have been very helpful. When they were young, they used to help stuff envelopes.

One of Judy's greatest satisfactions about her business is that she creates her own products. She enjoys creating something and putting it into motion. "It's like having a baby," says Judy. She also stated that, "I don't like someone telling me what to do — I feel boxed in. This is another reason why I enjoy being my own boss."

If Judy had to do it all over again, she would do it the same way. However, she feels she would not have waited as long to understand the importance of marketing and advertising. She says she could have made a lot more money much earlier. "People who go into small business with the idea of making a fast buck are wrong," says Judy. "It is hard work and you have to build it brick by brick. You also have to take risks and you must spend money in order to make it." Realistic goals, states Judy, are another important factor and "Be sure to give a new product time to catch on."

Judy's future goal is to build the business and then sell it in order to use the money for venture capital, particularly for other small businesses.

Judy is optimistic about her business and feels it will be even better next year. She noted, "I believe there are always opportunities to enter a small business. Every set of changes sets up new opportunities."

Judy Diamond's advice to those planning their own business was, "Be prepared to take a risk. If you're security conscious, forget it and take a job with the government. Be sure to develop some plans and stick with them. Business fails due to a lack of plans." One final point that Judy stressed was "to build an image of quality for yourself and you can do this on your stationery and business cards, etc." She has found this latter advice to be very important in the future of any developing business.

Linda M. Donato of Rockville, Maryland

Linda is the President and owner of a building contracting firm called Lindy Contractors and Associates, Inc. This is the largest woman-owned construction business in the area. Linda has been in business for almost two years.

It is difficult to ascertain how much time Linda works each week, because she also has a full time job for Johnson & Johnson Architects as an administrator. Linda estimates that she works about 80 hours per week on both her job and her business. That makes Linda a very busy person.

In order to get started, Linda borrowed $5,000 and also put in some of her own money. In order to get sales paid on time,

Linda occasionally borrows from herself. It took approximately two months before she broke even. Since Linda feels she started on a shoestring, she says her "biggest challenge was finances. My paying attention to figures was my primary reason for my success in bidding costs." Linda did approximately the same kinds of things for Johnson & Johnson and now uses this experience in her own business.

Linda joined the National Association of Women Business Owners after her own business was established. The Small Business Administration helped her considerably. She attends many seminars and enjoys them tremendously. In addition, Linda has applied for her AA Minority Status. This status is accorded those who have been deprived of government business. As a woman in the construction business Linda feels that she is discriminated against because few women are taken seriously in this business." She feels that she has been working diligently and knows the field. If she receives this status, she will be the first woman to achieve this status in a male-dominated field. This means she will not have to bid on government business, but she will be able to negotiate. Linda has done all her homework in this regard. If Linda gets this status, she hopes to expand her business and employ thousands of people.

Mr. Johnson of Johnson & Johnson has been most helpful with technical questions concerning her venture.

Linda has three daughters and they are all supportive of her and she expects that her older daughter will be involved in the business some day.

Linda suggests that anyone considering a career in small business take advantage of any courses that SBA offers. She says that "I do not have a college education and never missed it. College can be a crutch." She thinks it is important to join various committees and groups in your community. She is active in the General Federation of Women's Colleges, PTA, church groups and is on the board of the country club.

Linda's greatest satisfaction is to be commended when the job is completed. She is optimistic about her own business and feels that she will be able to expand in the very near future.

Linda feels that it is a good time to go into a business if you know what you are doing and prepare for it. Linda is a firm believer that "you can do anything if you believe you can do it."

Joseph Fortuna of Bethesda, Maryland

Joseph is the sole proprietor of Fortuna, Inc., a shoe and luggage retail store with repair services in the rear of the store. He has been in business for 36 years and has 12 employees. When he started in business, his son, then age ten, worked part-time during the school year and full-time during the summer months. "Over the years, 700 young people have worked for me part-time during the school year and during the summer," Joseph proudly states. Joseph's wife also supervises when he is not available.

When Joseph was a boy, he worked for his Dad who owned a shoe shop. When he was old enough to go out on his own, he received a six month apprenticeship with O'Sullivan Rubber Company. Joseph called on the supply house and the shoe shops. "I saw the difference between a successful shoe shop and those who just hang on," stated Joseph. He decided he wanted a business related to shoes; a shoe store in the front and service in the back. Joseph attributes "all of my ideas to my father, grandfather and great-grandfather — they planted the seed!"

The first decision Joseph had to make was location; either the center of Washington or the suburbs, i.e., Bethesda, Maryland. A successful businessman suggested that Joseph locate in the suburbs because a business can grow with the community. Bethesda now has a thriving business district, however, 36 years ago things were very much different.

Joseph borrowed $1,200 from the supplier of his equipment and he also had a small amount of his own capital. When Joseph bought the business there were outstanding jobs to be done which had been paid in advance. Joseph felt that he " ... had a moral obligation to honor them. Word got around that I was honest, a person of integrity and one who did a good job." Joseph used equipment which was not the most expensive and broke even financially within a year.

During most of Joseph's business years, Joseph worked six days a week for 12 hours a day. However, he derives great satisfaction from having his own business. He affectionately states that "The people who come into my store are my friends as well as my customers. They helped me when I needed them. I love my customers and my employees."

Joseph hopes to do many new things in the future which he has not been able to do because of the pressure of his work. He has found time to help someone else start their own business in Newport, Rhode Island.

Mr. Fortuna keeps up-to-date with business in a number of ways. He is active in the National Luggage Association and attends conventions where merchandise is displayed. He also recently attended a brainstorming meeting to improve the quality of luggage.

Joseph feels that if he had to do it all over again, he would do it differently. He "would try to form a small business company with other people to work together and move ahead more rapidly."

Joseph Fortuna has some good advice to men and women considering a career in small business. He emphatically states, "If you are lazy, don't go into small business. Expect to be at the job most of the time so the business does not go off course. Don't try to keep up with the Joneses. Build the business, mind your course, keep costs down, and don't buy expensive equipment until the business warrants it."

Fortuna believes his business will be better next year because new articles are expensive. Therefore, there will be a greater need to use repair services.

Joseph has some further suggestions for those who are considering a small business career. He feels that most high schools, junior colleges and colleges offer courses on most areas of interest. He suggests that you get a part-time job in the particular business in which you are interested. Even if you work at a minimum salary, the experience is very important.

Another important suggestion made by Joseph is to join worthwhile organizations in your community such as Lions, Rotary, Kiwanis, Chamber of Commerce, etc. Sponsor or be a part of a team for youth sports. Joseph emphatically stated, "Help youth — they are the customers of tomorrow."

Edie Fraser of Washington, D.C.

Edie Fraser is the chief executive of a corporation known as Fraser and Associates Public Relations firm. It is probably the largest company of its kind in the Washington, D.C. area operated by a woman, and it has been going strong for close to six years.

Edie started this business realizing that a "different kind of public relations firm was needed, one with a public policy approach in developing advocacy support." Its need is certainly obvious, since there are currently 31 employees.

Edie started her firm with approximately $25,000 of her own money. She sublet space in order to get going at a reasonable cost. "I did not believe in over-extending myself or getting into a deficit situation," stated Edie. She added, "I was convinced that I would make a profit the first year and I did, even though it was a small profit." She broke even in about six months.

To the question who was her greatest help, Ms. Fraser responded that many people have helped in different ways. To name a few, she noted, "external business colleagues that I respect and our own Board of Directors. My husband has been very supportive." She also mentioned that her parents were small business people and the encouragement from her father was probably one of the reasons she is in business today. She also expressed a great deal of admiration for her legal and accounting help and noted, "one of the prerequisites in my establishing this business is that I had an attorney and accountant that I really respected."

What Edie likes most about her small business is "being your own decision-maker, having a sense of creativity and being able to reap the benefits of your profits." Edie also noted that there is a feeling of camaraderie and enthusiasm that you can establish in a small business because there is no bureaucratic framework fostering the attitude that something *cannot be done.* Instead, she stated, "You really develop the attitude that it can and will be done."

Ms. Fraser receives a lot of satisfaction. She puts in about 70 hours a week. "Work fascinates me," she noted, and she enjoys proving to herself how unique her efforts can be. She also enjoys the risk-taking involved in the daily decision-making process so important to her business.

Edie re-emphasized how much her family has contributed to her business success and stated her husband has been "very, very supportive in the pursuit of her career."

Edie has set high standards for herself, and her firm, and has listed her future goals as follows:

1. To be the most successful public relations firm in the United States dealing with public policy issues.

2. Really make a lot of money-not only for myself, but for all of our top employees, and really reaping the benefits.

3. To enjoy professional and personal satisfaction and peace of mind. We can enjoy the fruits of the sustenance of what we do every day.It is a learning experience.

4. Helping as counselors to chief executive officers, which is not typically the case in our business.

To keep up with her field, she attends workshops and seminars as much as she can. "The problem in small business is that you can't because of time limitations. I have taken Japanese lessons because we have a lot of Japanese clients. I try to speak as often as I can, particularly where I am going to make money for speaking. I have attended SBA workshops and have also spoken there. My dad is part of the *SBA Score Program.* He loves it. If every retired business executive could do like my dad, there would be less problems with small business."

If she had to do it all over again, she would not have done anything differently. Edie also provided some excellent tips to others just getting ready to start their own business:

1. "You have to have the right personality traits, including preseverance. You have got to have a business sense. If you have the acumen and commitment to succeed, go ahead, but make sure you do it because it is not easy.

2. Get professional advice, legal advice, tax advice, accounting advice, the whole thing and listen to their advice.

3. Realize in the first couple of years you are going to make a terrible commitment of time and energy. If you are not willing to do it, do not go into small business. You are responsible for a lot of people and their families, their worries and frustrations and you must be able to accept them as well as the laurels and the pleasures of all the success. I think that entrepreneurial support is what we are seeking in making a society great. Small business is beautiful if you are really willing to put the energy, enthusiasm and professionalism behind the commitment. To create something, build it and seeing the finished product is very gratifying."

While Ms. Fraser believes her business will be better this coming year, she didn't know whether this is a good time to go into a small business, but emphasized "it all depends on the type of business you are planning and the type of person you are."

Edie's closing thoughts were enthusiastic and to the point. She stated, "I do think that small business is the backbone of society. One has to be very certain of establishing goals that are obtainable. Whether it is a product or a service, build a solid people-base behind it. You will never be successful unless you build a team of people that are committed to the same objectives that you are. There is the process of planning goals and reassessing what you have acheived on a continual basis. This is very important. If you aren't willing to take the frustrations of it, you ought to be in something else." It was very easy to understand why Edie Fraser is fascinated by business and the satisfactions she described to us, as well as why she is a success.

Jerry Grissett of Washington, D.C.

Jerry had always wanted to own his own business. He owns a combination delicatessen and record shop called Gerry G's Deli and Records, Inc. He had been in business about three months (when this interview took place) and has two employees. Jerry works about 40 hours each week.

In order to get started, Jerry saved $25,000 and used it to develop his business. Since this is a young business, Jerry has not broken even as yet, and all of his profit goes back into the business. However, Jerry said he is "not really going into the hole and that the business is going well."

Jerry likes being in his own business because "I have something I can call my own. I don't have to worry about being without a job when inflation takes over, I don't have to worry about getting fired or being laid-off. I always have something to fall back on. It means security to survive these times." Jerry's greatest satisfaction in owning a small business is having to answer to himself and *no one else.*

Jerry feels that his business would be a more difficult struggle without the help and support of his family. "I really have a nice family," he boasts.

Jerry attends seminars, which he feels will aid him in the development of his small business, and is reading materials to help him in his business.

Jerry had some important advice for those thinking of starting their own business. He stated, "Don't do it like I did — I did it the hard way! I went into it blind." Jerry advises anyone getting into business "to have all the necessary paperwork done before you open your doors. I had to learn day-by-day. Make sure you know what you are doing and when the going gets rough, hang in there. If you stay in and pray to the Lord to hear your prayer, you will find that if you have faith, you will succeed."

"People will tell you a lot of things, but you will never know about business until you're in it yourself," said Jerry. He feels that his business will be better next year because he has a lot to offer and his new ideas could only improve the company.

Jerry has some additional advice for those interested in going into business. He suggests that you "start out small, feel your way slowly and build. Be sure to use your time wisely and don't try to move too fast. Expand your business as you have the money." He also said that, "You have to forget about your personal life. Run your own business and don't have someone else run it for you. Small business is not a piece of cake as I thought it would be before I opened my business."

Jerry's enthusiasm and warmth came through loud and clear and being fairly new to the business world he knows he will succeed. He also realizes he has a lot of hard work and long hours in front of him.

Walter Grossmann of Fairfax, Virginia

Walter is the sole proprietor of an antique business. He is an antiquarian/appraiser who specializes in communicational antiques, such as books, newspapers, stereo cards, photographs and trade catalogs.

Walter has a disability called cerebral palsy but this has not been a handicap as far as his ability to be an antique dealer. His reasons for being in his own business are many. "I wanted to be independent — to make it on my own and I proved to myself that I could." He went into this business because of his interests in reading materials. "I also enjoy meeting the public and I come from a background of independent business people. I guess that accounts for my wanting to deal with people."

"You could easily get started in the antique business for around $2,000." Walter keeps overhead costs low by exhibiting at antique shows and by personal contacts with museum staff who may have an interest in some of his antiques. He pointed out that you can support yourself well in the first year of business, if you are careful in what you buy. "This is important in a depressed economy."

Walter went into business with little help from others. He adds that many antique dealers were always willing to answer his questions and share ideas with him. He is impressed with antique dealers' attitudes toward newcomers to the business and advises others interested in the antique business to ask questions of other dealers, "chances are they will give you good answers."

The hours of his business will vary, but on the average he spends about 50-65 hours a week, depending on the type of antique show he may attend. He does travel quite often from city-to-city doing shows or engaging in buying, "but the hard work is worth it." Walter attends about 25 shows each year, but plans to cut down on this kind of schedule and do more individual selling to curators of museums. He uses part-time help to assist him in the various functions of his business, as needed.

Walter receives a lot of satisfaction from his current status as owner of his own business. "I feel better about myself, my whole image has changed for the better." He deals with people from important museums. Walter tells proudly of recent sales of old newspapers, stereo cards and books to the White House and other collectables to the Smithsonian Institution in Washington, D.C. He deals with some pretty important folks and they are "apparently impressed with the items I have brought to them for their collections."

Walter has also enjoyed the extensive traveling to the various antique shows and views this as if each show were a vacation. He attributes his enjoyment of his particular business and his success on having learned "a correct attitude" from his family who were business people who dealt with people.

Walter's future goals include developing more accounts with individuals and museums interested in the collectables he discovers. He will probably limit his travel to special selected shows and buying trips.

Walter keeps up with information in his trade by close observation at antique shows. He is self-taught at this business and feels that careful examination of his items is the most important feature he had to learn. "Each show that I attend is an education in itself."

Walter had quite a bit of sound advice for others thinking about starting their own business and he related his thoughts to those with a disability. "Be careful about the area of business you are going into and make sure there is a market for your item. Keep good records, once you start your business. Don't be afraid to try it on your own, especially if you have a disability. Despite all the laws in favor of the handicapped, a person with a handicap may have a lot of trouble getting a good job. Being your own boss bypasses many of these employment problems. Now you can decide what you will do and how you will do it.

"Don't worry about accessibility to antique shows. Most of the time, there is easy access into the buildings or other areas used for the shows. I often see people in wheelchairs running their exhibits, so health problems need not be a barrier to developing this kind of business."

Walter's business has been doing well over the past three years. His philosophy should inspire others. His final comment was especially significant to others with a disability. He advised, "Don't just do what people say you should do, because too often they stress your limitations. People with disabilities can do many things and they shouldn't live down to the expectations others place on them, but should try to live up to their own abilities."

Joan and Roger Henebry of Annandale, Virginia

The husband and wife team of Joan and Roger Henebry are partners in a six year old business known as "Performance Marketing." They specialize in automatically typed personal letters, mailing list maintenance, mailing services, including signing, folding, inserting, sorting and stamping mail for delivery, typing of reports and manuscripts, direct mail advertising and fund raising counseling and services. Joan's experience included a range of clerical and artistic skills, while Roger's background was in direct mail advertising, marketing and fund raising. This seems to be a perfect marriage of skills and abilities to successfully operate their own business.

Joan started the business on a small scale about six years ago when she decided to stay home while their daughter was still in school. Joan was typing personalized letters and doing other clerical tasks at home. "I really didn't make much money, but it gave me something useful to do and developed my skills and I also learned new methods. I also enjoyed meeting other people. In those days, many of the contacts were made by Roger."

Once they went into business together, the initial costs were for equipment, advertising, an automatic typewriter and art supplies. During the first two years, these expenditures cost around $10,000. The first three years did not see a huge profit, but there were definite tax advantages to having a small business in the home. They currently do not have any employees and will contract out work that they can't do themselves. "We have reached a plateau in the amount of business we can handle and are a comfortable size business. We also enjoy working ourselves and don't want the responsibility of hiring, payrolls, taxes, paperwork and laying people off." Roger notes that "we like being small and try to control the size of our business."

Joan and Roger get a lot of satisfaction working out of their home. "We work harder now than we have ever worked, but on our slow days we can do things we want to, such as going to the beach or museums when others are at work. Sometimes we each work about 60 to 70 hours per week. This amounts to a 10 or 12 hour day.

In their business, Joan and Roger enjoy the fact that they can earn more money than they could on a salary, since there is more net income left after taxes. Joan also added, "and you don't have to please some dumb boss that may know less than you do about the work. We also get a lot of satisfaction knowing our work is good." Their repeat business attests to this fact.

In order to keep up with new items and methods in their work, they attend "direct mail shows" and computer business shows. "You really need to stay current, since clients are always asking for new and bettery ways to do things. The need for education never stops in this business. Four times per year our computer software changes enabling us to do jobs faster."

Joan and Roger gave some good advice to persons thinking of going into this business. "You have to know the field first." Roger had 25 years' experience in the direct mail business and his contacts were of key importance in their current success. Roger noted that, "Direct mail is a highly specialized field and while we do have some fancy equipment, we need to be good at other aspects as well since we consult with clients and assist in writing effective letters and other types of mail appeals." The personal touch is also a must in this line of work. People need to trust you and have confidence in your products. This means delivering the job when promised and making sure that everything is done right.

They also stressed the importance of knowing your contacts. Each time a new person comes into a company that you deal with, you have to "resell yourself" to that person.

"Much of our work comes to us through recommendations. When a person who has been dealing with us leaves their job, they usually take us with them." This alone tells you something about Joan and Roger's business and what they see as important factors in their success.

Future plans include the use of the latest equipment to make their job easier and their products even better.

Kenneth Rosen of Rockville, Maryland

Ken is the sole owner of a corporation called the American Candy & Tobacco Wholesalers, a wholesale candy and tobacco business. His corporation was formed under "subchapter S" of the Internal Revenue Code which provides for a tax savings, especially when beginning a small business.

Ken had worked for a large wholesale tobacco company for a few years and gained significant managerial experience. He felt very comfortable about this type of wholesale business. When he heard that the company for which he worked was being sold to another company, Ken decided to try his hand at his own wholesale business. Ken had often thought about owning his own company, but now the time seemed right.

To get started, Ken needed around $70,000, and relied on his own personal reputation to raise the needed capital. He didn't need much equipment. In fact, a small truck for picking up stock and delivery was the major item. Ken depended on quick turn-around of his merchandise. That is, "buying it today and selling it today on a cash-on-delivery basis." He notes that he went directly to the manufacturer rather than buying his goods from suppliers. This saved time and money and established important contacts.

Ken did well from the day he started business, since overhead costs were minimal. After three years as his own boss, he now has twelve employees.

Ken spends about 65 hours per week tending his business. For the first six months of business, 100 hours per week was usually the rule.

When asked who was his greatest help in starting out, Ken states, "I can't point to anyone but myself. I had no one else to depend on and it was a frightening decision to make."

Ken states that his wife has certainly made a difference in his success in business. "She has been my biggest booster and has always been a source of encouragement to keep on trying." Ken's wife, Myra, has also kept him aware of his limits and the need to slow down when he was working too hard.

Ken indicates that "my stepfather was a great inspiration to me — he ran his own business, although different from mine. He helped me to see the merits of hard work and determination."

Ken's satisfactions about his own business are many. He notes that "gathering together a group of employees and seeing an efficient and viable organization that runs well with or without me is gratifying." Ken feels that he is the most expendable person in the business. He can now leave it for short periods of time and "it runs as smoothly as if I were still there." Another key satisfaction is that it affords him an income that allows him to do more of the things he likes to do.

When asked about future plans, Ken would like to diversify over the next five to ten years by developing other business to adapt to changes in markets and buying habits. "The new business would be natural extensions of products we now sell." He will be monitoring the change in the market on an ongoing basis.

Ken keeps up with the events and changes in the wholesale business by going to association conferences about twice per year. It was difficult to get away for meetings in the first two years of business. He is a member of the National Candy Wholesalers Association (NCWA) located at 1425 K Street, N.W., Washington, D.C. 20005. "For those fairly new in this business and with no colleagues to talk with, the NCWA was a valuable source of information. They were always willing to assist me and often helped me to get over the isolation I felt, since you can't go to competitors for trade secrets."

Ken wouldn't have done much differently were he to start over again. "I did it the traditional way — lots of hard work and determination."

Ken did indicate that one should set realistic goals and keep close track of progress. Perhaps he might not have pushed himself as hard during the first two years. "You can get caught up in a whirlpool of constant work and pushing yourself and this can ruin family relationships and your health." The answer, he feels, was to set both short and long-term goals and watch your progress.

Ken gives a number of tips to those starting their own business. He advises against bringing your spouse into the business. "If your spouse is working, it is important to have the security of at least one steady income. If both your incomes are dependent on the business, it could be dangerous, especially during the start-up period.

For those persons thinking about entering a small business, Ken feels "there is no better time than now to start." More and more large companies are diversifying and buying up smaller businesses and "as these companies get larger, they tend to lose control over some local markets and gaps in the local market occur. There is always room for some small business person to fill these gaps." In this case, Ken stated, "smallness means better relationships and more business."

Being small has other advantages, Ken noted. "You can solicit the business of large companies without feeling intimidated. Many people are willing to give the newcomer a chance since, quite often, the person you are going to can identify with your situation. But, you have to take a chance and try to sell the larger companies. You have nothing to lose and you need to take chances and try."

Ken has an interesting philosophy about hiring and employees. He doesn't deal with his employees in the traditional way. "People want more than an income these days. They also want security. You get what you pay for — I don't believe in hiring cheap help and I get better people who want to work, try harder and who are trustworthy. Many of my employees work more than a forty-hour week for no additional pay, since all are on salaries. The incentive is that there is profit-sharing among all employees."

Ken, at age 29, provides a number of excellent insights into what makes his small business successful. His personal philosophy and characteristics have a lot to do with this success. He has built a solid team of employees, based on trust, a lot of common sense and the desire to do the best possible job for his accounts. Throughout the interview, his enthusiasm, self-confidence and integrity came through very loud and clear.

McDonald Robinson of Washington, D.C.

McDonald Robinson is the sole owner of the AAAA Driving School. He started his business in 1972 and has one full-time employee. He employs from one to nine people, depending upon need.

McDonald earned an instructor's license in order to drive because he likes the idea of being his own boss. He initially worked for another driving company and made very good money. Therefore, he decided to go out on his own.

In order to get started, McDonald purchased a car with driver controls. This cost him $200. He also needed about $150 more for a license and fees in order to get established. Because of the limited capital needed to get started, he met his expenses in the first month.

McDonald works from 60 to 120 hours a week. He emphatically states, "I like being in my own small business because I'm the boss. I am in charge of myself. If you are not a self-starter, don't go into small business. If you want Saturday and Sunday off, don't go into small business."

McDonald feels that his family has not made a difference in his success. He states, "It would be easier if I had a wife and family. A wife is an indispensable part of a small business."

His future goal is for bigger and better things. "Ultimately, I hope to own my own carwash," states McDonald. He also feels that business will be better next year.

He does not attend formal meetings, but does discuss techniques with people who have driving schools. There are no formal driving associations in this area, he noted.

Mr. Robinson's advice to men and women considering a career in small business is to ask yourself what kind of work you want to do. He believes, "You must enjoy your work, enjoy doing it yourself and enjoy being in control." He also suggests that you get a good lawyer and a good accountant, someone who knows your type of business, including the laws.

McDonald feels everyone should take a chance. "Don't be afraid of failure — give it a start — you can't tell until you try. When things are bleak, believe you can succeed. Make up your mind you can do it, or go back to a nine-to-five job."

Lois Ornstein of Rockville, Maryland

Lois is the sole owner of Plants, Etc., which has been operating for seven years and employs five people on a full and part-time basis. Her business consists of growing house plants, making special arrangements of these plants, selling and providing maintenance of plants to homes and offices.

Lois went into this business "mainly because of the thrill of making things grow." It also allows her greater freedom of movement. "I didn't like being in one location all of the time and I also like to be my own boss."

Lois got started using her home as a base of operations and needed only around $100 for plant care equipment. As she expanded her business, Lois needed another $1,000 for interior landscaping items and for opening accounts at nurseries. Lois explains that she broke even financially within two weeks, owing to the small initial investment. Currently, she works about 40 hours per week. This will vary, depending on the season.

Lois indicated that her former employer was her greatest help. He shared his knowledge of plants, how they are grown and the type of care needed for different greenery. He also introduced her to the nursery and plant growers, a most important group of contacts, especially if you are going into business for yourself.

Lois receives her greatest satisfaction from handling all aspects of the business, including the buying, bookkeeping, traveling and physical work. She also enjoys getting around and meeting people in both buying and sales. It is a particular source of satisfaction "to have people tell me that they can now grow healthy plants and keep them alive for long periods of time."

Married with three children, Lois indicated that her family has made a tremendous difference in the success of her business. Since she operates out of her home, "It takes a lot of patience, understanding and cooperation of other family members. They have helped quite a bit and I can always rely on either the children or my husband to help with the heavier items to be moved around or loaded onto our van."

Plans for the future include expanding the business to renting plants on a short-term basis and setting up floral decorations at parties. "I may even add a greenhouse onto our house, since I will need more room to grow plants throughout the year."

Lois subscribes to a number of journals for the trade in order to keep up with the latest methods and gain new ideas. For more technical advice on plants and their growth, she contacts the Agricultural Center of the University of Maryland, a free service.

Lois' advice to others thinking of starting their own business was, "know your subject matter! You must be prepared to learn about the business even if it means volunteering. Once you are in business, be tolerant of customers and not too authoritative, since they need your advice. You must often act as educator and teacher to your clients when it comes to care and feeding of plants."

To enter this type of business, Lois states, "you need to enjoy dealing with people — the product you sell is basically yourself and your knowledge of plants. You should also have the desire to see things grow, since you are dealing with life itself."

There you have it — brief personal capsules from a sampling of the interviews with men and women who describe some of the ins and outs and present advice for those who plan to start their own business. The information is real and comes from the experts — they did it on their own. They made mistakes, but they also made some good decisions — they also stuck with it.

We don't expect you to follow exactly in their footsteps, but we hope their ideas and advice will provide an inspiration for you to give it your best shot. Good fortune!

Structured Interview Format Sheet

By Dr. S. Norman Feingold
And Dr. Leonard G. Perlman

1. Name of business.

2. Name of owner. Check one:

   ☐ Partnership
   ☐ Corporation
   ☐ Sole Proprietor

3. Why did you go into small business in this particular endeavor?

4. How many dollars did you need to get started?

5. How long have you been in business?

6. Who was your greatest help?

7. How many employees do you have?

8. What do you like most about being in your own small business?

9. How long did it take before you broke even financially?

10. How many hours a week do you work?

11. What gives you the greatest satisfaction having your own small business?

12. Does your family help make a difference in your business success?

13. What are your future goals?

14. Do you attend meetings or seminars or go to school to help you keep up-to-date?

15. If you had to do it all over again, would you do it the same or differently?

16. What advice would you give to those men and women considering a career in small business?

17. Comments — tell us anything you feel is important that we can share with the readers of this book.

18. Do you believe that your business will be the same, better, or worse this coming year?

19. Is this a good time to enter small business?

20. What is your philosophy of small business, and do you have any words of wisdom to people who are considering a small business career?

References

A Directory of Federal Government Business Assistance Programs for Women Business Owners, U.S. Small Business Administration, Washington, D.C. April, 1980.

Checklist for Going Into Business. Small Business Administration, U.S. SBA, 1977 (Pamphlet)

Facts About Small Business and the U.S. Small Business Administration, Washington, D.C. March, 1979.

Franchise Opportunities Handbook, Department of Commerce, U.S. Government Printing Office, Washington, D.C., July, 1980.

Henderson, C. in *Hearings on the Future of Small Business in America.* Report No. 95-1810, Committee on Small Business, House of Representatives, Washington, D.C., November, 9, 1978.

Levenson, R. E. *Problems in Managing a Family-Owned Business*, Management Aids No. 208, SBA, Washington, D.C., 1978.

Metcalf, W. O. *Starting and Managing A Small Business of Your Own*, Third Edition, Vol. 1, U.S. Small Business Administration. U.S. GPO Catalog No. SBA 1.15:1/3, 1973.

Russell, J. S. "Let's Get Bullish About Small Business," *Journal of Career Education*, Vol. 6, No. 4, June, 1980, pp. 302-306.

White House Commission on Small Business, A Report. Washington, D.C.
   1980.

*Women's Handbook: How SBA Can Help You Go Into Business. Office
   of Management Assistance,* Small Business Administration, U.S. GPO,
   1979: 6-295-853.

Yankelovich D. (An article) "Are You Taking Risks With Your Life,"
   Parade Publications, Inc. New York, May 24, 1981.

Special Considerations

Women In Small Business:
Guidance For Women And Counselors
Working With Minorities

The senior author of this book had the pleasure of planning and participating in a Career Guidance Leadership Training Conference for counselors working with minorities and women interested in small business. This took place in the spring of 1978. It was partially funded by the National Alliance of Businessmen (NAB) and sponsored by the National Association for Industry — Education Cooperation, along with B'nai B'rith Career Counseling Services, the Small Business Administration, the National Graduate University and members of SCORE. This program became a prototype seminar for these target populations and was attended by 60 representatives from school systems, government, private agencies and small business. It was found that a ratio of two women, interested in small business, to one counselor is a suitable arrangement in this type of intensive seminar.

The seminar stimulated many other programs of this type across the country and a number of recommendations came out of this project which are worthwhile mentioning. For example:

- The recruitment of participants should be carefully planned and should include a mix of women already successful in small business, as well as those interested in planning a career in small business.

- Two days seems to be an appropriate period of time for this type of seminar.

- Minority groups should be involved in planning all phases of the seminar.

- The conference leader should be alert to planning follow-up activities, e.g., reconvening the same group after an interval of about six months.

- Only a few men were present and it is worthwhile to keep the numbers of men present purposely low so that the "for women only" orientation is kept intact.

- The ratio of two to one is believed to be an effective one, that is one counselor to every two women already in business or interested in small business.

To learn of special conferences or seminars, check with your local SBA Field Office, as well as local newspapers (those that list special programs, courses, etc.).

Resource Bibliography

Other Books You May Find Helpful...

There are numerous books and publications concerning every phase of business. Some are very detailed and dwell on specifics such as how to manage employees in a business to the use of computers to enhance your venture. The following bibliography is provided for your information. Most of these books are available at local libraries. If you have difficulty locating any of these titles, write directly to the publisher.

Auerbach, Sylvia, *A Woman's Book of Money: A Guide to Financial Independence.* Paperback. Doubleday. 1976.

Cheever, Raymond C., *Home Operated Business Opportunities for the Disabled.* Accent Special Publications, Cheever Publishing, Inc., P.O. Box 700, Bloomington, IL 61701. 1977.

Chenning, Peter C., *The Career Alternative: A Guide to Business Venturing.* Hawthorn Books, Inc., New York, 1977.

Cooper, Ken, *Nonverbal Communication for Business Success.* AMACOMA, A Div. of American Management Associations, New York, 1979.

Finn, Richard P., *Your Fortune in Franchises.* Contemporary Books, Inc., Chicago, 1979.

Hewitt, Geof, *How To Be Successfully Self-Employed — Working For Yourself.* Rodale Press, Inc., Emmaus, Pa., 1977.

Lasser, J. K., *How To Run A Small Business.* McGraw-Hill Book Co., 1974.

Kamoroff, Bernard, *Small-Time Operator.* Bell Springs Publishing, Laytonville, California, 1977.

Loffel, Egon W., *Protecting Your Business.* McKay Company, New York, 1977.

Lowry, Albert J., *How To Become Financial Successful By Owning Your Own Business.* Simon and Schuster, New York, 1981.

Naumes, William, *The Entrepreneurial Manager in the Small Business, Text, Readings, and Cases.* Addison-Wesley Publishing Co., Philippines, 1978.

Phillips, Michael and Salli Rasberry, *Honest Business: A Superior Strategy for Starting and Managing Your Own Business.* Clear Glass Publishing Company, San Francisco, 1981.

Rubin, Richard L. and Philip Goldberg, *The Small Business Guide to Borrowing Money.* McGraw-Hill Book Company, New York, 1980.

Smith, Brian R., *How To Prosper In Your Own Business.* The Stephen Greene Press, Brattleboro, VT, 1981.

Steinhoff, Dan, *Small Business Management Fundamentals*, McGraw-Hill Book Co., Second Edition, New York, 1978.

Seder, John W., *Credit and Collections*, McKay Company, New York, 1977.

Government Publications

Directory of Federal Government Business Assistance Program for Women Business Owners, SBA, Dept. of Commerce, *April, 1980.*

Directory of State Small Business Programs, SBA, Office of Chief Counsel for Advocacy, July, 1980.

Minority Business Development (A Guide to Federal Assistance Programs), U.S. Dept. of Commerce, Minority Business Development Agency, August, 1980.

Directory of Reaching Minority and Womens' Groups, 3rd Edition. Gov't Printing Office, Washington, D.C., 1979.

Small Business Development Center Policy Manual, SBA, September, 1980.

Small Business Subcontracting Directory, (Published Annually), Office of Procurement and Technical Assistance, SBA, Washington, D.C.

The Regulatory and Paperwork Maze — A Guide for Small Business, SBA, Office of the Chief Counsel for Advocacy, Washington, D.C., 1979.

Listing of Periodicals/ Magazines/ Newsletters

Small Business

American Journal of Small Business
In Business
Journal of Small Business Management
Small Business News (Small Business Association of New England)
Small Business Reporter (Bank of America, San Francisco)
Venture
Voice of Small Business (National Association of Small Business)
Enternational Entrepreneurs. (Santa Monica, California)

Women

Executive Female
Working Woman
Women's Business Enterprise Division (an SBA publication)

Minorities

Black Enterprise
Journal of Minority Business Finance
Hispanic Business

161

Others Not Classified Above

Business in Brief (Chase Manhattan Bank)

Business Week (a weekly periodical)

Center for Community Economic Development Review

Dun's Review

Forbes (bi-weekly)

Fortune (semi-monthly)

Economic Outlook Quarterly (Organization for Economic Cooperation and Development)

Index

Business Periodicals Index (Monthly) H. W. Wilson Company. This is a subject index covering 160 periodicals in the areas of business, finance, advertising, marketing and related topics.

Bibliography

Small Business Information Sources: An annotated bibliography National Council for Small Business Management Development, 1976. Can be ordered from NCSBMC, University of Wisconsin Extension, 929 North Sixth Street, Milwaukee, Wisconsin 53203

For your information we have listed a variety of periodicals that are concerned with business from many aspects. You may find them at libraries, business schools, etc.

Accounting

Accounting Review

Journal of Accountancy

Kiplinger Tax Letter

Automation and Computers

Datamation

Journal of Systems Management

Word Processing Systems

Book Trade and Libraries

American Libraries

Publishers Weekly

Banking and Finance

American Banker
Barron's
Financial World
Journal of Minority Business Finance
SBIC Venture Capital Service
Venture Wall Street Journal

General Interest

Changing Times
Consumer Reports
Kiplinger Washington Letter
Federal Times

International Trade

Employment and Earnings
Industrial Development
Monthly Labor Review

Area Trends in Employment and Unemployment (U.S. Department of Labor)

Glossary of Commonly Used Business Terms

T he following list of terms commonly used in the world of business is excerpted from the *Prebusiness Workshop Workbook*, a publication of the U.S. Small Business Administration, 1978. It should be noted that these definitions are not intended to be the only or complete definitions, but are adequate for clarifying these often used terms.*

accountant — *one who is skilled at keeping business records.* Usually, the name "accountant" refers to a highly trained professional rather than one who keeps books. An accountant knows how to set up the books needed for a business to operate and he can help a business owner understand what the business records mean.

account — *a record of a business transaction or "deal".* When you buy something on credit, the company you are dealing

---

*U.S. GPO: 1978-726-843/1612

with sets up an "account". This means they set up a record of what you buy and what you pay. You will do the same thing with any customers to whom you extend credit. At the bank, you will also have an "account", again a record of what you deposit and withdraw.

accounts receivable — a record of what is owed to you. All of the credit "accounts" — the record of what each customer owes you — taken together are your "accounts receivable". Even though you don't have the money in hand, that money which is owed to you is an *asset,* just as money in the bank is an asset. Your "accounts receivable" is something you have to know in order to know what your business is worth at any time. Of course, your accounts receivable must be collected to become a real asset.

analysis — breaking an idea or a problem down into its parts or a good examination of the parts of anything. In business you must "analyze", that is make an "analysis", of a problem before you can decide on the best solution. Let's say that your problem is some item that isn't selling well. You "make an analysis " by gathering all the facts as to why the item is not selling. Maybe you make a list of things which might be wrong or ask questions like: is the price right? What have customers said about the item, are the packages or displays dirty or unsightly, is the thing old fashioned or out of date? Does it do the job it is supposed to do? Do your customers have any need for it? And anything else you can think of which might help you explain why it doesn't sell. When you look at any problem closely — examine all its parts — what might be done to solve the problem should be clearer in your mind.

asset — anything of worth that is owned. Your personal assets (not counting your abilities) are the money you have in your pocket or in the bank, whatever is owed to you, any securities which you own, the property you own, whatever part of your home that you own, your furniture and appliances and all the miscellaneous things which you personally own. The assets of a business are just the same: money in the bank, accounts receivable, securities held in the name of the business, property or buildings, equipment, fixtures, merchandise for sale or being made ready, supplies and all things of value which the business owns.

articles of incorporation *— a legal document filed with the state which sets forth the purposes and regulations for a corporation.* These papers must be approved by the appropriate state office before a corporation legally exists and is allowed to do business. Each state has different requirements and the procedures are complicated so it is usually necessary to hire a lawyer specializing in corporate law to set up and get approval for a corporation.

bad debts *— money owed to you that you can't collect.* A business should never give credit or loan money to anyone who is not a good risk. But you can't be positive you are going to collect everything from those you do give credit or money to. You have to estimate in advance about how much you are not going to be able to collect and allow for it. You must set up a *bad debt allowance.*

balance *— the amount of money remaining in an account.* The total of your money in the bank after accounting for all transactions (deposits and withdrawals) is called a "balance". Also, the amount of money you owe a creditor or a customer owes you is called a "balance".

balance sheet *— an important business document which shows what a business owns and owes as of the date shown.* Essentially a "balance sheet" is a list of business assets and their cost on one side and a list of liabilities and owner's equity (investment in the business) on the other side with the amount for each. The liabilities include all that the business owes. If the balance sheet is figured correctly, the total assets will equal the total liabilities plus the owner's equity.

bookkeeping *— the process of recording business trans-actions in the accounting records.* It is very important to keep *accurate and complete* financial records and a good book-keeping system will be a great help.

break-even point *— where the income is equal to the outgo.* The level of business at which the revenue (income) exactly equals the expenses (outgo). It is important to know the break-even point so you can figure your profit on your estimated sales.

budget — *a plan expressed in money terms.* How much money do you need to run the business? How much money do you think will be coming in? A budget is a guide in helping you decide to spend money or not. (see plan)

business venture — *taking financial risks in a commercial enterprise.* The reason for risking your money, of course, is the hope of making a profit on your investment. One should always understand that there is a chance of losing money as well as making it — particularly when a business is new. Successful businesspersons have learned that they can control the risks by practicing good management and getting good advice from bankers, accountants, lawyers and business associates.

capital — *available money to invest or the total of accumulated assets available for production.* Put another way, your capital for going into business is the total of your property and money resources which you can make available for the business and whatever you will need to live on while getting the business going. Later on, if your business is successful, the business will accumulate "capital" in the form of property, goods and money (including securities).

capital requirement — *a list (or schedule) of expenses which must be met to establish a business.* Even before a business is started, the owner should start keeping records. One that is very important is a list of expected expenses and initial costs in order to establish how much capital must be invested to keep the business operating financially. Such a list must include all expected costs and have a margin of extra for the unexpected. What happens to many small businesspersons is that they fail to figure on all the expenses and costs which must be met. One of particular importance (and often forgotten) is the amount of money you will need for living expenses until the business starts earning a profit.

cash — *money in hand or readily available.* Currency — hard money, bills and negotiable securities (like checks) — in your cash drawer is cash. But so is the money you can draw on demand — your bank accounts or savings accounts also represent "cash". Cash is what you must have to keep a business going and it isn't unusual for even a very successful business to run out of "cash", particularly as the business is growing. Keeping a supply of "cash" is very important so good managers plan ahead on their cash needs.

cash discount *— a deduction that is given for prompt payment of a bill.* Even though the amount seems small, some where about 2%, when figured over a year it is important. A 2% discount for paying within 10 days is the same as getting 36% interest on your money for the year. (See terms of sale). Example: it costs 2% more if you wait the full 30 days, so those 20 days = 2%. Use 360 days for a year (for simple math) divide by 20 = 18 time periods × 2% = 36% per year.

cash receipts *— the money received by a business from customers.* "Cash receipts" are to a business what food and water are to anything living. An animal can live on its stored up food for only so long and then if it doesn't get more, it dies. A business will die, too, if it does not have a regular, sufficient flow of cash. A business can survive just so long on its stored up capital. Businesspersons preserve their capital as much as possible and try to control their cash receipts so that the business can continue.

contract *— an agreement regarding mutual responsibilities between two or more parties.* In business law a "contract" exists when there has been a meeting of minds — whether or not the contract is written. However, contracts are usually in written form but should never be taken lightly because they legally bind the parties to the agreement. Any business contract should be examined by a lawyer who know business law. Even with legal help, a contract should be read thoroughly and signed only after you fully understand what you are signing. One word of caution — many sales forms or order blanks are binding contracts and should not be signed unless the terms of the agreement are well understood.

controllable expenses *— those expenses which can be controlled or restrained by the businessperson.* Some of the costs of doing business can be postponed or spread out over a longer period of time. For example, depreciation on equipment is a "controllable" expense in the sense that it isn't required if one puts off obtaining new equipment until the level of business is such that it can support the new purchase and its depreciation allowance.

chain of command — *the proper lines of authority between the head of an organization, its managers and supervisors and its workers.* It is well understood that there needs to be direct lines of authority in a military organization so that each person understands to whom they report and from whom they take orders. The same is true in a business organization although this doesn't mean that one should run a business like an army unit where commands are not to be questioned. What it does mean is that a good manager will make sure that employees understand the order of authority and the method of communicating with management. In every well organized business there should be a direct line of authority which everyone understands. Sometimes a chain of command chart is useful in making this clear.

corporation — *a business venture comprising a group of individuals treated by the law as an individual.* A business corporation is an artificial personage, created by a state charter, which can do business as a separate entity the same as individuals can do in a sole proprietorship or a partnership. The corporation acts on its own through its officers and is empowered to make contracts and carry out business activities like an individual. Unlike other types of ownership, the shares of a corporation may be owned by a number of persons.

co-signers — *joint signers of a loan agreement, pledging to meet the obligations in case of default.* When you ask someone to "co-sign" a note, you are asking them to share a debt with you if you can't pay it back. They guarantee the loan will be paid back and the lender can take legal action to take their property if they refuse to pay. Borrowing money this way is a considerable obligation for the co-signer and should not be entered into lightly by either the borrower or co-signer.

credit — *credits and debits are used in bookkeeping to record transactions.* To credit is to place an entry on the right side of an account. A credit in an asset account makes it smaller. A credit in a liability account makes it larger. Another definition: the business owner's reputation for prompt payment of obligations, as in "a good credit rating."

debit — *debits and credits are used in bookkeeping to record transactions.* To debit is to place an entry on the left side of an account. A debit in a liability account makes it smaller. A debit in an asset account makes it larger.

debts — *that which is owed.* If you borrow money, buy something on credit, or receive more money on an account than is owed, you have a "debt" — an obligation to pay back whatever amount of money or goods is involved. Going into "debt" was once considered a sin but can be a useful and often necessary way of doing business. A "debt" though is a bad thing when it is larger than the ability of the borrower to repay and must always be carefully considered before it is made.

default — *failure to pay a debt or meet an obligation.* Any debt is a trust and failure to pay it is a violation of a high obligation. If you "default" you demonstrate that you are untrustworthy and unreliable — two damaging attitudes toward your reputation. In business such a reputation can, and probably will, cost you business, restrict your credit and lose you valuable creditors and business friends.

demand — *an order to comply with an obligation.* In business we speak of paying on "demand". This simply means that the obligation must be satisfied immediately when requested. Contracts are often written with a "pay on demand" clause. This means just what it says, the debtor must pay when asked if the terms of the contract agreement have been met.

depreciation — *a decrease in value through age, wear or deterioration.* You have all heard it said that an automobile "depreciates" as soon as it is driven off the lot. It becomes a "used" car immediately and is worth something less to a buyer than when it was brand new. All of the equipment which you buy for a business is the same way — it begins to depreciate immediately and is worth something less as it continues to be used. Depreciation is a normal expense of doing business which must be taken into account. As a new piece of equipment is purchased it is set up as an item in a "depreciation account" whereby it can be expensed over a period of time. There are laws and regulations governing the manner and periods of time that may be used for depreciation inasmuch as the rate of depreciation effects income and capital on which a business pays taxes.

economic — *pertaining to money or financial matters.* We speak of "economics" as the management of resources whether we are talking about a nation, city, a business or an individual. Business itself is a subject of economics and the economic situation affects every business in some way. A small businessperson does well to have a basic understanding of economics because it is such an important matter in the conduct of business.

enterprise — *a business firm or a business undertaking.* The word "enterprise" means any hard, dangerous or important undertaking or project. Its a good name for a business because a successful business takes all these things.

embezzlement — *to steal or take by fraud another's property for one's own use.* This dishonest act is one of the great perils of doing business. Seemingly trustworthy people sometimes are moved to steal from their employers and associates. Many businesses have been unable to survive the effects of such acts. There are three ways to protect a business against the possibility of embezzlement — careful selection of those people who are the best risks, business practices which make embezzlement difficult, and business insurance or bonding against any loss that may occur.

entrepreneur — *a person who organizes and manages a business.* This is a French word borrowed from that language and now a part of regular English. Its popularity probably comes from its grand sound as benefits anyone who has the initiative to create and run a business.

equity capital — *venture money.* In order to go into business you will most certainly have to lay it on the line. You put up savings or property when you go into business and you do it in hopes of getting a good return. Unfortunately, some people who have worked hard and protected their savings magnificently allow themselves to be dazzled by the prospect of their own business and make their investment foolishly. Most often they have little but heartache and debts to show for their effort. So it is very important to consider carefully before investing in your own business and to take all the steps you can to assure a business success and the protection of your "equity capital."

factors — 1. *something which contributes to a result.* 2. *a finance company specializing in high risks loans (usually at high interest rates).* English is full of words with more than one meaning. Here there are two meanings which apply to business. The first has to do with "facts" or "factual things" which are a part of any subject. We speak of the "factors" in borrowing money and what we mean is the individual considerations or facts which the banker or loan officer must know in order to approve a loan. The second meaning of "factor" is quite different and has to do with money lenders who make a business of loaning money for a short time and for purposes where the risks may be high. Factors who loan money to a business, usually require collateral and may exercise control of your business decisions.

financing — *obtaining money resources.* Businesses usually have to obtain financing at some time — either to go into business or expand operations (hopefully not just to stay in business). The time to set up relationships with those who might finance your business is before you need the money. Maybe you won't ever need to finance anything but that would be most unusual so you would be well advised to lay the groundwork for it early.

financial statements — *documents that show your financial situation.* Two major statements are needed to cover the information necessary to run a business and get financing. (Income statement and balance sheet.) In order to borrow any appreciable amount of money, the lender will require you to prepare an accurate financial statement. Even if not required for a loan, you need them to help you make plans and decisions, as well as showing you how you are doing.

fixed expenses — *those costs which don't vary from one period to the next.* Generally, these are expenses that are not affected by the volume of business. Rent, for example must be paid whether or not any business is accomplished. Fixed expenses are the basic costs that every business will have each month.

franchise (franchisor, franchisee) — *a right or privilege to deal in a certain line or brand of goods and services.* A franchising company (franchisor) is in the business of "selling" businesses or brands to small businesspersons. Usually, the franchisor and the businessperson who agrees (franchisee) enter into a binding contract where the franchisor supplies the product, materials and a certain amount of know-how and the franchisee agrees to handle the product exclusively and run the business according to certain standards prescribed by the franchisor. Such a relationship may be mutually advantageous but is a long term arrangement that should be carefully examined before accepted.

functional — *performing a function or carrying out a characteristic action.* In the sense in which the word is usually used, it describes a thing which is more useful than ornamental and that is related to its basic function. In business, we speak of a "functional" organization and it simply means an organization around the activities which the business engages in rather than the more formal "line management" organization. A "functional" organization implies that it has specialists who function as managers rather than managers who only manage and are not specialists.

gross — *overall total before deductions.* Another way to put it is that "gross" means the whole amount. A businessperson has to learn early the difference between "gross" and net figures. Many people beginning in business get fooled by the gross figures. For example, a business shows a substantial "gross" profit but by the time additional expenses are deducted the amount of the "net" profit is small. Another meaning of "gross" is something that is "very wrong" and that's exactly what it is if you get confused on what gross figures really mean.

income — *money coming in.* In a business sense, "income" is really pretty much the same for the business as for an individual. One's income is all the money received before anything is taken out and that's what it is in a business enterprise. One must not confuse the gross income of a business with his personal income (net income) from the business. As clear as that should appear to be, many small businesses have failed because the owner was misled into thinking the business was doing better than it really was.

income statement — *a financial document that shows how much money (revenues) came in and how much money (expenses) was paid out.* Subtracting the *expenses* from the *revenues* gives you your *profit* and all three are shown on the income statement. The statement should cover some definite time period.

industry ratio — *the standard or "average" percentage of expenses spent by firms in a similar type of business (i.e. firms in the same industry).* These "industry ratio" figures are very important guidelines for a business. It is not that you ought to spend exactly the same percentage as the average for your business but by comparing costs with what many other businesses spend, you can look for areas that seem out of line. If, for example, you are spending just half as much for advertising as the industry ratio, it would be well to consider if additional advertising might be helpful in building sales.

interest — *the cost of borrowing money.* Just as you are interested in a return on your investment in your business, return on investment is of concern to the lender of money. Banks and loan companies are businesses like any other. They have to receive a profitable income or they can't attract money, expand and provide the services which banks must provide. Of course, any interest you pay comes right off the top of your income and is profit that you can't make for yourself. Shop for a good price on "interest" as you would for anything you buy and get advice on how to figure the real interest.

inventory — *a list of assets being held for sale.* If you are in a retail business, the stock you have on the shelves is "inventory" but then so are your available supplies, goods received or stored and any expendable items on hand. As a regular part of the bookkeeping process inventory must be periodically counted because any inventory is a part of your current assets needed to figure what the business is worth.

invest — *lay out money for any purpose from which a profit is expected.* One way to evaluate whether an investment in a business is worthwhile is to consider what you would receive on that same amount of money put into a low risk investment. Certainly, the prospects should clearly be for a much greater return if the money is risked in a business.

lease — *a long term rental agreement.* A "lease" arrangement is mutually advantageous to both the lessor (renter) and the lessee (one who rents). The agreement gives the landlord assurance that the property will be rented and protects the renter because it assures that the business property will not be rented out from under the business. It is a good idea to have lease options for extending the rental periods. However, one word of caution — businesses often find that they are in trouble because they did not plan on sufficient space but were bound by a lease which they could not get out of.

liability insurance — *risk protection for actions for which a business is liable.* Insurance that a business carries to cover the possibility of loss from law suits in the event the business or its agents were found at fault when an action occurred. It protects the business investment.

limited partnership — *a legal partnership where some owners are allowed to assume responsibility only up to the amount invested.* The idea for a limited partnership is that some investors may put up money for a business venture without being directly involved in its operation and so are not held responsible for the debts of the other partners beyond the possible loss of the money they have invested.

line position — *a place of authority in a "line" organization.* In a "line position" the person involved is organizationally responsible only to the man directly above him in the organization.

liquidate — *to settle a debt or to convert to cash.* This literally means to do away with. In a business sense it means to do away with a debt by paying it or to do away with assets by selling them and thus turning them into hard cash.

loan — *money lent at interest.* A lender makes a "loan" with the idea that it will be paid back as agreed and that interest will be paid as a sort of "rent" for the use of the money.

management — *the art of conducting and supervising a business.* It isn't enough to just invest money in a business — the business must be nurtured, protected and helped along to success. Managers do more than manage people, which most everyone understands, for they must also manage things. Another way to look at it is that "management" is the exercise of judgment in the affairs of the business.

marketing — *all the activities involved in buying and selling a product or service.* You must know most of the following things to market successfully:

Who is going to buy?
What is it they want?
Where will they go to get it?
How much will they pay?
How much will they buy?
Who else sells it?
How will you sell it?
How much profit do you want?

merchandise — *goods bought and sold in a business.* "Merchandise" or stock is a part of inventory. In usage merchandise has come to mean anything movable that may be sold or traded.

motivation — *strong influence or incentive.* Motivation is the thing which moves a person to do something. "Motivation" may be something of which the individual is not even aware. A whole field of business psychology has grown up around motivation research — the hidden reasons why people buy things.

net — *what is left after deducting all charges.* (See "gross").

nonrecurring — *one time; not repeating.* "Nonrecurring" expenses are those involved in starting a business which only have to be paid once and will not occur again.

obsolescence — *declined in value because of replacement by new and/or better things.* A business owner has to be aware of changing patterns in the things which people buy. People have a way of wanting whatever is the latest or the newest in most things so you will do well not to overstock items which tend to change style.

objective — *something toward which effort is directed; something to accomplish.* It's interesting that "objective" also means realistic and we might say that "objectives" are realistic goals that we set.

operating costs — *expenditures arising out of current business activities.* In other words, your "operating costs" for any period of time are what it costs you to do business — the salaries, electricity, rental, deliveries, etc., that were involved in performing the business dealings.

operating ratios — *the relationship of costs from business activities.* What percentage of your costs went for rent? How does it compare with other businesses like yours? These are facts which a business needs to know if it is efficient and not wasting resources.

operating organization — *the plan for doing business.* The management structure as opposed to the legal structure of a firm is its operational organization.

organize — *to put in order.* A good manager can "organize" just about anything — people into a work force, bills into a payment schedule, or merchandise into a display plan. There is a kind of logic to everything and using that logical pattern in business affairs can make just about any task a lot simpler and easier.

owner-manager — *one who owns and operates a business.* One of the greatest assets which an "owner manager" has is flexibility to meet problems. There is no need to call a committee together or consult the board of directors to take action. Being a good owner manager is among the highest of callings and is one of the most satisfying of endeavors.

ownership organization — *the legal structure for a business.* How a business is organized legally depends upon how it is owned. If one person owns it — it's a proprietorship (usually), if several own jointly as owner-managers — it is a partnership unless incorporated. If many people own a business — it most certainly is some form of a corporation.

partnership — *a legal business relationship of two or more people who share responsibilities, resources, profits, and liabilities.* Partnerships are built on mutual trust and friendship, but should still have the agreement in writing.

payable — *ready to be paid.* One of the standard accounts kept by a bookkeeper is "accounts payable". This is simply a list of those bills which are current and due to be paid.

personnel — *persons collectively in the employ of a business.* As a small business grows, it will need people to handle the expansion of business and carry out the work of the business. Your personnel are a part of your business and deserve consideration as full fledged members of the firm even though they may not share in the firm's ownership and profits.

plan — *a plan is a formal decision to do something, then figuring out how you are going to do it before you start.* You must answer the questions of What? Where? When? How? and Why? You should *plan first* then do. (See budget).

pledge — *to bind by a promise, to give possession of something of value as security on a loan.* There has to be a great deal of trust between parties doing business — indeed it seems doubtful that business itself could proceed without it — it is the basis for all credit transactions, most business agreements and the general conduct of commerce. For the most part, we accept the "pledge" of other people about most business things without question and happily they keep their promises. However, another kind of "pledge" is sometimes necessary which calls for a more formal arrangement, particularly where sizeable amounts of money are involved. In these cases the borrowing party "pledges" (usually in writing) to give possession of some of his capital assets if he is unable or does not meet the terms of his obligation.

posting — *to enter in an account.* Literally, "post" means to give a position to something so when you "post" figures in a ledger, you are assigning them their right position in the firm's account books.

pricing — *to set the selling price.* One of the most difficult jobs in business is selecting the right price. If the price is set too high the customers won't buy. Too low a price and you lose profit. Pricing should be done very carefully. You have to consider how much profit you need, what your competition is charging, and how much your customers are willing to pay.

principal — *property or capital assets as opposed to income; also, one who is directly concerned in a business enterprise.* This is still another of those confusing words with more than one meaning but if you really consider that it means "the first in importance" whether we are talking about people or capital assets the meanings make more sense. Therefore the money you invest in a business is the first in importance — principal — and if you are investing money and/or effort in business you area "principal".

profit — *financial gain; returns over expenditures.* Simply put, "profit" is what you've got left after paying for everything. Hopefully, the profit represents a good return in the investment in a business plus a sort of reward-payment for good management. But never take profit for granted — it can be disappointing.

profit and loss statement — *a list of the total amount of sales (revenues) and total costs (expenses).* The difference between revenues and expenses is your profit or loss. It is also called an "income statement".

profit margin — *is the difference between your selling price and your costs.* A lot of factors affect profit margin both inside and outside the business. A reasonable profit margin is necessary to remain in business.

proprietorship — *subject to exclusive ownership.* A "proprietor" is one who owns a business and a business owned by one person is called a "proprietorship".

ratio — *the relationship of one thing to another.* A "ratio" is a short cut way of comparing things which can be expressed as numbers or degrees. For example, we say that a green grocer has a 10 to 1 loss ratio on lettuce and that's a short cut way for saying that for every 10 heads of lettuce that the grocer buys, on the average, he loses one head that doesn't sell or spoils before it can be sold and so has to be thrown away. Ratios of this kind are keeping figures over a period of time — for example the grocer may have learned his loss "ratio" by keeping track of how many heads of lettuce he sold during the month and counting those he threw away. The "ratio" here is figured by dividing the number lost into the number sold.

receivable — *ready for payment.* When you sell on credit, you keep an "accounts receivable" as a record of what is owed to you and who owes it. In accounting, a "receivable" is an asset — it represents money that is owed to you. As such "receivables" are listed as a current asset in the balance sheet.

regulations — *rules or laws (affecting a business).* It is accepted in our system of government that the state has the obligation of protecting citizens so government sets up laws which prevent injury to citizens. Some of these have to do with business practices and must be followed to avoid penalties. Of course, many such regulations benefit the small businessperson.

reserve — *that which is held back or stored for future use or in case of emergency.* The success or failure of many young businesses depends upon their abilities to weather a financial crisis. Even though you plan financial needs in great detail, unforseen expenses are likely to occur sometime so you should have sufficient "reserves" to meet an emergency.

retail — *selling directly to the consumer.* Selling in large quantities to dealers for resale is a "wholesale" activity while selling in small quantities directly to people who will use the product is called "retail". There is some confusion brought about by advertising which says, discount, cut-rate or "wholesale prices" but these operations are really "retail" as long as they are selling in small amounts to the general public.

secured — *protected or guaranteed.* "Secure" means to make a thing safe so when we speak of a "secured loan" we mean to make it safe or protect it by putting up something of value as collateral, as a guarantee of repayment.

service business — *a retail business which deals in activities for the benefit of others.* If you go to a doctor or lawyer you will be sent a bill marked "for services rendered". In that sense the doctor or lawyer is engaged in a "service business" the same as a laundry, auto repair shop or that part of a filling station business concerned with tire repairs.

share — *one of the equal parts into which the ownership of a corporation is divided.* A "share" represents a part ownership in a corporation. How many "shares" you hold represents how much ownership you have. Of course, you can own "shares" in a firm without participating directly in the business. But in a small business, even if it is a corporation, the chances are that the owners participate or share the management responsibilities.

site — *a plot of ground set aside for a particular use.* The business "site" may or may not be owned by the business owner and it is often better to rent a "site" when a business is getting started. For many businesses, particularly retail businesses, the proper "site" is most important because the location of the business may determine the number and kinds of available customers.

stabilizing — *to make stable; to be less subject to ups and downs.* Like a ship on the ocean, a business may run into a "rough sea" of changing conditions. The business "stabilizes" when it is not affected by these changes or when the conditions themselves are less fluctuating. Successful businesspersons look for "stabilizing" methods to smooth out the ups and downs — either by diversifying into products which are more "stable", eliminating the factors which cause the ups and downs — particularly the downs — or by operating on a level that minimizes the effects of the fluctuations.

statistics — *a collection of accurate numerical data; classified facts which can be stated in numbers.* There are "statistics" of interest to a businessperson in every community. The local census figures are "statistics" as are the physical count of the number of businesses in a particular place. A business gathers "statistics" by counting the number of customers coming into the store on a given day. Statistics are useful to a small business because they are some of the facts needed to base good decisions.

stock — *an ownership share in a corporation, another name for a share; another definition, accumulated merchandise.* The things which a merchant has available for sale is referred to as "stock" and when those things are put out for display, we say the shelves are stocked.

taxes — *a business is subject to a wide variety of taxes many of which are quite different from individual taxes.* The types of taxes, methods and timing of payment, and to whom paid should be checked with an accountant, the taxing authorities, city, county, State and Federal.

terms of sale — *the conditions concerning payment for a purchase.* Very important source of saving. For example, 2/10; N/30 terms means that if payment is made within ten days you can take a 2% discount otherwise you must pay in full within 30 days.

trade credit — *permission to buy from suppliers on open account.* When you buy business supplies on credit you are really borrowing from the supplier — you have the loan of whatever he is selling you until it is paid for. Often the supplier extends this service for a period of time (usually 20 to 30 days) without charging interest but it is not uncommon for him to charge interest if the amount is large and the time for repayment is extended. "Trade credit" is useful to small businesspersons and they should make it a point to keep their reputation good so that they may continue the practice.

transfer — *to remove from one place to another or from one person to another.* One of the main services of banks is to allow the efficient "transfer" of funds. The whole business of checks is a convenient way to accomplish the transfer of money without the need for actually transferring the money physically.

tangible — *something that is real.* Literally, "tangible" means that the thing is such that you can touch it but the meaning for business is something which can be seen and evaluated. We speak of "tangible" assets and we mean those real or touchable assets that have a value and can be converted, if need be, into cash. The "intangible" assets of a business would be those things which may be of value but can't be measured or objectively evaluated, as for example, the good will that a business has built up.

volume — *an amount or quantity (of business).* The "volume" of a business is the total it sells over a period of time.

wholesale — *selling for resale.* (See retail for explanation).

APPENDIX 1

Definitions of the Size of Business[1]

Small Business	Employment Size	Asset Size	Sales Size
Independent Contr.	0	0	Under $100,000
Family Size	1-4	Under $100,000	$100-500,000
Small	5-19	$100-500,000	$500,000-1 million
Medium	20-99	$500,000-5 million	$1 million - 10 million
Large	100-	$5 million - 25 million	$10 million - 50 million
Total Small Business	0-500	$0 - 25 million	$0 - 50 million
Medium Business	500-900	$25 million - 100 million	$50 million - 250 million
Large Business	1,000 +	$100 million+	$250 million+
Government Size Business	10,000+	$2 billion+	$2 billion+

Note: These research definitions are proposed by the Office of Economic Research for general research purposes. Researchers may find it difficult to obtain data broken out by these size categories and should feel free to proceed with the best data available.

---

[1] From U.S. Small Business Administration, January, 1980.

185

APPENDIX 2

List of All SBA Counseling Notes

Selected COUNSELING NOTES are found in the Following Appendix.

To receive COUNSELING NOTES not available in this book write to SBA*.

CN - 101 — Building Service Contracting
CN - 102 — Service Stations
CN - 103 — Catering
CN - 104 — Radio/Television Repair Shop
CN - 105 — Retail Florist
CN - 106 — Franchised Businesses
CN - 107 — Hardware Store or Home Center
CN - 108 — Small Volume Home Building
CN - 109 — Starting a Travel Agency
CN - 110 — Restaurants
CN - 111 — Sporting Goods Store
CN - 112 — Drycleaning
CN - 113 — Carwash
CN - 114 — Beauty Salon
CN - 115 — Pest Control
CN - 116 — Marine Retailers
CN - 117 — Retail Grocery Store
CN - 118 — The Nursery Business
CN - 119 — The Wholesale Nursery Business
CN - 120 — The Garden Center Business
CN - 121 — The Landscape Business
CN - 122 — Apparel Store
CN - 123 — Pharmacies
CN - 124 — Retail Photography Store
CN - 125 — Office Products
CN - 126 — Automotive Parts & Accessories
CN - 127 — Motels
CN - 128 — Paint & Decorating Centers
CN - 129 — Interior Design Services
CN - 130 — Fish Farming
CN - 131 — Day Care Centers
CN - 132 — Men's Outerwear
CN - 133 — Bicycles
CN - 135 — Roofing Contractors
CN - 135 — Printers
CN - 136 — Fabricare
CN - 137 — The Bookstore

CN - 138 — Home Furnishings
CN - 139 — Handbags
CN - 140 — Bake Shops
CN - 142 — Ice Cream
CN - 143 — Recreational Vehicles
CN - 144 — Real Estate
CN - 145 — Sewing Centers
CN - 201 — Breakeven Points for Independent Trackers

*** These materials are free of charge ***

---

*NOTE: When writing for any of these *Counseling Notes* include the number and name of the business and mail to:

Small Business Administration
Office of Management Information and Training
Washington District Office
1030 15th Street, N.W.
Suite 250
Washington, D.C. 20417

APPENDIX 3

Twenty Four Selected Counseling Notes

The following Counseling Notes are provided for your convenience and information in a variety of potential businesses that have widespread applicability in the United States.

Building Service Contracting	(CN-101)
Catering	(CN-103)
Radio-Television Repair Shop	(CN-104)
Retail Florist	(CN-105)
Franchised Businesses	(CN-106)
Hardware Store or Home Center	(CN-107)
Home Building, Small Volume	(CN-108)
Travel Agency	(CN-109)
Car Wash	(CN-113)
Pest Control	(CN-115)
Garden Center Business	(CN-120)
Landscaping Business	(CN-121)
Apparel Store	(CN-122)
Retail Photography Store	(CN-124)
Office Products	(CN-125)
Automotive Parts and Accessories	(CN-126)
Interior Design Services	(CN-129)
Fish Farming	(CN-130)
Bicycles	(CN-133)
Fabricare Center	(CN-136)
Bookstores	(CN-137)
Bake Shops	(CN-140)
Ice Cream Stores	(CN-142)
Sewing Centers	(CN-145)

NOTE: While these Counseling Notes are reviewed and updated periodically one or more years may have passed from the most recent updating. For this reason some of the dollar amounts indicated in the notes will be low due to the high inflation rates of the past few years. It would be wise therefore, to add an average of twenty percent to all figures given as either costs or income. Using this rule-of-thumb you will reach a close estimate of the current dollar amounts as described in these notes. You will also need to take into account the planned location of any given type of business. Some areas of the nation will have a lower cost of living rate than others. As such, goods and services and expected income from a business will reflect the location accordingly.

Building Service Contracting: A Building Service Contractor provides janitorial services and other building maintenance services — window cleaning, carpet shampooing, floor and wall maintenance, and the like — on a contract basis. Other services performed by contractors can include lighting maintenance, pest control, parking lot maintenance, and security services. Most building service contractors perform their services by negotiating for an account, but some accounts are obtained through the bidding process.

The contractor must be able to estimate the labor time involved in cleaning the building to the client's specifications. Labor is the largest cost to the contractor and total labor costs including taxes, unemployment and workmen's compensation, and other fringe benefits can approach 70 percent of the total contract price. Other factors to consider when estimating include the cost of equipment and cleaning supplies, overhead (office expenses, insurance, transportation costs, etc.), and the contractor's profit.

Capital investment requirements for entering the building service contracting industry are fairly low compared to other industries. Investment must be made in office supplies and cleaning equipment. Commonly used major equipment includes floor buffers, carpet shampooers, industrial vacuum cleaners, and wet/dry vacuums. Other necessary expenses include mops, buckets, brushes, and assorted floor finishes and cleaners.

The initial capital also must contain enough reserves to provide working capital (cash) sufficient to cover the first few months' payroll. Since there is often a time lag between paying the employees and receiving the account's payment, a contractor must pay the employees from his reserves. The trend across the country has been to bill at the beginning rather than the end of the month of service, but there is still a lag in payments.

According to a recent study by the Building Service Contractors Association International, a firm needs approximately $350,000 in gross sales to generate a net, after-tax income of $10,000. That net income figure does not include the owner's salary, which is accounted as one of the firm's expenses.

Although it is fairly easy to enter building service contracting, the industry as a whole has a high rate of business failures. These are commonly attributed to poor accounting procedures, under-bidding in an attempt to win contracts, over-extension of resources, and cash shortfall.

Usually, building service contracting businesses are located in or near a city, as an urban area provides more opportunities for accounts. Points to consider when choosing a site are the number of existing buildings and buildings under construction, the number of potential clients, the amount of competition, and the demand for various maintenance services.

Most small contractors market their services through personal contacts. Many have designed a sales brochure telling about the company which is personally given to the potential customer to study or is mailed to the potential customer with a cover letter. Many contractors also place an ad for their company in the yellow pages of the telephone directory. Advertising can be done by using an attractively-designed letterhead and putting the company insignia on company uniforms and trucks.

In most cases there are no licensing requirements governing the building service contracting industry. Federal regulations having the greatest effect on the industry are the Occupational Safety and Health Act (OSHA) and the Equal Pay Act.

For Further Information

Building Service Contractors Association International
1750 Old Meadow Road, McLean, Va. 22101

Building Services Contractor. Bimonthly. $6 a year. MacNair-Dorland Company. Inc. 101 West 31st St., New York, N.Y. 10001

BSCA Bulletin. Monthly. $18 a year. BSCA International. 1750 Old Meadow Road. McLean, Va. 22102

Maintenance Supplies. Monthly. $7 a year. MacNair-Dorland Company, Inc. West 31st St., New York, N.Y. 10001

Sanitary Maintenance. Monthly. $10 a year. Trade Press Publishing Company. 407 East Michigan St., Milwaukee, Wisc. 53201

Small Business Reporter. "Building Maintenance Services," Vol. 12, No. 3, 1974. $1 at any Bank of America office.

(Revised by Ellen Balderson, Building Service Contractors Association International, McLean, Virginia)

Catering: Catering represents an expanding segment of the rapidly growing food and beverage industry of the United States. The function of the caterer is to supply whatever is needed for the execution of events at a specific time and location where food is an important element of the occasion. Mobile caterers are projected to increase food and drink sales by 9.5 percent in 1979. The gain is lower than that experienced in previous years because the industrial work force will be growing at a very low rate, perhaps as low as 1 percent. This area of the food service industry could be particularly vulnerable in 1979 if the economy takes a downturn.

The three basic types of caterers include the banquet hall, which means that the caterer provides the location, the locational caterer, who goes to the customer's site, and the mobile caterer, who operates a vehicle designed to carry prepared food to various locations and serves from the vehicle. However, the basic success factor for any food service contractor still lies in the ability of each to see the needs of the community and to adapt the operation to meet those needs.

The amount of capital required to start a catering service is determined by the type of operation chosen. Large caterers, who have the capacity to provide all the food, equipment, and personnel necessary to support a function of 100 to 200 persons will need around $100,000 of capital funding. Naturally though, the smaller mobile caterer will be able to initiate operations with a much smaller investment. Profits in the business are fairly average, returning a 2 to 5 percent net on sales with the major expense items being food, labor and equipment maintenance and/or rental.

For marketing purposes, catering relies chiefly upon the word of mouth reputation as the most effective means of attracting customers. This is one reason why caterers need to be selective of their personnel, emphasizing service with quality rather than accepting too many jobs which could over-extend their capacities. Other methods of promoting the catering service include the commercial advertisement of telephone directory, magazines, newspapers, and direct mail campaigns to churches, community organizations, and so forth. In advertising it is important to remember that even though business functions are growing rapidly it is still the individuals who constitute the major portion of the market with private parties, wedding receptions, and a variety of other occasions.

In beginning the catering service, it is often better to start with a cold menu, only adding hot items as the business develops. This is because hot items require more equipment and skilled experience in delivering. At the bare minimum, the starting caterer will need only one range-oven combination until sales are established and he/she can invest in more equipment. Other kitchen equipment to be purchased includes refrigerators, freezers, slicers, and dining appointments, all of which will require proper and systematic maintenance. The light equipment, which refers to all equipment for the guest service, and includes linen, tableware, glasses, novelties, and the paper service is also a necessary addition. For delivery purposes one may either invest in a van or a panel truck.

Future trends in the industry indicate that because of inflation many people can no longer affort catering services for the traditional occasions. Business and professional tax deductible events will require more catering services and it is felt that caterers who have on-premise restaurants will not be as severly affected in the years ahead as those who only cater. Prospective caterers should evaluate their position and seek to adapt to market trends.

For Further Information

Catering Handbook, Edith and Hal Weiss. 1971. $14.50. Aherns Publishing Company, Inc., New York, N. Y.

Convenience and Fast Food Handbook. Thorner, Marvin E. 1979. $23. NRA.

Profitable Catering. Axler, Bruce. 1974. ITT Educational Publishing, Indianapolis, Indiana.

(By the National Restaurant Association, Chicago, Illinois)

Radio-Television Repair Shop: The owner manager of a radio-television repair shop wears many hats. He must combine technical ability in electronics with management proficiency in the areas of planning, organizing, directing, decision making, coordinating, and controlling. It is for this reason that the prospective owner-manager should have some commercial education with coursework in accounting, finance, marketing, and management.

Capital investment requirements have grown rapidly in recent years with the current normal standard of $6000 to $9000 per technician employed in the business. Generally you may expect cost of sales (parts and labor) to average 53.2 percent of net sales, with operating expenses approaching 41.0 percent leaving operating profit to be almost 5.8 percent (NARDA 1977). Sufficient working capital is usually considered to be in the current ratio range of 2 to 1 (current assets/current liabilities).

Equipment selection, or fixed asset investment, will vary with the size of the business, number and types of brands serviced, and whether equipment is bought new or on a depreciated basis. The types of equipment needed for operations include a service truck, repair parts for service calls, kits of modules for particular brand servicing, test equipment for both service calls and shop use, and finally office equipment for administrative work. For the smallest shop the minimum cost that can be anticipated is around $12,000.

In the marketing area one of the most important problems to be solved is the selection of the shop location. It is important to evaluate both the automotive traffic availability of parking for the areas in consideration, the opportunity to erect a commanding sign, the number of homes in the trade area, the proximity of competitive shops, as well as other census data pertinent to site selection. However, once the site is selected sales will become more a function of aggressive sales and advertising tactics. The owner manager should seek to maximize sales going to the customer via effective ad campaigns so that the customer automatically responds to the shop whenever a radio-television repair problem arises.

Radio-television repair shops are subject to normal commercial regulations on the State and municipal level with sales licenses, commercial permits, etc. One recent legislative issue however bears mention, the Magnisom-Moss Act of 1975, which will probably effect the servicing of warrantees and thus mean uniform regulation of industry in relation to guarantees made on products or servicing.

Recent trends for the industry show increased competition for the smaller shops because of an increased tendency towards repair shops with larger staffs, more highly technical equipment, and lower unit operating costs. The era of the smaller shop is closing and it will become necessary for the radio-television entrepreneur to enter the field at a higher operating level in order to be competitive price-wise.

For Further Information

National Association of Retail Dealers of America
2 North Riverside Plaza
Chicago, Illinois 60606

Elements of Service Management
NARDA
318 W. Randolph Street
Chicago, Illinois 60606

Small Business Management Fundamentals. Steinhoff. 1974. McGraw Hill Inc., New York

"Starting and Managing a Small Business of Your Own." *Starting and Managing* Series No. 1 3rd Edition. Small Business Administration, Washington, D.C.

Stereo. Published Quarterly. Norman Eisenberg, editor. The Publishing
House. Great Barrington, Massachusetts 01230.

TV Communications. Monthly. Paul S. Maxwell, editor, P.O. Box 1317.
Englewood, Colorado 80110.

(By John Gooley, National Association of Retail Dealers of America, Chicago, Ill.)

Retail Florists: Florists Shops provide an opportunity to
achieve both pleasure and profit for the person who enjoys
working with plants and flowers. It is a business that deals
with perishable products and incurs deadlines as well as
peaking during holiday periods. As in any business, the key
success factor is management ability. As a manager,
knowledge of fresh flowers, green plants, soils, plant
nutrition, insect and disease control, light and temperature
requirements, etc., will need to supplement management
skills in purchasing, pricing, and marketing. Many State
colleges offer two or four year programs in floriculture and
experts recommend an additional three or four years of
practical experience before initiating your own retail outlet.

For financial purposes the most recent Census of Retail
Trade by the Bureau of the Census indicates retail florists
achieved over $1.6 billion in sales distributed among nearly
25,000 establishments. Using the same data average sales
compute to be over $66,000 per operating florist with the
median sales level being slightly below the $50,000 level. It is
generally felt that a minimum of $12,000 is needed for initial
investment requirements with an additional margin of six to
nine months of operating capital for the small shop's initial
expenses. The small shop can expect costs to average about 47
percent of sales for cost of goods sold, 38 percent of sales for
operating expenses, leaving about 15 percent gross profit
before taxes for owner's salary and return on investment.

Product mix for sales in the florist industry are cyclical in
that flower arrangements are popular in certain periods with
green plant sales gaining demand in other years as is the
current case. Florists should strive to locate in communities
where average income is sufficient to support the types of

floral products they wish to sell. Therefore, if the area is a young community sales for entertaining and general home use will be large; whereas flower shops located in older communities have more business in arrangements for sickness or sympathy motivations. To generate sales the yellow pages and direct mail advertising are the most effective methods and other techniques include major commercial wire transmitting systems for sales to distant locations (AFS, Florafax, FTD, and Teleflorist).

The equipment needs of the shop itself are relatively simple. The main item, a refrigerator, should be maintained in the 38° to 42° F range and 80 percent + humidity depending upon types of flowers. Designing tables, a wrapping table, showcases, sinks with a water supply are also essential and need to be figured into initial setup costs. In addition, the prospective owner will want to investigate the legal aspects of operating the shop. Normally, a municipal license and State sales tax certificate will be required except in cases of greenhouse operations. The exception is that for the 30 percent who maintain greenhouses some State agricultural departments will require inspection of these operations.

Future trends appear promising for the florist industry with sales expected to double to $6 billion by 1985. With the current green plant demand, most florists are targeting their marketing towards the 25 to 45-year old college educated consumer in the suburbs. Consequently, florist shops are increasingly locating in shopping centers where they can take advantage of higher income communities and large traffic flows. In addition, however, a large portion of the floral market is being taken by non-retail florist stores (food and hardware) which in 1972 sold two-fifths of the total market. This, coupled with another trend toward retail florist chains, projects increased competition for the floral sales dollars.

For Further Information

Society of American Florists Association
901 North Washington St.
Alexandria, Va. 22314

Florists Transworld Delivery
29200 Northwestern Highway
P.O. Box 2227
Southfield, MI. 48076

Teleflora, Inc.
2400 Campton Blvd.
Redondo Beach, Ca. 90278

Florafax International, Inc.
P.O. Box 45745
Tulsa, OK 74145

American Floral Services, Inc.
P.O. Box 12309
Oklahoma City, OK 73112

(Prepared by Management Assistance with information supplied by Perry A. Russ, Society of American Florists, Alexandria, Virginia.)

Franchised Businesses: Franchising, frequently and inaccurately described as an industry or business, is neither. It is a *method* of doing business, of marketing a product and/or service, which has been adopted and used in a wide variety of industries and businesses. There is no simple, single definition of franchising.

Franchise arrangements have been subdivided into two broad classes: product distribution arrangements in which the dealer is to some degree, but not entirely, identified with the manufacturer/supplier; and entire business format franchising, in which there is complete identification of the dealer with the buyer.

In recent years, the traditional areas of franchising, automobile dealers, service stations and soft drink bottlers, have been augmented by the entry and expansion of other industries such as food service, accounting, retailing, employment, motels and hotels — even real estate. The growth in the franchising sector of the economy has been rapid and in 1979 the U.S. Department of Commerce estimates total retail sales by franchised outlets will top $180 billion.

Under the franchise system an individually owned business is operated as though it were part of a large company, complete with a trademark, uniform design, equipment and standardized services or products. In an era of tight money, greater competition and large chain growth, franchising offers distinct advantages to the small entrepreneur as compared with a totally independent business.

The buyer of a franchise has the advantage of the franchisor's experience in site selection, management, advertising, accounting, and product research and development and thus starts his business with a greater degree of efficiency, proven products or methods and a higher expectancy of profitability.

But it is important for the franchisee to examine himself to be certain he is "right" for the business and to determine if he can accept the degree of direction and the long hours and hard work necessary for success.

Depending on the type of franchise, the initial investment can vary from a few thousand dollars to upwards of $200,000 and royalty fees can range from nothing to 18 percent of gross sales. Profits can vary nearly as widely. Yet franchising affords a greater degree of security and a better chance for success than individual ownership for those willing to devote the time and effort to their business.

Prospective franchisees must investigate any franchise offering thoroughly before signing any contracts and should seek competent legal returns on little investment and high pressure sales tactics which tend to discourage the franchisee from seeking legal and accounting advice.

In addition to their own qualifications and motivations, prospective franchisees should examine carefully the franchisor's business and the industry of which it is a part, with particular attention given to profit projections, costs, training and start-up aid, location and territory, operating assistance and controls, renewal and termination, and the provisions of the contract.

Prospective franchisees today are afforded a much greater degree of protection than they were even a few years ago. Responsible franchisors, working through the International Franchise Association, have backed full disclosure of all elements of the franchise offering and have sought uniformity of State laws and regulations dealing with disclosure. Today 12 states accept a "Uniform Franchise Offering Circular" in which franchising companies present in great detail facts regarding their companies and their franchises. The Federal Trade Commission adopted a similar "Circular" providing equal protection in all the states effective July 1, 1979.

Whether or not a franchisee's state has a franchise disclosure law, any responsible franchisor will provide a copy of the statement. Other private and public sources of information and help, are the U.S. Small Business Administration, the local Better Business Bureau office, Chamber of Commerce, and the International Franchise Association.

For Further Information

Franchise Handbook: *A Complete Guide to Selecting, Buying and Operating.* Jan Cameron. 1970. $6.95. Crown Publishers, Inc. 419 Park Ave., South, New York, NY.

Franchising in the Economy 1973-75. Prepared by Bureau of Domestic Commerce, U.S. Department of Commerce, Washington, D.C. 20203.

Investigate Before Investing: Guidance for Prospective Franchisees. Fels and Rudnick. 1974. $5. International Franchise Association, Washington, D.C. 20036.

Franchise Index/Profile. *Small Business Management Series* No. 35. Prepared by the Small Business Administration. Available from the Superintendent of Documents, Washington, D.C. 20402.

(Revised by Joseph L. Koach, CAE, Executive Vice President, International Franchise Association, Washington, D.C.)

Hardware Store or Home Centers: Hardware stores and home centers provide tools, merchandise and know-how for do-it-yourself home improvement, repair, and maintenance. Larger stores with broader lines have largely dispelled the "man's store" image. A hardware store or home center's competive position in any trade area depends largely on how well the owner keeps up with the changing life style of families in the trade area and maintains a sales floor and merchandise mix that serves their needs.

Most such stores operate as a proprietorship. The successful owner devotes 12-14 hours a day to the business, participates in local, social, and civic affairs, and devotes major efforts toward the financial and personnel phase of retailing.

Financial Requirements and Returns

Local conditions, codes, competition, etc., will obviously influence financial requirements, however, as a rule, a new owner will need about $30 per square foot of store area, excluding lease costs. This normally will break down about as follows: Inventory $18; Fixtures $3.50; Registers, trucks, etc. $2.50; Working capital $5. Lease costs will average about $3.50 per square foot. Any new owner should expect to operate a minimum of from 12-16 months before reaching the break-even point.

The owner can expect to operate on a margin of about 34 percent with a pre-tax net profit on sales at store maturity of approximately 5 percent and a pre-tax net profit on investment of around 17 percent. An active owner's return on investment averages approximately 36 percent.

"Franchise" Influence In Hardgoods Distribution

Approximately 85 percent of all hardware stores and home centers operate under a "franchise" arrangement with their wholesaler. They purchase goods at highly competitive prices and most major suppliers also provide advertising assistance, management data and operating statistics. In order to share in such "franchise" benefits, the retailer must follow strict operational plans and, in some cases, invest in the wholesale firm.

Getting Started In The Business

Key elements in starting a hardware business are location, merchandise mix, and service performance. Any newcomer to the business wil find reliable assistance in selecting a good location and salable merchandise mix. Service performance will be judged by customers served.

Legal Requirements

A hardware store or home center owner operates under well defined local, state, and federal laws which will not be a major element in the store's success or failure.

Industry Trends and Outlook

The hardware/home center industry is experiencing rapid growth. Social and economic factors all appear to be giving the home handyman, who relies heavily on such stores, a stronger role in the future. There are many signs that the hardware industry, which has always been a stable one and will continue to grow.

For Further Information

National Retail Hardware Association
770 North High School Road
Indianapolis, Indiana 46224

The above organization can provide a list of many helpful publications or direct you to one of its twenty-three affiliated organizations around the nation.

(Revised by Jack Rice, Director of Educational Services, National Retail Hardware Association, Indianapolis, Indiana)

Small Volume Home Building: The home building business in the past has offered an attractive opportunity for small businesspeople. Over half of the new single-family homes provided in the United States have been constructed by small volume builders. The small volume builders construct an average of 20 homes a year, many are built on site for specific buyers. Others are constructed, or "spec" built in anticipation of a buyer.

Traditionally, small builders learn the business from experience in the building and construction trades. However, in today's housing industry abilities beyond trade skills are needed. Marketing, finance, land acquisition, negotiation, work coordination (including planning, forecasting, and subcontracting), accounting, and other skills are required. It is also important that builders keep up with the latest industry developments in cost saving devices, federal housing programs, and local construction regulations. Builders must be familiar with interest rate trends and mortgage market developments. The small builder must be aware of all national forces that eventually will effect local housing markets.

There are basically two types of single-family builders, the custom builder and the speculative or tract builder. Basically both operate out of homes or small offices. The custom builder obtains a contract to build a house for a fixed fee or percentage over cost. The builder may use subcontractors on every phase of construction.

The "spec" builder who builds in hope of finding a buyer should plan to have enough working capital to live on for two years. The "spec" builder will need down payment for land, which usually costs 20 percent of the house sales price. The builder will need to arrange for a construction loan in order to build the "spec" house. A good credit rating is essential because builders are personally liable on all loans and notes. Ideally, the home builder should make a net profit before taxes of 10 percent.

Equipment needs vary with the scale of a builder's operation. Most builders need a pick-up truck, electric generator, storage space, possibly a heating device, and eventually an office and associated equipment.

Small businesspeople have been the backbone of the single-family home building industry. In recent years, however, changes such as rising materials costs, reshaped those elements that in the past brought builders success.

As a result of these changes, the successful builder must conduct some form of market research before beginning a new project. Basically, market research is defining the housing needs of the region the builder services (or market) in terms of price and specified types of housing people desire. Typical marketing research endeavors would include analyzing the reasons for the success or failure of a competitor's recent project, researching the age and income distributions of the population in an area and from it predicting future trends. For example: if an increasing number of young married couples are moving into a community, the housing needs of the community will rise. A builder might then try to learn the income distribution of this group. This data will then give a contractor a clue to the specific type of housing and price range that will respond to the needs of these young couples. When the builder feels a survey has correctly been completed, plans can then be developed for both the types of housing to be constructed and also the sales promotion activities to follow.

Builders may be required to be licensed and to follow local building codes. Specific information in these areas generally can be obtained from local authorities. The latest mortgage and Federal agency information is available from the National Association of Home Builders, Morgage Bankers Association, Federal Home Loan Bank Board, and local savings and loan associations.

For Further Information

Federal Home Loan Bank Board
101 Indiana Avenue, N.W.
Washington, D.C. 20552

Mortgage Bankers Association of America
1125 15th Street, N.W.
Washington, D.C. 20005

National Association of Home Builders
15th and M Streets, N.W.
Washington, D.C. 20005

How to Start Your Own Small Business, Drake Publishers, Inc., New York, 1973.

Construction Company Organization and Management, George E. Deatherage, McGraw Hill, 1964.

"Business Plan for Small Construction Firms," *Management Aid* No. 221. Small Business Administration, U.S. Government Publications (Free)

"Starting and Managing a Small Business of Your Own," *Starting and Managing* Series No. 1:15:1, Small Business Administration, Superintendent of Documents, Washington, D.C. 20402.

(By David J. Rollison, Director of Business Management, National Association of Home Builders)

Starting a Travel Agency: The dynamic growth of modern travel has created many technical problems for the traveling public and with them the need to consult well-informed and highly qualified experts — travel agents — to plan, arrange and coordinate travel. Average travelers faced with a myriad of alternatives for transportation, accommodations, and other travel services, must depend upon the professional travel agent to guide them wisely and honestly.

There are currently more than 15,000 independent businesses in the United States and Canada which devote all, or substantially all, of their time and effort to the promotion and sale of travel and related services. These agencies employ more than 60,000 trained personnel. The travel agency industry is a highly specialized, intricate and serious business — far from the occasional misconception of being a continuous round of carefree traveling.

Therefore, anyone intending to enter the travel agency field should realize that it is an exacting profession requiring specialized knowledge and skills, adequate financing, devotion and willingness to serve the public in the best traditions of business and ethical conduct.

Despite the large number of travel agencies in the U.S. and Canada, there are relatively few sources of formal training and education for a person desiring to enter the industry. Although on-the-job training in an existing agency has been the most common source of experience, there are other sources of education available to aspiring travel agents. Several schools offer correspondence courses designed to give a basic understanding of travel agency operations. For example, the American Society of Travel Agents (ASTA) offers the ASTA Travel Correspondence Course.

Day and night courses are often offered by trade schools, travel agencies, and other organizations. In addition, many junior colleges and several universities offer courses in tourism and travel management both on the undergraduate and graduate level.

An agent, by definition, is one who is officially appointed by a principal or many principals. By principals we mean airlines, shipping lines, railroads, and so forth. Some principals, hotels and tour operators, appoint agents on an informal basis while others, notably the airlines and many shipping lines, appoint agents through one of several Conferences. Without such appointments an agent cannot receive commissions. Each conference establishes its own criteria for approval and the applicant must meet the standards pertaining to financial responsibility, business experience, and so forth.

The amount of capital required to open an agency varies. Several Conferences have certain requirements for minimum financing.

It is a travel agent's responsibility to serve the public with various travel services. A travel agent provides a wide range of unbiased travel advice; arranges transportation; arranges for hotel, motel and resort accommodations, meals, sightseeing, transfers of passengers and luggage between terminals and hotels; prepares individual itineraries; arranges reservations for special interest activities; and handles and advises on many details involved in modern-day travel.

Once an agency is established, familiarization trips, provided through airlines and tourist offices, give travel agents an opportunity to visit many new points of interest or to get reacquainted with established resort areas so that they may become the most knowledgeable travel people in the world.

For Further Information

ASTA Travel News. ASTA Travel News, Inc., 488 Madison Ave., New York, N.Y. $10 year.

Guide to Buying, Selling and Starting a Travel Agency. Travel Library, P.O. Box 249, La Canada, CA 91011.

The Travel Agent. American Traveler, Inc., 2 West 46th St., New York, N.Y. $5 yearly.

Travel Trade. 605 Fifth Avenue, New York, N.Y. 10016. $5 yearly.

Travel Weekly. Ziff Davis Publishing, One Park Ave., New York, N.Y. 10016. $9 yearly.

(Revised by Richard Ramaglia, American Society of Travel Agents, Inc., New York, N.Y.)

Carwash: The carwash industry is one of the fastest growing segments in the automotive service field. Types of carwash are: (1) self-service spray wash, (2) Exterior automatic with car stationary or drivethrough, and (3) Exterior only full service conveyor.

The investment will vary depending on type installation. In keeping operating cost to a minimum the industry trends is toward more automation. More equipment means more maintenance, requiring the operator to possess or employ someone with mechanical aptitude. The selection of proper equipment can mean the difference between profit and loss. The size of the operation, land, building and expected volume determine the type of equipment to be used. Equipment manufacturers of distributors often will assist the prospective carwash operator in the proper layout, sizing and evaluation of an existing operation, as well as in the establishing of a new installation.

According to a recent National Carwash Council survey, self-service operations usually require a minimum of three to four bays to provide a good profit base. Current industry trends are running to even larger (8-12 bay) units. Total cost per bay ranges from $10,000 to $15,000 with metered price ranging from 50¢ to 75¢ for 4-5 minutes. An operator of a well managed self-service carwash in a good location can expect return on investment to range from 30 percent upwards, depending upon volume, utility and maintenance costs.

Typical investment figures, exclusive of land and building, for an exterior automatic carwash run from $20,000 to $70,000, depending upon type of equipment purchased. Washes at these installations can usually be purchased from $1.25 to $2.25. A typical exterior only installation is the in-bay associated with a conventional service station. Operators easily wash 65 to 150 cars per day by offering either a free wash with a fill-up of gasoline, or by charging a normal price with or without a gas purchase.

Full service conveyorized tunnel facilities usually have a gasoline tie-in. Depending on amount of equipment they range from 50 to 150 feet in length. A full service tunnel can cost between $80,000 to $350,000. To justify this expense it should wash as many as 4500 cars monthly and pump approximately 70,000 gallons of gas. Generally, cost of sales average about 41 percent of gross, while operating expenses may reach 30 percent.

Capital investment is substantial and makes site selection important. A successful carwash is generally a neighborhood business requiring a population density in the vicinity of 20,000 within its primary drawing area (2-3 miles radius). Before establishing a carwash a detailed appraisal examining the city, neighborhood, location, traffic, prevailing weather and economic strata and habits of expected patrons should be conducted. It's generally preferable to locate a carwash on a heavily travelled street. A neighborhood with average to above average income where there's a predominance of vehicles less than four years old is another supportive factor.

Carwash installations require an above average amount of electrical and plumbing costs. The accepted life of a carwash building is 15 to 20 years. While maximum life expectancy of carwash equipment ranges from 5 to 8 years.

Prospective carwash operators should check out local zoning requirements as they relate to carwash installations. Rules and regulations issued by the Environmental Protection Agency concerning carwash effluent, Federal Energy Administration regarding prices, Fair Labor Standards Act pertaining to minimum wage legislation, and the Occupational Safety and Health Act regarding employment and consumer safety must be complied with by the carwash operator.

For those interested in entering the carwash industry the following sources may be helpful:

For Further Information

National Carwash Council
7 S. Dearborn Street
Chicago, Illinois 60603

American Clean Car, 500 N. Dearborn Street, Chicago Illinois 60610

Auto Laundry News, 17 Sherwood Place, Greenwich, Connecticut 06830

Self Service Car Wash News, 13224 Newport, No. 6-B, Tustin, California 92680.

Car Wash Express, P.O. Box 2451, Bassett Branch, La Puente, California 91746

(By Larry Guariniello, National Carwash Council, Chicago, Illinois)

Pest Control: Pest control is normally confined to include the building and its immediate surroundings and does not include tree spraying, lawns and ornamental shrubs, mosquito control, forestry, or agricultural crops.

Job estimation in pest control is similar to other trades in that the owner-manager must be able to discern the costs of labor, materials, supplies, equipment, general overhead costs, maintenance, depreciation, and all other expenses that are incurred in running the business. Guidelines on these types of expenses can be obtained from Association membership.

The capital investment requirements vary with the type of work performed. The National Pest Control Association defines the work categories and the estimated start up costs as follows.

1. Insects and Rodents — Start up costs including chemicals and the equipment for their use — approximately $150. This type of operation would normally be conducted out of a person's home, and use the family car.

2. Termite Control — Start up costs for chemicals and equipment will vary from $800 to $1200 plus a specialized vehicle (van or pickup truck) will be required.

3. Fumigation — Start up costs for chemicals and equipment would be approximately $3,000. Fumigation services are not recommended for the beginning because of the high set-up costs, complexity, and insurance requirements.

In all cases of equipment selection it is strongly recommended that equipment be purchased from a pest control operator-supplier who has in-depth knowledge of the equipment and chemicals.

Insurance rates for general pest and termite control will cost about $500 to $700 and fumigation about $3,000.

The industry is made up of about 8,000 firms. Fifty firms have annual sales in excess of one million dollars. Eighty to eighty-five percent of the businesses have sales less than $100,000. A 1976 productivity survey shows the average technician produces about $32,000 in revenue per year. It would normally take a new business three to five years to attain this sales level.

The industry is seasonal, particularly in the colder Northern states. Expenses are higher and profits are lower in the colder regions. During the peak season (between April and July) the pest control operator may work 10 to 14 hours a day, six or seven days a week.

Location of business is of little importance because the operator performs his services on the customer's premises.

Marketing — The new firm is advised to use a Yellow Pages ad, solicit referrals from customers, canvas, and advertise in local media.

Laws and regulations applying to the pest control operators are stringent. In addition to the usual laws which apply to business, the pest control operator is regulated under the Federal Insecticide, Fungicide and Rodenticide Act (FIFRA). This law controls the manufacture, distribution, and use of all pesticides. Many states require pest control operators be certified as competent or work under the direct supervision of a certified PCO. Certification is obtained by passing an examination in each category of work the operator wishes to do.

Industrial future of the pesticide business indicates modest growth, 12 to 14 percent (including inflation) per year. Growth is accomplished by the addition of new markets, deeper penetration into existing markets, and by increased service to present customers.

For Further Information

National Pest Control Association, Inc.
8150 Leesburg Pike, Suite 1100
Vienna, Virginia 22180

Pest Control Technology, P.O. Box 12356, Cincinnati, Ohio 45212

Pest Control Magazine, 9800 Detroit Avenue, Cleveland, Ohio 44100

(By Robert J. Kerber, DBA, College of Business, Illinois State University, Normal, Illinois in cooperation with Alan M. Leopold, General Manager, National Pest Control Association, Inc., Vienna, Virginia.)

The Garden Center Business: A typical Garden Center (retail nursery) consists of a building with display, office, and storage spaces located on a sales yard large enough to exhibit bulky items such as shrubs and peat moss. In addition, there may be a greenhouse and a lath house in a shaded area. Some garden centers operate a highly seasonal business, virtually shutting down in the winter months. Others expand their operations — inventory and services — so as to operate year-round. Some provide landscape services.

Very small garden centers may have only the owner-manager working year-round. Almost all garden centers expand their work force with part time employees during peak seasons. It is estimated that one full time employee is needed for every $50,000 in sales. The owner-manager of a small nursery may expect to spend a large part of his or her time doing things that the manager of a larger firm would not be doing. As a result such an owner-manager can expect to work very long hours during the peak days and weeks of the season.

It is essential that the owner-manager, or some other employee(s), have a substantial knowledge about the technical aspects of the products being sold. Such knowledge extends to plants and soil, fertilizers, insecticides, and plant diseases.

A knowledge of state and local regulations dealing with plant quarantines and other restrictions is necessary. Local zoning laws must be investigated and complied with.

An adequate system of recordkeeping must be maintained, not only for income tax purposes, but primarily for the information it supplies the owner-manager in terms of planning for financing and marketing.

A characteristic of virtually all nursery people is that they enjoy working with plants and they derive a great deal of satisfaction from producing healthy vegetation. A large amount of outside work is required. Many nurserypeople think of the nursery business as a way of life rather than as a business or a place of employment.

The volume of sales that will be necessary to generate a satisfactory income for the owner-manager, depends on a variety of factors. However, the following percentages derived from reports of retail operators for 1976 (for firms with less than $200,000 in sales) give some indication of the possibilities.

Cost of goods sold will be 50 percent of sales leaving a gross margin of 50 percent. The gross breaks out as follows: selling expenses 26 percent; managerial expenses 5 percent; administrative expenses 6 percent; miscellaneous expenses 3 percent; and profit before income tax 10 percent.

The amount of investment required will vary depending on the scale of operations. The cost of the land will depend on its location, and the cost of the building will depend on how extensive it is. Sales tend to be concentrated in two peak seasons. Spring is stronger than the fall. The spring peak ranges from February through April in the South, and April through June in the North. Inventory turnover is seldom more than once a year. Therefore, an inventory of $40,000 to $50,000 must be provided at the beginning of the spring season to develop sales of $100,000. A firm with a good credit rating can expect to finance part of this inventory with trade credit.

Site location is important to the garden center because of its availability to potential customers, and its attractiveness for advertising. A spacious corner lot with adequate off-street parking, located on a well-traveled road in a suburban setting is desirable. In spite of a good location, it still is necessary to advertise. Advertising costs run about 5 percent of sales for established firms, but should be higher for new centers.

For Further Information

The American Association of Nurserymen
230 Southern Building
Washington, D.C. 20005

The American Nurserymen Publishing Company
310 South Michigan Ave.
Chicago, Ill. 60604

Horticultural Research Institute
230 Southern Building
Washington, D.C. 20005

Small Business Administration
Washington, D.C. 20416
Counseling Note No. 118, "The Nursery Business"

Small Business Administration
Washington, D.C. 20416
Counseling Note No. 119, "Wholesale Growing"

Small Business Administration
Washington, D.C. 20416
Counseling Note No. 121, "The Landscape Business"

(By Professor Eric W. Lawson, Syracuse University, Syracuse, New York, in consultation with the American Association of Nurserymen)

The Landscaping Business: A Landscape Firm is one which basically places environmental plants in the ground according to a plan which is designed to enhance the appearance of the area. The firm also may prepare the plan and sell the plant and other materials used. The scale of operations varies from a one crew — three person, one truck — firm to a firm with many pieces of heavy earth moving equipment, cranes and a large work force. A variant of the above pattern has grown up in recent years and consists of a landscape maintenance firm which provides service for established lawns and plantings to residential, commercial, industrial, and governmental customers on an annual basis. Many landscape firms are part of or are affiliated with either garden centers or nursery growers, or both.

Typically, the manager of a landscape firm has a substantial knowledge of environmental plants. Not only must there be knowledge of technical matters relating to soil and fertilizer, but also some artistic judgment with respect to present and future color, shapes and sizes of plants used. The work is performed out of doors and at times involves considerable physical effort. The owner-manager of a small operation must participate in this activity. Since the results are constantly on display the landscape manager must have a keen sense of pride.

Three factors should be considered in determining location: firm should be established in a well populated, expanding area; traveling distance to customers' property; and whether a retail outlet is in operation, or may be in the future. The base of operations must be large enough, at a minimum, to store a truck, necessary hand tools and equipment, plants, and supplies. Many landscape firms build patios, fences and other landscape objects for which raw materials must be supplied and may require additional storage space.

The minimum capital needed to start a landscape business must cover the cost of a truck and tools plus any inventory made necessary by the absence of convenient suppliers. The maintenance of an inventory increases the chance of success because it assures the availability of materials and reduces costs. In addition to the above basic requirements, there must be enough working capital to pay wages and other operating costs and carry the receivables until the contract jobs are completed and paid for. Since wages and other operating costs vary widely throughout the country, it is not possible to estimate a representative figure. A cash flow covering at least three months of peak operations should be calculated and the indicated amount made available.

Profit potentials can be estimated from the following typical relationships: cost of goods sold, labor and material run about 67 percent of gross sales to produce a gross margin of about 33 percent. This typical margin of 33 percent breaks down as follows: selling expenses 8 percent; administrative expenses 17 percent; and profit before taxes 8 percent.

The landscape firm must develop names of prospective customers and sell its services on a continuing basis. A good reputation will develop sales for an established firm. Advertising is important.

The market is competitive. It is necessary that a landscape manager know what job costs are, including allowance for indirect costs and for costs incurred during the idle season. Hence, a good record system and a knowledge of how to use it is essential.

For Further Information

The American Association of Nurserymen
230 Southern Building
Washington, D.C. 20005

The National Landscape Association
230 Southern Building
Washington, D.C. 20005

The American Nurserymen Publishing Company
310 South Michigan Ave.
Chicago, Ill. 60604

The Horticultural Research Institute
230 Southern Building
Washington, D.C. 20005

Small Business Administration
Washington, D.C. 20416
Counseling Note No. 118, "The Nursery Business"

Small Business Administration
Washington, D.C. 20416
Counseling Note No. 119, "Wholesale Growing"

Small Business Administration
Washington, D.C. 20416
Counseling Note No. 120, "Retail Garden Centers"

(By Professor Eric W. Lawson, Syracuse University, Syracuse, New York, in consultation with the American Association of Nurserymen)

Apparel Store: The success of an Apparel Store depends a great deal on knowledge gained through previous experience in retail sales, buying, finance, and managerial positions. A minimum of two years is recommended. In addition, some formal training in business, merchandising, and management will prove beneficial.

A prosperous store owner also needs selling ability and a winning personality. Those who genuinely like people and enjoy selling clothes can build the warm and congenial atmosphere essential to the small store success. In addition, the new owner must be energetic and enthusiastic — willing to work at least 10 hours a day, six days a week — and contend with a multitude of problems.

The National Retail Merchants Association has determined that the average apparel store can expect the following operating expense ratios when cost of goods sold is 59.2 percent of sales, leaving 40.8 percent for gross profit:

Gross profit		40.8
Wages	18.0	
Rent	5.0	
Advertising	3.0	
Other expenses	11.1	
Total expenses		37.1

These figures will vary by area, type of store, and other factors.

Investment requirements for an apparel store vary with types of apparel. They range from $44,150 to $76,450 for a hypothetical store with floor space of 2,000 sq. ft. and annual gross sales of $250,000. These totals are itemized as follows:

Fixtures and Equipment	$ 3,310 - $ 6,590
Premises	12,690 - 23,410
Opening costs	8,150 - 11,450
Inventory	20,000 - 35,000

Selected Balance Sheet Ratios

Cash as percent of assets	7.3
Inventory as percent of assets	52.0
Long term debt as percent of total liabilities	21.0
Short term debt as percent of total liabilities	14.4

A word of caution: the store owner should have cash reserve for at least three months' operating costs, preferably one year, after start-up costs have been met. It is a rare new business that makes a profit the first year.

When selecting a desirable location, factors to be considered are prospective customers, trade competition (will area's population and sales volume support an additional new store), and visibility/accessibility (busy pedestrian traffic, good visibility, adequate parking).

Development of a unique or distinctive image carried out through all facets of the store's operation is beneficial in attracting the selected market segment. A "differential advantage" will justify the new opening and make the store stand out from other competition. A major problem for a new retailer is source of supply. Many apparel retailers use a resident buying office which screens manufacturers' lines and recommends those lines or items that offer the best style and value. New smaller stores may experience difficulty in obtaining services of resident buying offices because of their small sales volume, but some offices do serve smaller accounts.

Although the established apparel store allocates 3 percent of gross sales to advertising, new stores may spend as much as 4 to 6 percent the first year of operation to focus public attention on image. Direct mail and newspapers receive the largest share of the advertising budget. The remaining dollars are used for radio, TV, fashion shows, and personal approach advertising.

The laws and regulations for apparel stores are generally the same as for other retail outlets. However, there are specific federal (and in some cases, state) laws and regulations covering apparel labeling and flammability. Information is available from the Federal Trade Commission, Washington, D.C., or the Attorney Generals of states. The IRS and state and local tax collectors should be contacted for information about tax and license requirements. The owner should become familiar with credit laws, shoplifting laws, and workmen's compensation.

For Further Information

National Retail Merchants Association
100 West 31st St.
New York, N.Y. 10001

Career Apparel Institute
1156 Avenue of the Americas
New York, N.Y. 10036

Stores Magazine, 100 West 31st St., New York, N.Y. 10001

Women's Wear Daily, 7 East 12th St., New York, N.Y. 10003

(By Professor Lowell Salter and Clarise Adkins, University of North Florida, Jacksonville, Florida, in consultation with Patrick Cash, National Retail Merchants Association, New York, N.Y.)

Retail Photography Store: The owner of a retail Photography Store must possess a strong understanding of business, a thorough knowledge of cameras and supplies, and good interpersonal skill for dealing with customers. These attributes are gained from experience with photography, selling, and business procedures. The field is very competitive because of the variety of outlets, yet opportunities exist for the dedicated and competent retailer. This vital industry is based on growth in sales greater than average. Growth comes from innovations in new camera and film technology, and the rapid increase of knowledgeable customers.

Total start-up expenditures for a retail operation are estimated to range from $63,000 to $117,000. Included in this total are: investments for fixtures and equipment ($5,000 to $12,000), opening costs ($3,000 to $5,000), store preparation ($5,000 to $15,000), inventory ($40,000 to $60,000), and working capital ($10,000 to $25,000).

Revenues are generated by sales of merchandise (85 percent) and photo finishing (15 percent). Operating expenses consume approximately 26 percent of available dollars with payroll taking 14 percent. Profit before taxes is about 4 percent on the average.

About 50 percent of photo store purchases are made because of pricing. Other factors are range of selection, reputation, service, and knowledge of equipment. As a result, adequate pricing is essential. The average mark-up over wholesale cost is 35 to 50 percent, but the ability of sales personnel to close a sale based on technical knowledge, reputation of the store, and availability of service plus good personal relations with customers, is becoming increasingly significant. Customer credit is a major concern and precautions against bad debts are necessary. The service charge for accepted credit cards may be worthwhile.

In addition, advertising plays an important role in attracting customers. New store owners generally benefit from professionally created flyers, advertising in the classified pages of telephone directories, and local newspaper advertising. The use of attractive store fronts and window displays using colorful enlargements are effective supplements to advertising.

Start-up of a retail business involves contacts with city, county, state and federal agencies. The most common issue is sales, income, and employee taxes. City or county governments may also require licenses. Contact the Chamber of Commerce in the particular area for specific details. The Internal Revenue Service and state tax bureaus should be contacted.

Forecasts of industry sales indicate continued growth through the next decade. The majority of camera purchasers are college educated, professional, between the ages of 25 and 44 with incomes between $15,000 and $25,000. This group is increasing in size. Although a competitive threat to the independent retailer exists in the form of chain outlets, the small dealer can prosper by emphasizing individual attention and personalized services backed up by knowledgeable business practices.

For Further Information

Photo Marketing Association
603 Lansing Avenue
Jackson, Michigan 49202

Small Business Reporter "Independent Camera Shops", Bank of America, Department 3120, P.O. Box 37000, San Francisco, CA 94137

Photo Weekly Magazine, Billboard Publications, 1515 Broadway, New York City, N.Y. 10036

Photographic Trade News Magazine, 250 Fulton Avenue, Hempstead, New York, N.Y. 11550

Wolfman Report on the Photographic Industry, Published by ABC Leisure Magazine, 130 East 59th Street, New York, N.Y. 10022

(By Professor John W. Bonge, Lehigh University, Bethlehem, Pa., in consultation with John W. Dancer, Photo Marketing Association, Jackson, Michigan)

Office Products: Office products dealers sell the major portion of business furniture and supplies and a substantial number of business machines used throughout the Nation. Most of the industry's sales, estimated between $12 and $15 billion annually, are made to commercial customers by outside salespeople. Some dealers rely on over-the-counter retail sales.

Typically, the office products dealer has a commercial selling background along with the basic fundamentals of financial management. Training in specific product uses and product line application is generally available from the manufacturer. Management and general sales education are offered by trade associations, training programs sponsored by government agencies, and adult education programs, presented at local educational institutions.

Initial capital requirements can be small. It should be noted, however, that many dealers have encountered serious problems with undercapitalization after doing business for several years. Starting capital requirements may include store and warehouse space, retail fixtures, and shelving and an initial inventory. Wholesalers have become an increasingly significant force in the industry in recent years, and this trend has tended to reduce the capital requirements for starting inventory. With an acceptable credit rating, it is possible to establish an account with a major wholesaler on an initial order of about $6,000. As the business grows, additional capital may be required for an expanded inventory, delivery vehicle, materials handling equipment, data processing equipment, and other growth-related investments.

Net profits for office products dealers averaged 3.87 percent of sales in 1976 on gross profits of 37.74 percent, according to a NOPA survey. Return on investment for this year was 19.13 percent, and 93 percent of those responding operated at a profit. Inventory is the largest cost item for the average dealer — usually about 60 percent of sales. Wages, including those of owners and officers, are the second largest at about 20 percent of sales.

Because most of the industry's sales are to commercial users, much of the industry's marketing activity consists of calls by outside salespeople on customers and prospects. Often, the owner is an important member of the outside sales-force. In recent years, much emphasis has been placed on training outside salespeople to develop solutions to office problems rather than simply take orders.

Telephone selling has become a major marketing technique in the industry as rising costs have made regular face-to-face calls on marginal accounts impractical. Advertising expenditures averaged .67 percent of sales in 1976. Many dealers spend more on advertising, however, especially those with a high percentage of consumer trade.

Equipment requirements vary depending on the type and amount of services the dealer wishes to offer. Normally, customers would expect some sort of maintenance and repair service. This type of service would require a service de-partment area, tools, test equipment, spare parts, and qualified repair people. Other steps in retail operations would include shelving, fixtures, and cash registers. Additional services may be provided the customers by either including the necessary equipment and personnel or, by sending the work to a vendor.

The industry's real growth rate has been about 6 percent annually. Office supplies have shown remarkable stability, while office furniture and machines have been more sus-ceptible to general economic fluctuations. The development of word processing and rapid expansion in the use of mini-computers has caused some concern in the office products industry. The gradual replacement of paper oriented document production and storage by electronic media could profoundly alter the traditionally paper-based industry.

For Further Information

National Office Products Association
301 North Fairfax Street
Alexandria, Virginia 22310

Geyer's Dealer Topics, 51 Madison Avenue, New York, N.Y. 10010

Office Products, Hitchcock Building, Wheaton, Illinois 60187

Office World News, 645 Stewart Avenue, Garden City, New York 11530

(By Robert J. Kerber, DBA, College of Business, Illinois State University, Normal, Illinois, in consultation with Mr. Robert Mueller, National Office Products Association, Alexandria, Virginia.)

Automotive Parts and Accessories: The automotive parts and accessories industry is an aftermarket phenomenon. In 1973, industry sales were estimated to be $66.2 billion: $25.3 for Parts, Tires, Batteries and Accessories (PTBA); $23.5 billion for Fuels, Lubricants and Additives (FLA); and $17.4 for Service. Sales for Parts, Tires, Batteries and Accessories are expected to grow from $43 billion in 1978, to $65 billion in 1982 and nearly $85 billion in 1985.

The Automotive Parts and Accessories Association (APAA) estimate that nearly 135,000 of 460,000 auto parts and accessories retail outlets are especially geared to serve the growing Do-It-Yourself Market which now stands at 40 million and growing at a 9.5 percent annual rate. APAA research attributes the continuing growth in the PTBA segment to 1) the shortage of mechanics, which now stands at a ratio of 238 cars to one mechanic instead of the 87 to 1 ratio recommended by maintenance experts; 2) the rising average age of passenger cars, at 6.2 in 1977 up from 5.5 years in 1969; 3) the popularity of vans and recreational vehicles and the strong trend for each owner to make his vehicle "unique"; 4) the intensifying trend to limit "extras" and accessories as standard equipment; and 5) the sharp rise in the number of adults, of both sexes, taking automobile maintenance courses at community colleges and in adult education courses offered by public school systems. The American Automobile Asssociation adds inflation and the general increase in service rates to the list.

The above data tend to indicate that the automotive parts business is going to be in a growth mode for sometime into the future and is likely to remain viable for even a longer period. Accordingly, it is reasonable to conclude that the industry has the kind of outlook which makes it attractive for new entrants into the business world.

The 1973 study made by Industrial Marketing Research, Inc. for APAA classified automotive aftermarket retail outlets and determined their market shares by product category. The tables below are based on some of their findings.

Class of Store	% of Total $ Volume	PTB&A %	FL&A %	Service %
Gasoline Service Stations	46.9	24.2	83.7	30.4
PTBA Dealers	16.6	37.2	1.9	6.4
Auto Repair Shops	8.9	6.4	2.2	21.8
Home-Auto Stores	2.6	5.4	0.9	0.8
	75.0	73.2	88.7	59.4

Selected Operating Characteristics

Class of Store	$ Avg. Sales	PTB&A % Sales	FL&A % Sales	Service % Sales
Gasoline Service Stations	144,000	19.8	63.1	17.1
PTBA Dealers	482,292	85.7	4.1	10.2
Auto Repair Shops	96,156	27.4	8.5	64.1
Home Auto Stores	177,732	79.8	11.9	8.3

A significant number of the retail outlets servicing the automotive aftermarket are operated under franchise. Nearly all gasoline service stations are operated under franchise. In recent years, the independents and non-company owned stations have had strong competition from the major oil companies. Nevertheless, the outlook and opportunity for small and independently owned businesses in this line will continue to be viable for an extended period.

A major problem of the industry is finding sales personnel having the wide range of technical knowledge needed to serve the growing Do-It-Yourself segment of the market. The problem is intensified by rising wage and salary levels.

Consequently, owners must utilize the self-service concept with generous utilization of point-of-sale explanatory materials. In part, this difficulty is overcome by packaging, which includes extensive and easy-to-understand explanations of the ways, places and times at which various products may be used.

Inventory control arising out of the wide variety of items carried is likely to pose a problem. Average-size volume dealers may carry between 15,000 and 20,000 items in the inventory. Inasmuch as PTBA stores normally carry large inventories of many high unit cost items, it has been estimated that between $35,000 and $50,000 is required to go into this business. Amounts and conditions vary widely among the franchise operations.

Stores which have machine shops and service bays should be especially aware of OSHA regulations and liability insurance considerations. IRS and local tax laws are generally the same for these establishments as they are for other types of retail outlets. Building and fire codes, as well as zoning laws, may include special provisions relating to service bays and the handling of petroleum products.

For Further Information

The Retail Automotive Aftermarket 1973 and *The 1976 National Survey of Maintenance Do-It-Yourself Study.* The Automotive Parts and Accessories Association, 1025 Connecticut Ave., N.W., Washington, D.C. 20036.

Health and Safety Guide for Auto and Home Supply Stores, National Institute for Occupational Safety and Health, P.O. Building, Cincinnati, Ohio 45202.

Home and Auto, 753 Third Ave., New York, N.Y. 10017

Automotive Marketing. The Chilton Company, Chilton Way, Radnor, Pa. 19089

Automotive Aftermarket News, 300 West Lake St., Chicago, Ill. 60606

(By Professor Carl M. Franklin, Professor Dinker S. Raval, and Sylvia L. Barner, Morgan State University, Baltimore, Maryland, in consultation with the Automotive Parts and Accessories Association Inc., Washington, D.C.)

Interior Design Services: The Growing Importance of Interior Design in America presents an expanding opportunity for qualified individuals. Offices and commercial establishments are cognizant of the direct contributions made by a professional approach to their design problems. The residential market continues to expand as owners of even more moderately priced homes and apartments rely increasingly on designer services.

Aside from these historical trends, contemporary society is now beginning to enter a stage where adaptive use of older buildings is becoming a preferred economic option. Together with the necessary support of architects and engineers, it is the interior designer who is becoming the most critical figure in effecting these successful conversions.

Few interior design businesses have ever been initiated by anyone other than a person qualified to perform the design services. Overhead considerations alone would certainly dictate that, initially, both the entrepreneur and the interior designer be the same person. In a normal growth pattern, subsequent additions would include the hiring of secretarial, bookkeeping, and drafting services and the eventual accommodation of assistant designers, often those specializing in certain design categories. But many of the world's most successful interior designers do not need to rely on a large scale operation in order to be amply rewarded for their efforts.

One should readily conclude that success in selling interior design services requires more than the undertaking of a business venture. One should in fact *be* an interior designer.

According to the American Society of Interior Designers (ASID), "a professional interior designer is one who is qualified by education and experience to identify, research, and creatively solve problems relative to the function and quality of man's proximate environment." By contacting ASID, prospects for interior design careers may learn the specific channels through which a person can achieve professional status. In general, requirements include education at an accredited college or professional school, a term of practical experience, and the successful completion of a qualifying two-day examination.

Not all practicing designers enter the field through ASID membership program. However, the professional organization does stand ready to counsel and guide those interested by providing lists of accredited schools, and other career-aid programs. Furthermore, the rise of consumerism in the country has given the appellation "ASID" following a designer's name distinguishing sign of professional credibility among the many self-styled amateurs purporting to have "a flair for decorating."

Interior designers receive compensation from their customers in various ways: by time charges, fixed fees per project or, by retaining trade discounts on ordered goods from wholesalers and manufacturers. Designers in demand today can earn as much as $65 to $75 per hour on a time charge basis in the average American city. Firms may also seek additional income by employing purchasing expertise, e.g., buying items for resale in current design projects.

Investment needed to begin business operations can also vary greatly. Is there to be an office, or a store-front operation displaying a representative retail inventory to capture the interest of walk-in traffic? Many professional interior designers began business careers operating from their own homes. Consultation are done on the customer's premises, and recognized designers are permitted access to certain wholesale showrooms in large market centers in order to show merchandise to clients. If the designer is not going to carry inventory, he should be prepared to maintain a library of sample wall coverings, floor coverings, fabric, texture and finishes.

The pursuit of a business career in interior design runs strongly along professional lines in much the same manner as does an architect's or engineer's. To begin one's own enterprise in the field is an option with a rewarding potential, but the achievement of professional status is a first priority.

For Further Information

American Society of Interior Designers
Membership Program Chairman
730 Fifth Avenue
New York, N.Y. 10019
(Write for information)

Business Guide for Interior Designers. Siegel, Harry. 1976. Watson-Guptill Publications. 1 Astor Plaza, New York, N.Y. 10036

(By C. Kent Slepicka, Director, American Society of Interior Designers, Washington, D.C.)

Bicycles: The retail bicycle business is divided into three basic segments: Two are the small bicycle sales and service shop and the wide variety of National and regional mass merchants and specialty stores for toys and sporting goods. The third segment, which has existed since 1974, is the retail sale of bicycles by major oil companies at local service stations.

The focus here is on the community bicycle shop which is divided into two varieties: the all purpose, large bicycle sale and repair shop, and the traditional "small town" operation.

A bicycle shop is usually open for business six days a week. There is not often a great deal of tension surrounding the sale of bicycles, but servicing customers has become increasingly difficult in recent years due to increased consumer demand.

It is desirable for a prosperous store owner to have mechanic experience or trained, experienced, personnel. A superior service and repair department can give a store owner the advantage of being successful over another shop that offers the same products. It is helpful to have prior business experience before entering the field.

Some ventures vary, but a bicycle retail shop's business is divided into 75 percent bicycle sales and accessories and 25 percent services and repair. One dealer estimated gross margin at 32 percent. Bicycle inventory (including parts and accessories) can create as much as 75 percent of total operating expense.

Vehicle and equipment selection and starting costs are arbitrary. In a small city opening operations would probably require between $40,000 to $50,000 for an inventory of 200 bicycles. Perhaps $20,000 would go to stock, $10,000 to overhead, and $10,000 to $15,000 more to offset six months to a year of a non-profit existence. A free-spending economy greatly influences bicycle sales.

December is traditionally the big month for Christmas bike buying, however, May, June, and July can be excellent sales months.

A recent survey by the National Bicycle Dealers Association in Chicago, Illinois, reveals the following approximate expenditures for annual gross income for participating bicycle dealers in 1977:

Rent	$ 4,343
Advertising	2,214
Inventory — Bicycles	25,367
Inventory — Parts and Accessories	13,893
Inventory — Other	7,503
Utilities	1,534
Insurance	1,227
Servicing Equipment — Tools	930
Physical Improvements and Maintenance	842
Salary for self	12,705
Total salary — Family	2,193
Total salary — all employees	7,806
Uncollectable Accounts Receivable	346
Total	$80,903

Although the local bicycle dealer views the mass merchant as primary competition, the local oil service station's new venture into the field of bicycle sales could become a serious threat. One oil company feels that there is a definite connection between bicycles and automobiles and the convenience that an oil service station can offer has been the largest factor in their business.

The best bicycle prospects appear to be the ten-speed light weight with turned down handle bars, with 26″ or 27″ wheels; a 3-speed touring light weight; and a brightly colored juvenile model of the motorcross and hi-rise variety.

Accessory sales and repair services have become an increasingly important aspect of the bicycle business due to new safety legislation. Federal officials have proposed bikeways, municipal traffic ordinances for bicycles, licenses for riders and bike education for students. Every state has individual laws for users of bicycles and some in the retail sales area. A store owner should be aware of the community's local ordinances that effect buyers.

During the past seven years the bicycle has outsold the automobile in America. More than 75 million bikes were sold while 72 million passenger automobiles entered the transportation mix. The outlook for annual bicycle sales will probably range between 9 and 10 million. The Bicycle Manufacturers Association feels there are at least 75 million potential bicycle customers and with the upcoming trend of energy conservation, the industry's future is a bright and fruitful one.

For Further Information

American Bicyclist Magazine, 461 8th Avenue, New York, N.Y. 10001

Bicycle Journal, P.O. Box 1570, Fort Worth, Texas 76101

(By Dr. Jack J. Gross and Suzanne Cunningham, Temple University, Philadelphia, Pa., in consultation with Philip J. Burke, Bicycle Manufacturing Association of America, Inc., Washington, D.C.)

Fish Farming: Aquaculture, possibly the oldest form of agriculture, is on the increase. Channel catfish, and other catfish, trout, abalone, and oysters are among the products of these special farming industries.

Fish farming can be profitable, but it is far from a get-rich-quick venture. Success depends on excellent business management, together with plenty of technical know-how, and the ability to keep up with changing technology. Risk is moderate-to-high. Experts emphasize the desirability of visiting successful farms before investing.

The total processed catfish sold in the United States for 1975 and 1976 was estimated to be 41 to 42 million pounds.

This includes the processed farm-raised catfish, catfish imports, and wild catfish. In 1977 an estimated 50,000 acres of U.S. catfish farms produced some 80 million pounds, live weight, of fish, which sold at an average of 55 cents per pound, a total sales value of $44 million. Farm-raised catfish accounted in 1977 for nearly 3 percent of all fish consumed in the U.S. Projections run as high as a tenfold increase by the year 2000.

The profitability of catfish farming is greatly influenced by available marketing alternatives, and selecting markets is an important part of fish farm management.

Many catfish farmers sell directly to wholesale processing plants, especially in the states of Mississippi and Alabama. Nationally, about 27 percent of the catfish production goes to this outlet. Some processors enter into lower contractual agreements with growers.

More than 40 percent of commercially grown catfish goes to recreational markets. Growers often set aside fee-fishing ponds on their farms and stock them heavily for public recreational fishing. They either collect a flat fee for fishing or charge the fisherman for what he catches. This marketing method usually brings the farmer top dollar for his product.

Some farmers choose to sell live or dressed fish to local buyers at the fish farm. About 31 percent of all fish sold are marketed in this manner, and some farmers find this method highly profitable.

A few fish farmers operate restaurants in which they serve some or all of the fish they produce. This can be very profitable if proper restaurant management is exercised.

For channel catfish farming, a recommended size farm is 60 land acres: 40 acres farmed intensively in ponds of 5 to 10 acres each, the rest in roads, dams, storage, and so on. Soil borings should be analyzed to make sure ponds will not require the added expense of linings to make them hold water. Ponds must be completely protected from any flood runoff, and the site must be protected legally from aerial crop spraying on adjacent land. In addition, there must be no toxic chemical residue from nearby recent operations. Drainage from the farm into existing streams is legally prohibited in some areas.

Water is crucial. High quality water must be abundant, even during the summer. Stream sources or wells may be used. However, water temperature, power and pumps, and protection from pollution, parasites, disease organisms, and undesirable wild fish, should be considered.

After land purchase the largest cost is pond construction, ranging from $500 to $5,000 and more, for earth moving, drainage, and grass cover. Cost of installing the water system depends on whether stream or well water is to be used, and on whether an oxygen-adding method is installed. The largest operating expenses are fingerlings and feed. Other expenses are chemicals for control of disease, parasites, weeds, and cost of maintaining ponds. During the first year there is no return on the capital investment.

For catfish raised in cages, the net return per acre was $333.28 before taxes, according to the Kerr Foundation, Inc. of Poteau, Oklahoma. This return came from sales of $1,200. Costs were $866.72 as follows: direct production costs $747.24, and fixed costs (including land, equipment, and cages) $119.48. (For further details see *Capital Cage Culture* published by the Kerr Foundation, Agricultural Division, Poteau, Oklahoma.)

The most serious risks can be divided as follows: variation in water quality, disease and parasitism, poor quality fingerlings, and vandalism and theft. Production risk and risk associated with marketing, can be controlled through good management. Price risk may occur, however, as consumers' tastes change, as competitors move into and saturate a market, or as other meat substitutes become significantly cheaper.

For Further Information

National Marine Fisheries Service
1 Union National Plaza, Suite 1160
Little Rock, AR 72201

Catfish Farmers of America
P.O. Box 2451
Little Rock, AR 72203

U.S. Department of Agriculture
Soil Conservation Service
Your local office

The Kerr Foundation, Inc.
Agricultural Division
P.O. Box 588
Poteau, OK 74953

(By Professor Joseph Barton-Dobenin and Professor Margaret W. Maxfield, Kansas State University, Manhattan, Kansas, in consultation with the National Marine Fisheries Service, Little Rock, Arkansas.)

Fabricare: Laundry and drycleaning services comprise the two major categories of the fabricare industry. This industry ranges from small coin-operated units through plants serving hospitals up to those processing commercial work. However, it is a service-oriented business very much dependent upon customers feeling confident that their clothing, draperies, or expensive precious rugs are in competent hands and will be cleaned effectively and without damage.

The scope of the industry lends itself to a modest beginning with a coin-operated laundry to which can be added similarly operated drycleaning units. However, statistics show that the owner-manager must be prepared to work 12 hours a day and do some after hours work at home. Success often depends upon a well-chosen location, such as in or near a shopping center, so that it can become a habit to visit the laundry/drycleaners in conjunction with buying necessities at the supermarket and drugstore. This criteria for a suitable location must be underscored by creating and providing good, consistent, quality service.

Across the industry, before-tax profits can be as high as 11 percent of total sales — the package plants (where all the equipment and work is done on the premises) is the more profitable. Supplies average a maximum of 10 percent of total sales, but labor costs run as high as 45 percent which emphasize the service nature of the industry. Figures suggest that the overall reputation of the industry is improving in that drycleaning sales were 12 percent higher in the first seven months of 1978 compared with all of 1977.

The major consideration for the selection of equipment should be the number of pounds-per-hour that the plant is planned to clean versus the desired sales volume. Trade associations and machinery manufacturers can assist in this determination. The layout and operation of the plant must comply with regulations administered by the Environmental Protection Agency (EPA) and the Occupational Safety and Health Administration (OSHA). In addition, some states require a special license to operate drycleaning equipment. The potential owner should carefully research and comply with these regulations.

As the industry is labor intensive, anyone entering the industry should not only have some general business experience, but should be capable of managing personnel. This skill is as necessary in ensuring that the sales staff are sensitive to the customer's particular concerns, as it is with those handling the items in the cleaning processes. Previous experience in laundry or drycleaning work is a wise investment of time and effort.

Advertising costs often have to be higher in a service-oriented business compared with retailing, but specialty work such as cleaning leather or other coverings, stain removal, and off-season "two-for-three specials" bring customers and increased profitability.

For Further Information

International Fabricare Institute
12251 Tech Road
Silver Spring, Md. 20015

Coinamatic Age. Bi-monthly. Free. Coinamatic Trade Publications, Inc. 259 Broadway, New York, N.Y. 10007

Coin Launderer & Cleaner. Monthly. $10 annually. The Scheldko Corp. 2528 Harrison St., Glenview, Ill. 60025

Drycleaners News. Monthly. Rate not listed. Drycleaners News Corp. 70 Edwin Ave., Waterbury Conn. 06722

(By Professor Allan B. Cowart and Donald Clause, University of West Florida, Pensacola, Florida, in consultation with Lynn Turrentine, International Fabricare Institute, Silver Spring, Maryland)

The Bookstore: Bookselling can provide a profitable business for those interested in sharing the worlds of literature, ideas, and art with others and in the management aspects of this type of business. Statistics indicate that nearly half the bookstores in the United States are financially unsuccessful.

Sales volume and good management are essential to bookstore profits. Most successful bookstores are run by owners who do most of the work themselves, hire a minimum of outside help, buy and control inventory wisely, and manage all other costs closely. Long store hours (commonly 50-60 open hours per 6-day week) and courteous personal attention to individual customer's desires are necessary.

A potential total sales volume of $100,000 to $150,000 per year is essential for independent operation of a successful bookstore. Such a bookstore averages 1,500 to 2,000 square feet of which 1,200 to 1,600 square feet is devoted to displaying and selling space. The shop is run by 3-4 full-time people and stock turnover averages 3.5 times per year.

The American Booksellers Association provides the following financial data for 1977:

Net total sales	$125,000	100.0%
Less cost of goods sold	83,250	66.6
Gross profit margin	41,750	33.4
Less expenses		
Rent (cost of space)	6,625	5.3
Owners' salary	9,250	7.4
Wages	9,125	7.3
Utilities	1,250	1.0
Advertising	1,250	1.0
Supplies	1,250	1.0
Depreciation	1,250	1.0
Postage	875	.7
Telephone	750	.6
Insurance	750	.6
Other expenses	5,250	4.2
Total expenses	37,625	30.1
Net Profit	4,125	3.3

A potential bookstore owner should first gain practical experience by working in a bookstore for at least six months to one year. This experience will lead to knowledge about small business management and accounting, reading published materials, taking courses, and talking to people in the business.

Careful selection of a community with room for the type of bookstore considered is a critical first step in locating a suitable site. Communities with high-income, well-educated populations of over 25,000 and including a high proportion of education institutions and professional employment make desirable locations for bookstores. Desirable sites also include premises in downtown business districts and shopping areas of high pedestrian traffic and close to ample parking.

Appropriate inventory selection will depend on available floorspace and the nature of customer traffic. Items commonly stocked include: hardback fiction and non-fiction books, mass market and trade paperbacks, publishers' remainders, magazines, greeting cards, stationery, diaries and calendars, gifts, games, and records.

Start-up capital needs may vary greatly depending on the condition of the premises rented, whether new or used furniture and fixtures are installed, and so forth. It is important that a detailed estimate of start-up/cash requirements be made. A typical estimate might be as follows:

Assumptions:

Expected annual sales $125,000, shop of 1,750 square feet, rent $3.50 per square foot per year, inventory turnover 3 times per year, gross profit margin 33 percent.

Beginning inventory	$27,900
Three months' rent	1,530
Furniture, fixtures	3,000
Prepaid insurance, utilities, fees	1,000
Leasehold improvements	2,500
Initial advertising	500
Cash reserve	2,000
Total initial cash needs	
Cash reserve	2,000
Total initial cash needs	$38,430

For Further Information

American Booksellers Association
112 East 42nd St., New York, N.Y. 10017

Manual on Bookselling, edited by Anderson and Smith (Harmony Books), N.Y., N.Y. $4.95

Publisher's Weekly. R. R. Bowker Company, 1180 Avenue of the Americas, N.Y., N.Y. 10036

(By Dr. Coenraad L. Mohr, Illinois State University, Normal, Ill., in consultation with Ms. Cyd Rosenberg, American Booksellers Association, Inc., New York, N.Y.)

Bake Shops: Baking as a business offers steady, year-round employment with little tendency to layoffs or closed shops due to weather. It is seldom monotonous because of the great opportunity for creativity. Bakers' salaries compare favorably with those in any of the skilled crafts or trades, with early morning to mid-afternoon hours. A baker may enter the field as an apprentice, as a part-time employee during school, as a member of a baking family or, as a graduate of a commercial baking course.

Retail bakeries have every reason to be optimistic about the future of the industry. Consumers are putting more and more emphasis on quality and variety and are more concerned with product ingredients. The growth of the industry is supported by the latest figures from the U.S. Department of Commerce which states that in 1978 retail bakery sales topped the $2 billion mark at $2,436 billion. The annual total for 1978 reflected a 12 percent jump over 1977.

To start a baking business of 2,000 square feet requires $150,000. Initial capital outlay, including basic equipment, would be about $50,000. With an annual sales volume of $90,000 to $125,000 per year, a person would realize a net profit of between 10 to 15 percent, depending on prevailing market trends in labor and overhead.

The prospective owner however, should not obligate himself beyond 8 percent of gross for equipment payments and should buy only the equipment needed for anticipated beginning volume. Allow for future needs so that when the time comes, space will be available.

Bakeries are subject to local, state and federal regulations. Particular attention must be paid to sanitation laws and practices. Wage and hour laws as well as Occupational Safety and Health Administration regulations must be considered. Licensing by local and state boards should be investigated and zoning laws should be checked by prospective owners. It would be advisable for a firm to engage the services of an attorney if there are questions on taxes, incorporation, intrastate/inter-state commerce, etc.

Location selection is dependent on factors such as: convenience, competition, and available parking space. Consider sites such as shopping centers that draw large numbers of retail customers.

The market outlook for bakeries for the next several years has to be considered excellent. Consumer interest in baked goods is up and the positive and negative effects of inflation appear to be a standoff. All indicators are showing the consumers' return to the neighborhood retail shop.

For Further Information

Allied Trades of the Baking Industry
5240 West Irving Park Road
Chicago, Ill. 60641

Associated Retail Bakers of America
6525 Belcrest Road
Hyattsville, Md. 20782

Westco Products
1654 Long Beach Ave.
Los Angeles, CA 90021

Bakery Production and Marketing, Gorman Publishing Company, 5725 East River Road, Chicago, Ill. 60631

(By Joan Barkley, Associated Retail Bakers of America, Hyattsville, Md.)

Ice Cream: The creation of ice cream and frozen desserts continues to grow. Over the past decade there has been a move towards fewer but larger manufacturers of ice cream, some of whom are engaged in other activities such as milk marketing. Profit margins are not large, so it is a challenge to small business to enter the industry. Nevertheless, there has been a recent increase in the number of ice cream products. Overall, there appear to be better opportunities for small manufacturers in the exclusive, rather than in the large retail markets, while consumer preferences by taste, income group, and local environment create a number of variables which have to be considered.

Ice cream manufacturing is not a homemade type of operation. It is highly regulated by federal, state and other local authorities who control ingredients, packaging, labeling and sanitation. Comparable regulations also apply to most frozen desserts. These regulations, coupled with the sophistication of ice cream manufacturing, which involves about twelve operations, create a production process using several items of equipment. Commercial manufacturing requires considerable skill.

Nationwide, the ice cream industry has gross profit of about 21 percent to 23 percent of sales and a net profit before taxes of 3.5 to 5 percent of sales. However, with the retailing of ice cream, greater net profits can be expected, that is, up to 10 percent from sales in convenience stores. If it is sold in a "direct — dipping store," for example, the traditionally old fashioned ice cream parlor — where multiple flavors of ice cream complemented by some desserts are carried — the net profit can be as low as 3 percent because of labor costs, costumes for servers and decor. Nevertheless, it is this style of retailing enterprise which is predicted to increase by over 20 percent in the next five years.

It is projected that ice cream consumption will continue to grow but capitalization for larger scale manufacturing on a competitive basis is considerable because of the concentration of production capacity and its alliance to comparable industries, like milk marketing. However, scope exists, with smaller capitalization, in the presently returning fashion of the specialty ice cream parlor.

For Further Information

The International Association of Ice Cream Manufacturers
910 — 17th Street, N.W.
Washington, D.C. 20006

The National Ice Cream Retailers Association
325 West Adams Street
Muncie, Indiana 47305

(By Donald Clause, University of West Florida's Small Business Development Center, Pensacola, Fla., in consultation with Robert Mulligan, Ice Cream Industry and Forrest Mock, National Ice Cream Retailers Association, Muncie, Ind.)

Sewing Centers: The retail fabric business has about 12,000 outlets throughout the United States. Total volume is in excess of $3 billion. Of this amount, approximately 25 percent of the stores are owned under individual proprietorship, partnerships or small corporations. It is an ideal business for a husband and wife or two women to open together. Quite often, a woman who enjoys sewing decides to open a fabric store herself. Depending on the location, the store may be open 6 or 7 days a week from 10:00 a.m. to 6:00 p.m. or, 10:00 p.m. if it is in a shopping center.

One of the main advantages in opening a fabric store is the flexibility in size, it can be as small as 600 to 700 square feet. The ideal fabric store size is from 1800 to 2500 square feet. Depending on the size, it can be operated by 1 or 2 owners and under 1200 feet, generally, it would not require additional personnel unless it is located in a shopping center where the hours are extra long.

Due to the competitive nature of the fabric business and the large number of items each store must carry. the fatality rate for new stores, without proper help, is as high as 85 percent. It is desirable that owner managers possess high level sewing skills and some business experience to be successful.

In today's economy an investment of $15 per square foot is needed for inventory and working capital. For instance, if a 1000 square foot store is contemplated, $15,000 should be available. Of this amount, $1500 would be used for patterns, $2000 for notions, and $8000 for fabric. The balance would be used for working capital. Unless a lot of money is available, fixtures should be made rather than bought. The average gross markup is 50 percent; average maintained net profit is 20 percent providing no outside sales management is employed.

The national average for selling space is $56 per square foot. Patterns have an inventory turn of .6 per year; fabrics of 2X per year; notions of 3 to 4 X's a year. When estimating expenses, no more than 10 percent of anticipated gross can be allocated between rent and advertising. A 1000 square foot store should do $56,000 average in its second year. Approximately $450 a month can be spent on rent and advertising.

Heavy chain store dominance in large cities is evident. The best likelihood for success of an independent sewing retailer is in cities of 25,000 or less. While there are stores of all types ranging from boutique to strictly promotional, depending on the trading area, it is desirable to carry middle to better priced fabrics. Knowledgeable service is a positive key for the store toward building a reputation and maintaining growth.

The future of the fabric industry is good. Women sew for a number of reasons, including creativity, economy, better fitting clothes, and as a hobby. Demographics of women who sew (age, geographic location, etc.) are available from the American Home Sewing Association.

For Further Information

American Home Sewing Association
350 Fifth Avenue, Suite 1312
New York, New York 10001

Fabricnews, 360 North Bedford Drive, Suite 314, Beverly Hills, California 90210

Homesewing Trade News, 330 Sunrise Highway, Rockville Center, New York 11570

Sew Business Magazine, 666 Fifth Avenue — 14th Floor, New York, New York 10019

(By Harold J. Fields, American Home Sewing Association Inc., New York, N.Y.)

APPENDIX 4

Resources: Business Guides and Handbooks

To obtain copies of any of the texts mentioned in this resource check with your local library. Many of these directories are expensive and you may only want to borrow them for short periods of time or use them directly at a library. This is not a complete listing, but a sampling of the kinds of materials available for your use in specific businesses. There are many others covering just about any business area.

Apollo Handbook of Practical Public Relations. Adams, Alexander B., 1970. Apollo Editions, 10 East 53rd Street, New York, NY 10022. This is for the non-specialist in public relations and is a guide to help you and your company sell your message to the public.

Credit Management Handbook. Credit Research Foundation, 2nd Edition, Richard D. Irwin Inc. 1818 Ridge Road, Homewood, Illinois 60430. Tells how to organize and operate a credit department and how to make credit decisions on all size accounts; how to collect overdue accounts and how to use credit ratings.

Marketing Handbook. Frey, A. W. Editor, 2nd Edition, Ronald Press Company, 79 Madison Avenue, New York, N.Y. 10016. This is a comprehensive reference describing the marketing of goods and services.

Office Management Handbook. Wylie, Harry L., Editor, 2nd Edition, 1972, Ronald Press Company, 79 Madison Avenue, New York, N.Y. 10016. Describes standard principles and practices for operating an office efficiently. Applies to any size office.

Production Handbook. Carson, Gordon B., Editor 3rd Edition. Ronald Press Company, 79 Madison Avenue, New York, N.Y. 10016. Describes in detail plant layout and location, production planning and control, quality control and manufacturing processes.

Purchasing Handbook. Aljian, George W., Editor, 1973, McGraw-Hill Book Company, 1221 Avenue of the Americas, New York, N.Y. 10020. Gives a complete description of a purchasing department showing the organization, management and operating procedures.

Directories

Very often businesses need a variety of information concerning products, buyers, trade associations, etc. The telephone books (Yellow Pages) are an excellent source for lists of particular products and services. The following are a few of these directories that you may find useful.

Guide to American Directories. Check for latest edition, B. Klein Publications, Inc., P.O. Box 8503, Coral Springs, Florida 33065. An excellent resource as it gives information on directories classified by industry, by profession and by function. A good way to find new markets or sources of supplies.

Encyclopedia of Associations. Vol. I, National Organization of the United States. Biennial. 12th Edition. Gale Research Company, Book Tower, Detroit, Michigan 48226. A comprehensive listing of trade, business, professional, labor, scientific, educational, fraternal, and social organizations in the U.S.

Dun and Bradstreet Reference Book. Published six times per year. This reference contains the names and ratings of nearly 3 million businesses located in the United States and Canada. For complete listings of available information write to Dun & Bradstreet Marketing Services, 99 Church Street, New York, N.Y. 10007.

Directory of Conventions. Successful Meetings, 633 Third Avenue, New York, N.Y. 10017. This provides a national listing of forthcoming conventions, conferences and trade shows.

Thomas's Register of American Manufacturers, 11 vols. Thomas Publishing Company, One Pennsylvania Plaza, New York, N.Y. 10001.

National Trade and Professional Associations of the United States and Canada and Labor Unions. Published annually, Columbia Books Publisher, 734 Fifteenth Street, N.W., Washington, D.C. 20005. Gives a list of names, telephone numbers, addresses, size of staff, etc. of more than 4,000 national business and professional associations.

Trade Names Directory. Crowley, Ellen, Editor, 1st Edition, 1976, 2 Vols. Plus supplements. This reference text identifies trade names for 106,000 consumer products and their manufacturers, importers, and distributors.

APPENDIX 5

References From The Small Business Information Directory

U.S. Small Business Administration

Current Issues Of The Bank of America's "Small Business Reporter"

Copies of Bank of America's Small Business Reporter may be purchased at a cost of $2 per copy from Small Business Reporter, Bank of America, Department #3120, P.O. Box 37000, San Francisco, California 94137. Use check or money order. **DO NOT SEND CASH.**

Business Operations

Understanding **Financial** Statements
Vol. 7 No. 11, 1974

How to **Buy or Sell** a Business
Vol. 8 No. 2, 1975

Personnel Guidelines
Vol. 14 No. 2, 1978

Franchising
Vol. 9 No. 9, 1978

Equipment Leasing
Vol. 14 No. 1, 1978

Marketing **New Product** Ideas
Vol. 10 No. 5, 1974

Steps to **Starting** a Business
Vol. 10 No. 10, 1976

Management **Succession**
Vol. 10 No. 12, 1976

Business **Management: Advice** from Consultants
Vol. 11 No. 3, 1973

Avoiding **Management Pitfalls**
Vol. 11 No. 5, 1977

Crime Prevention for Small Business
Vol. 13 No. 1, 1977

Beating the **Cash Crisis**
Special Issue, 1975

Financing Small Business
Vol. 13 No. 7, 1977

Advertising Small Business
Vol. 13 No. 8, 1976
Cash Flow/Cash Management
Vol. 13 No. 9, 1977

Business Profiles

The **Handcraft** Business
Vol. 10 No. 8, 1976
Home Furnishings Stores
Vol. 11 No. 2, 1972
Health Food Stores
Vol. 11 No. 2, 1976
Independent **Liquor** Stores
Vol. 11 No. 4, 1977
Building Contractors
Vol. 14 No. 3, 1978
Mail Order Enterprises
Vol. 11 No. 7, 1977
Bars & Cocktail Lounges
Vol. 11 No. 9, 1977
Bookstores
Vol. 11 No. 6, 1979
Property Management
Vol. 13 No. 10, 1977
Apparel Stores
Vol. 12 No. 2, 1974
Coin-Operated Laundries
Vol. 14 No. 4, 1979
Restaurants and Food Services
Vol. 12 No. 8, 1977
Hairgrooming/Beauty Salons
Vol. 12 No. 9, 1977
Dry Cleaning Services
Vol. 13 No. 2, 1975
Consumer **Electronic Centers**
Vol. 13 No. 3, 1975
Gift Stores
Vol. 13 No. 4, 1975
Auto Supply Stores
Vol. 13 No. 5, 1976
Mobilehome Parks
Vol. 13 No. 6, 1976
Establishing an **Accounting** Practice in California, 1975
Establishing a **Dental** Practice in California, 1977
Establishing a **Medical** Practice in California, 1977
Establishing a **Veterinary** Practice in California, 1974

U.S. Department of Commerce's Urban Business Profile Series

Profiles of urban businesses are for sale at listed prices by the Department of Commerce, Publications and Distribution, Rm. 1617, Entrance, 14th & E St., N.W., Washington, D.C. 20230, Tel. (202) 377-5494.

Beauty Shops (25¢)
Bowling Alleys (30¢)
Building Service Contracting (30¢)
Children's Infants' Wear (25¢)
Contract Construction (30¢)
Contract Dress Manufacturing (25¢)
Convenience Stores (25¢)
Custom Plastics (30¢)
Dry Cleaning (25¢)
Furniture Stores (25¢)
Industrial Launderers & Linen Supply (30¢)
Machine Shop Job Work (30¢)
Mobile Catering (25¢)
Pet Shops (25¢)
Photographic Studios (25¢)
Real Estate Brokerage (25¢)
Savings & Loan Assn. (25¢)
Supermarkets (30¢)
Preparing a Business Profile (25¢)

Miscellaneous Publications

National Cash Register Co.
2301 Research Blvd.
Rockville, MD 20850
(301) 948-4700
"Expenses in Retail Business" Free on request

Dun & Bradstreet
1901 N Ft. Myer Dr.
Arlington, VA 22209
(703) 841-9500
"Key Business Ratios in 125 Lines," *"Cost of Doing Business, Partnerships & Proprietorships,"* *"Cost of Doing Business, Corporation,"* *"Failure Records thru 1980"* Free on request.

Dun & Bradstreet
P.O. Box 803
Church St. Station,
New York, NY 10008
(212) 285-7417
"Pitfalls in Managing a Small Business" $1.50

The Accounting Corporation of America
1929 First Ave.
San Diego, CA 92112
"Barometer of Small Business" Midyear Edition, $6. Year Book, $10.

Robert Morris Associates
Credit Division
1432 Philadelphia Nat'l. Bank Bldg.
Philadelphia, PA 19107
"Statements Studies" Annual, $15 plus $1.50 for postage and handling.

Council of Better Business Bureaus, Inc.
1150 17th St., N.W.
Washington, D.C. 20036
(202) 862-1200
(Ask for Publication Order Form)

References From The Small Business Information Directory

U.S. Small Business Administration

Federal Government Agencies

Department of Commerce

14th between E & Constitution Ave., N.W., Washington, D.C. 20230
Library, 7th floor, Main Commerce Building
Information on: Reference Materials............ (202) 377-5511
Bureau of Business Development, Rm. 3826
Information on: Markets; Industry Data...........(202) 377-3176
Franchising ....(202) 377-3873
Bureau of Export Development
Information on: Exporting ....(202) 377-4566
Office of Export Development
Information on: Trade Opportunities Programs.... (202) 377-2665
Bureau of the Census
Federal Office Bldgs. 3 & 4, Suitland, MD 20233
Information on: Business Census,
Trade Statistics..................(301) 763-7564
National Technical Information Svc.
5285 Port Royal Rd., Springfield, VA 22161
Information on: Tech Data/Reports, Mag Tapes/
Periodicals ....(703) 557-4650
Patent Office, 2021 Jefferson Davis Hwy
Crystal Plaza, Bldg. 3, Arlington, VA 20231
Information on: Patents and Trademarks ....(703) 557-3080
Ombudsman, Special Asst. to the Scty., DC 20230
Information on: Help with Federal Gov't. ....(703) 377-3176

"Franchise Opportunities Handbook," @ $4.75 (GPO) &
"Franchising in the Economy 1975-1977" @$1.50 (GPO)
Census of Populations and Housing: 1970" @$4.25 (GPO); "Retail
Trade: Sales Size" @$2.25 (GPO); *Retail Trade: Single Units and
Multiunits"* @$2.25 (GPO)

Department of Defense

Ofc. of Under Secretary of Defense, (R&E), Rm. 2A340
Pentagon, Washington, D.C. 20301
Information on: Federal Procurement Procedures (703) 697-1481
Ask for *"Selling to Military"* & *"Small Business and Labor
Surplus Area Specialists Designated to Assist Small and
Minority Businesses"*

Department of Labor

Wage & Hour & Public Contracts Div., Rm. 904,
6525 Belcrest Rd., Hyattsville, MD 20782
Information on: Federal Minimum
Wage-Hour Law .... (301) 436-6767

Department of the Treasury

Internal Revenue Service
Information on: Taxpayer Service for
New Businesses .... (202) 488-3100
(Ask for *"Your Business Tax Kit"* Free)
Rm. 701, 1201 E St., N.W., Washington, D.C. 20226
Information on: Info. & Assistance
(DC & MD) .... (202) 376-0038*
Skyline Ctr., 5205 Leesburg Pike,
Bailey's Crossroads, VA
Information on: Info. & Assistance (VA) .... (703) 557-9230
Bureau of Customs
Customs District Director & Customhouse,
Dulles Int'l. Airport, PO Box 17423, Washington, D.C. 20041
Information on: Custom Rates & Import Requirements
& Quotas .... (703) 566-8338
"Exporting to the United States" @$1.70 (GPO) . (703) 471-7150

*DO NOT CALL DURING TAX SEASON.

Federal Trade Commission

Pennsylvania Ave. & 6th St., NW, DC 20580
Office of Public Information
Information on: "List of Publications" .... (202) 523-3598
Bureau of Consumer Protection
Information on: Consumer Complaints .... (202) 523-3727
Div. of Legal & Public Records
Information on: Trade Practices & Regulations
(Franchises) .... (202) 523-3598
(Ask for FTC Buyer's Guide 4, *"Franchise Business Risks"*)

General Services Administration

Business Service Center, Reg. 3
Rm. 1050, 7th & D Sts., SW, Washington, D.C. 20407
Information on: "Doing Business with the Federal Government" &
the *"Federal Buying Directory"* .... (202) 472-1804
(Ask for SF 129, Bidders Mailing List Application)

Interstate Commerce Commission

12th & Constitution Ave., N.W., Washington, D.C. 20423
Information on: Information & Regulations........ (202) 275-7252

Securities and Exchange Commission

500 N. Capitol St., Washington, D.C. 20549
Information on: Public Information Consumer
Affairs ....(202) 523-3952

Library of Congress

Register of Copyright Ofc., Bldg. 2
Crystal Mall, 1921 Jeff. Davis Hwy., Arlington, VA 20540
Information on: Copyrights ....(703) 557-8700
National Referral Center, Thomas Jefferson Bldg.
Rm. A-5227, 2nd & Independence, SE, Washington, D.C. 20540
Information on: Referral Service.................(202) 426-5670

Government Printing Office

710 N. Capitol St., Washington, D.C. 20402
Information on: Government Publications .... (202)783-3238
Great Hall, Entrance, 14th & E St., NW, Washington, D.C. 20230
Information on: Sales and Distribution ....(202) 377-3527
Rm 120, USIA Bldg., 1776 Pa. Ave., NW, Washington, D.C. 20547
(202) 724-9928
Rm. 2817, State Dept., 21st & C Sts., NW, Washington, D.C. 20520
(202) 632-1437
Rm. E172, Pentagon Concourse, Washington, D.C. 20310
(202) 577-1821

D.C. Government

Dept. of Manpower, 500 C St., NW, Washington, D.C. 20001
Information on: Job Bank (Place Vacancies).......(202) 724-3785
Information on: Employment Svcs. & Job
Training (CETA) ....(202) 724-3800

APPENDIX 6

Free Management Assistance Publications

Below is a list of SBA's free **MA**s (Management Aids),
SMAs (Small Marketers Aids), and **SBB**s (Small Business
Bibliographies). **MA**s and **SMA**s provide recommendations
for handling management problems and tips on business
operations. **MA**s are generally aimed at manufacturing
businesses, **SMA**s at retail and service firms; however, many
of both **MA**s and **SMA**s provide information of use to
owner managers of all types of businesses.

SBBs list key reference sources for a variety of business
management topics. These sources include books,
pamphlets, and trade associations.

To get copies of the publications listed, check the titles you
want and fill out the order blank below. New and revised
titles are printed in bold type.

NOTE: On the following page there is
        a breakdown of the publications
        by topic.

To receive copies of the available publications listed, **call toll free 800-433-7212
(Texas only call 800-792-8901),** or check the titles desired, complete this order blank
and return it to:

U.S. Small Business Administration
P.O. Box 15434
Fort Worth, Texas 76119

Name_____
                          (Please Print or Type)

Street_____

City/State/Zip_____

MAs (Management Aids)

___ 170. The ABC's of Borrowing
___ 171. How to Write a Job Description
___ 178. Effective Industrial Advertising for Small Plants
___ 186. Checklist for Developing a Training Program
___ 187. Using Census Data in Small Plant Marketing
___ 189. Should You Make or Buy Components?
___ 190. Measuring Sales Force Performance
___ 191. Delegating Work and Responsibility
___ 192. Profile Your Customers to Expand Industrial Sales
___ 193. What Is the Best Selling Price?
___ 194. Marketing Planning Guidelines
___ 195. Setting Pay for Your Management Jobs
___ 197. Pointers on Preparing an Employee Handbook
___ 200. Is the Independent Sales Agent for You?
___ 201. Locating or Relocating Your Business
___ 203. Are Your Products and Channels Producing Sales?
___ 204. Pointers on Negotiating DOD Contracts
___ 205. Pointers on Using Temporary-Help Services
___ 206. Keep Pointed Toward Profit
___ 207. Pointers on Scheduling Production
___ 208. Problems in Managing a Family-Owned Business
___ 209. Preventing Employee Pilferage
___ 211. Termination of DOD Contracts for the Government's Convenience
___ 212. The Equipment Replacement Decision
___ 214. The Metric System and Small Business
___ 215. How To Prepare for a Pre-Award Survey
___ 216. Finding a New Product for Your Company
___ 217. Reducing Air Pollution in Industry
___ 218. Business Plan for Small Manufacturers
___ 219. Solid Waste Management in Industry
___ 220. Basic Budgets for Profit Planning
___ 221. Business Plan for Small Construction Firms
___ 222. Business Life Insurance
___ 223. Incorporating a Small Business
___ 224. Association Services for Small Business
___ 225. Management Checklist for a Family Business
___ 226. Pricing for Small Manufacturers
___ 227. Quality Control in Defense Production
___ 228. Inspection on Defense Contracts
___ 229. Cash Flow in a Small Plant
___ 230. Selling Products on Consignment
___ 231. Selecting the Legal Structure for Your Business
___ 232. Credit and Collections
___ 233. Planning and Goal Setting for Small Business
___ 234. Attacking Business Decision Problems With Breakeven Analysis
___ 235. A Venture Capital Primer for Small Business
___ 236. Tips on Getting More for Your Marketing Dollar
___ 237. Market Overseas With U.S. Government Help
___ 238. Organizing and Staffing a Small Business
___ 239. Techniques of Time Management
___ 240. Introduction to Patents
___ **241. Setting Up a Pay System**
___ **242. Fixing Production Mistakes**

SMAs (Small Marketers Aids)

SBBs (Small Business Bibliographies)

___ 1. Handicrafts
___ 2. Home Businesses
___ 3. Selling by Mail Order
___ 9. Marketing Research Procedures
___ 10. Retailing
___ 12. Statistics and Maps for National Market Analysis
___ 13. National Directories for Use in Marketing
___ 15. Recordkeeping Systems — Small Store and Service Trade
___ 18. Basic Library Reference Sources
___ 20. Advertising — Retail Store
___ 29. National Mailing-List Houses
___ 31. Retail Credit and Collections
___ 37. Buying for Retail Stores
___ 53. Hobby Shops
___ 55. Wholesaling
___ 64. Photographic Dealers and Studios
___ 66. Motels
___ 67. Manufacturers' Sales Representative
___ 72. Personnel Management
___ 75. Inventory Management
___ 79. Small Store Planning and Design
___ 80. Data Processing for Small Businesses
___ 85. Purchasing for Owners of Small Plants
___ 86. Training for Small Business
___ 87. Financial Management
___ 88. Manufacturing Management
___ 89. Marketing for Small Business
___ 90. New Product Development

Topic Listing

Accounting MA 224, SMA 126, SMA 140, SBB 10, SBB 15
Advertising and Public Relations MA 178, MA 224, MA 244, SMA 157, SMA 160, SMA 161, SMA 163, SMA 164, SMA 169, SBB 10, SBB 20, SBB 29
Borrowing/Raising Equity MA 170, MA 235, MA 250, SMA 147
Budgeting MA 220, SMA 146, SMA 164
Computers MA 250, SMA 149, SBB 80
Credit and Collections MA 118, MA 232, SBB 10, SBB 31
Crimes Against Business MA 209, SMA 119, SMA 129, SMA 134, SMA 137, SMA 151
Display (Retail) SMA 157, SMA 161, SBB 10, SBB 79
Equipment (Manufacturing) MA 212, MA 244, MA 249
Exporting MA 237, MA 247
Employees (See Personnel)
Financial Management MA 206, MA 220, MA 229, MA 232, MA 234, MA 235, SMA 126, SMA 130, SMA 140, SMA 146, SMA 147, SMA 164, SMA 165, SBB 15, SBB 87
Form of Business (Legal) MA 223, MA 231
Government (Doing Business With) MA 204, MA 211, MA 215, MA 227, MA 220
Government (Regulations) MA 217, MA 219, MA 223, MA 224, SMA 118, SMA 139, SMA 142, SMA 170, SBB 10

APPENDIX 7

U.S. Small Business Administration

Local Field Offices Throughout the United States

Regional Offices

Region I

Regional Office
Small Business Administration
60 Battery March, 10th floor
Boston, Massachusetts 02110

Region II

Regional Office
Small Business Administration
26 Federal Plaza, Room 29–118
New York, New York 10007

Region III

Regional Office
Small Business Administration
231 St. Asaphs Road
1 Bala Cynwyd Plaza, Suite 646 West Lobby
Bala Cynwyd, Pennsylvania 19004

Region IV

Regional Office
Small Business Administration
1375 Peachtree Street, N.E.
Atlanta, Georgia 30309

Region V

Regional Office
Small Business Administration
Federal Building
219 South Dearborn Street, Room 838
Chicago, Illinois 60604

Region VI

Regional Office
Small Business Administration
1720 Regal Row
Regal Park Office Building, Room 230
Dallas, Texas 75235

Region VII

Regional Office
Small Business Administration
911 Walnut Street, 23rd floor
Kansas City, Missouri 64106

Region VIII

Regional Office
Small Business Administration
Executive Tower Building
1405 Curtis Street, 22nd floor
Denver, Colorado 80202

Region IX

Regional Office
Small Business Administration
450 Golden Gate Avenue
Box 36044
San Francisco, California 94102

Region X

Regional Office
Small Business Administration
710 2nd Avenue, 5th floor
Dexter Horton Building
Seattle, Washington 98104

District Offices

Region I

District Office
Small Business Administration
Federal Building
40 Western Avenue, Room 512
Augusta, Maine 04330

District Office
Small Business Administration
Federal Building
87 State Street, Room 204
P.O. Box 605
Montpelier, Vermont 05602

District Office
Small Business Administration
55 Pleasant Street, Room 213
Concord, New Hampshire 03301

District Office
Small Business Administration
150 Causeway Street, 10th floor
Boston, Massachusetts 02114

District Office
Small Business Administration
One Financial Plaza
Hartford, Connecticut 06103

District Office
Small Business Administration
57 Eddy Street, 7th floor
Providence, Rhode Island 02903

Region II

District Office
Small Business Administration
26 Federal Plaza, Room 3100
New York, New York 10007

District Office
Small Business Administration
Federal Building, Room 1071
100 South Clinton Street
Syracuse, New York 13260

District Office
Small Business Administration
970 Broad Street, Room 1635
Newark, New Jersey 07102

District Office
Small Business Administration
Chardon and Bolivia Streets
P.O. Box 1915
Hato Rey, Puerto Rico 00919

Region III

District Office
Small Business Administration
231 St. Asaphs Road
1 Bala Cynwyd Plaza, Suite 400 East Lobby
Bala Cynwyd, Pennsylvania 19004

District Office
Small Business Administration
Federal Building
1000 Liberty Avenue, Room 1401
Pittsburgh, Pennsylvania 15222

District Office
Small Business Administration
Oxford Building
8600 LaSalle Road, Room 630
Towson, Maryland 21204

District Office
Small Business Administration
109 North 3rd Street, Room 301
Lowndes Bank Building
Clarksburg, West Virginia 26301

District Office
Small Business Administration
1030 15th Street N.W., Suite 250
Washington, D.C. 20417

District Office
Small Business Administration
Federal Building
400 North 8th Street, Room 3015
Box 10126
Richmond, Virginia 23240

Region IV

District Office
Small Business Administration
Federal Building, 600 Federal Place, Room 188
Louisville, Kentucky 40202

District Office
Small Business Administration
404 James Robertson Parkway, Suite 1012
Nashville, Tennessee 37219

District Office
Small Business Administration
Providence Capitol Building, Suite 690
200 E. Pascagoula Street
Jackson, Mississippi 39201

District Office
Small Business Administration
908 South 20th Street, Room 202
Birmingham, Alabama 35205

District Office
Small Business Administration
Federal Building
400 West Bay Street, Room 261
P.O. Box 35067
Jacksonville, Florida 32202

District Office
Small Business Administration
2222 Ponce De Leon Blvd., 5th floor
Coral Gables, Florida 33134

District Office
Small Business Administration
1720 Peachtree Street, N.W., 6th floor
Atlanta, Georgia 30309

District Office
Small Business Administration
230 S. Tryon Street, Suite 700
Charlotte, North Carolina 28202

District Office
Small Business Administration
1801 Assembly Street, Room 131
Columbia, South Carolina 29201

Region V

District Office
Small Business Administration
1240 East 9th Street, Room 317
Cleveland, Ohio 44199

District Office
Small Business Administration
Federal Building, U.S. Courthouse
85 Marconi Boulevard
Columbus, Ohio 43215

District Office
Small Business Administration
575 North Pennsylvania Street, Room 552
New Federal Building
Indianapolis, Indiana 46204

District Office
Small Business Administration
Federal Building
219 South Dearborn Street, Room 437
Chicago, Illinois 60604

District Office
Small Business Administration
477 Michigan Avenue
McNamara Building
Detroit, Michigan 48226

District Office
Small Business Administration
212 East Washington Avenue, 2nd floor
Madison, Wisconsin 53703

District Office
Small Business Administration
12 South 6th Street
Plymouth Building
Minneapolis, Minnesota 55402

Region VI

District Office
Small Business Administration
1001 Howard Avenue
Plaza Tower, 17th floor
New Orleans, Louisiana 70113

District Office
Small Business Administration
611 Gaines Street, Suite 900
Little Rock, Arkansas 72201

District Office
Small Business Administration
Federal Building
200 N.W. 5th Street, Suite 670
Oklahoma City, Oklahoma 73102

District Office
Small Business Administration
5000 Marble Avenue, N.E.
Patio Plaza Building, Room 320
Albuquerque, New Mexico 87110

District Office
Small Business Administration
1100 Commerce Street, Room 3C36
Dallas, Texas 75242

District Office
Small Business Administration
One Allen Center
500 Dallas Street
Houston, Texas 77002

District Office
Small Business Administration
222 East Van Buren Street
P.O. Box 9253
Harlington, Texas 78550

District Office
Small Business Administration
727 E. Durango, Room A–513
Federal Building
San Antonio, Texas 78206

Region VII

District Office
Small Business Administration
1150 Grande Avenue, 5th floor
Kansas City, Missouri 64106

District Office
Small Business Administration
Mercantile Tower, Suite 2500
One Mercantile Center
St. Louis, Missouri 63101

District Office
Small Business Administration
New Federal Building
210 Walnut Street, Room 749
Des Moines, Iowa 50309

District Office
Small Business Administration
19th & Farnum Street
Empire State Building, 2nd Floor
Omaha, Nebraska 68102

District Office
Small Business Administration
110 East Waterman Street
Main Place Building
Wichita, Kansas 67202

Region VIII

District Office
Small Business Administration
721 19th Street
Denver, Colorado 80202

District Office
Small Business Administration
Federal Building
125 South State Street, Room 2237
Salt Lake City, Utah 84138

District Office
Small Business Administration
Federal Building, Room 4001
100 East B Street
P.O. Box 2839
Casper, Wyoming 82602

District Office
Small Business Administration
Federal Office Building, Room 528
301 South Park, Drawer 10054
Helena, Montana 59601

District Office
Small Business Administration
Federal Building
657 2nd Avenue, North, Room 218
P.O. Box 3086
Fargo, North Dakota 58102

District Office
Small Business Administration
National Bank Building
8th & Main Avenue, Room 402
Sioux Falls, South Dakota 57102

Region IX

District Office
Small Business Administration
3030 North Central Avenue, Suite 1201
Phoenix, Arizona 85012

District Office
Small Business Administration
301 E. Stewart
Box 7527, Downtown Station
Las Vegas, Nevada 89101

District Office
Small Business Administration
350 S. Figueroa Street, 6th floor
Los Angeles, California 90071

District Office
Small Business Administration
880 Front Street
Federal U.S. Building, Room 4–S–38
San Diego, California 92188

District Office
Small Business Administration
211 Main Street, 4th floor
San Francisco, California 94105

District Office
Small Business Administration
300 Ala Moana
P.O. 50207
Honolulu, Hawaii 96850

Region X

District Office
Small Business Administration
1005 Main Street, 2nd floor
Continental Life Building
P.O. Box 2618
Boise, Idaho 83701

District Office
Small Business Administration
915 Second Avenue
Federal Building, Room 1744
Seattle, Washington 98174

District Office
Small Business Administration
1016 West 6th Avenue, Suite 200
Anchorage Legal Center
Anchorage, Alaska 99501

District Office
Small Business Administration
1220 S.W. Third Avenue
Federal Building
Portland, Oregon 97204

District Office
Small Business Administration
Court House Building, Room 651
P.O. Box 2167
Spokane, Washington 99210

APPENDIX 8

U.S. Department Of Commerce — List Of Regional Offices

REGION I (ME/VT/NH/MA/CT/RI)
Secretarial Representative Helen M Keyes
Deputy Secretarial Representative John J Parla
Secretary Karen Durante
441 Stuart Street 7th Floor
Boston Massachusetts 02116
(Area Code 617) 223-0695
FTS 223-0695
Telecopier 223-0699

REGION II (NY/NJ/VI/PR)
Secretarial Representative Bernard H Jackson
Deputy Secretarial Representative Alfred A Funai
Secretary Della Haft
Federal Bldg rm3722
26 Federal Plaza
New York New York 10007
(Area Code 212) 264-5647
FTS 264-5647
Telecopier 264-9399/9248

REGION III (PA/DE/MD/WV/DC/VA)
Secretarial Representative Dianne L Semingson
Deputy Secretarial Representative Linda A Sadler
Secretary Delores DeMayo
William J Green Federal Bldg
600 Arch Street rm10412
Philadelphia Pennsylvania 19106
(Area Code 215) 597-7527
FTS 597-7527
Telecopier 597-0676/2409

REGION IV (KY/TN/MS/AL/FL/GA/NC/SC)
Secretarial Representative Paul E Hemmann
Deputy Secretarial Representative James R Westlake
Secretary Joyce Baston
1365 Peachtree Street
Suite 300
Atlanta Georgia 30309
(Area Code 404) 881-3165
FTS 257-3165
Telecopier 257-2026

REGION V (OH/IN/IL/MI/WS/MN)
Secretarial Representative Loren A Wittner
Deputy Secretarial Representative Kent Wiley
Secretary Alyce G Schmale
CNA Bldg rm1402
55 East Jackson Blvd
Chicago Illinois 60604
(Area Code 312) 353-4609
FTS 353-4609
Telecopier 353-2418

REGION VI (LA/AR/OK/NM/TX)
Secretarial Representative Edward L Coker
Deputy Secretarial Representative Thomas C Adams
Secretary Loyce Coolidge
Federal Bldg rm9C40
1100 Commerce Street
Dallas Texas 75242
(Area Code 214) 767-8097
FTS 729-8907
Telecopier 729-8443

REGION VII (MO/IA/NE/KS)
Secretarial Representative Louis Gene Bickel
Deputy Secretarial Representative Wallace Green
Secretary Genevieve Ford
Federal Bldg rm1844
601 East 12th Street
Kansas City Missouri 64106
(Area Code 816) 374-3961
FTS 758-3961
Telecopier 758-5112

REGION VIII (CO/UT/WY/MT/ND/SD)
Secretarial Representative Stephen L R McNichols
Deputy Secretarial Representative Edman J Gleed
Secretary Beverly A Ward
Title Bldg rm515
909 17th Street
Denver Colorado 80202
(Area Code 303) 837-4285
FTS 327-4285
Telecopier 327-2968

REGION IX (AZ/NV/CA/HI)
Secretarial Representative Allen C Haile
  Deputy Secretarial Representative Mary Dee Beall
    Secretary Frances Smith
        Federal Bldg Box 36135
        450 Golden Gate Avenue
        San Francisco California 94102
            (Area Code 415) 556-5145
            FTS 556-5145
            Telecopier 556-3238/7826

REGION X (ID/WA/OR/AK)
Secretarial Representative Leonard W Saari
  Deputy Secretarial Representative Robert P Meredith
    Secretary Esther McDonald
        Federal Building rm3206
        915 Second Avenue
        Seattle Washington 98174
            (Area Code 206) 442-5780
            FTS 399-5780
            Telecopier 399-4470/5353

For Information: *Write to Regional office that represents your State.*

APPENDIX 9

U.S. Department of Labor, Regional Offices*

Information about employment and training activities may be obtained from your State Job Service/Employment Service, from the Employment and Training Administration, U.S. Department of Labor, Washington, D.C. 20213 or from the offices of the Regional Administrator, ETA, whose addresses and states served appear below.

Location and states served

John F. Kennedy Building, Boston, Mass. 02203
Connecticut, Maine, Massachusetts, New Hampshire, Rhode Island, Vermont
(617) 223-6439

1515 Broadway, New York, N.Y. 10036
New Jersey, New York, Puerto Rico, Virgin Islands
(212) 399-5445

P.O. Box 8796, Philadelphia, PA 19101
Delaware, District of Columbia, Maryland, Pennsylvania, Virginia, West Virginia
(215) 596-6336

1371 Peachtree Street, N.E., Atlanta, GA 30309
Alabama, Florida, Georgia, Kentucky, Mississippi, North Carolina, South Carolina, Tennessee
(404) 881-4411

230 South Dearborn Street, Chicago, Ill. 60604
Illinois, Indiana, Michigan, Minnesota, Ohio, Wisconsin
(312) 353-0313

Griffin and Young Streets, Dallas, Texas 75202
Arkansas, Louisiana, New Mexico, Oklahoma, Texas
(214) 749-2721

911 Walnut Street, Kansas City, Missouri 64106
Iowa, Kansas, Missouri, Nebraska
(816) 374-3796

1961 Stout Street, Denver, Colorado 80294
Colorado, Montana, North Dakota, South Dakota, Utah, Wyoming
(303) 837-4477

450 Golden Gate Ave., San Francisco, CA 94102
Arizona, California, Guam, Hawaii, Nevada
(415) 556-7414

909 First Avenue, Seattle, Washington 98174
Alaska, Idaho, Oregon, Washington
(206) 442-7700

---

*From the *Directory of Local Employment Security Offices*, U.S. Department of Labor,
Employment and Training Administration, 1979. GPO-269-073

APPENDIX 10

State Vocational Rehabilitation Agencies

For person with various handicaps: The following list should be used to locate the office nearest to you — call or write for further information:

Alabama

J. W. Cowen
Director
Division of Rehabilitation and Crippled Children Service
P.O. Box 11586
Montgomery, Alabama 36111
(205) 281-8780

Alaska

Michael C. Morgan
Director
Division of Vocational Rehabilitation
Pouch F. Mail Station 0581
Juneau, Alaska 99811
(907) 586-6500

Arizona

Thomas G. Tyrrell
Administrator
Rehabilitation Services Administration
Dept. of Economic Security
1400 W. Washington Street
Phoenix, Arizona 85007
(602) 255-3332

Arkansas

E. Russell Baxter
Commissioner
Arkansas Dept. of Human Services
Rehabilitiation Services Division
P.O. Box 3781
Little Rock, Arkansas 72203
(501) 371-2571

California

Edward V. Roberts
Director
Dept. of Rehabilitation
830 K Street Mall
Sacramento, CA 95814
(916) 445-3971

Colorado

Mark E. Litvin, Ph.D.
Director, Division of Rehab
Dept. of Social Services
1575 Sherman Street, 5th Floor
Denver, Colorado 80203
(303) 839-2652

Connecticut

James S. Peters, II, Ph.D.
Associate Commissioner
State Dept. of Education
Division of Vocational Rehab.
600 Asylum Avenue
Hartford, Connecticut 06105
(203) 566-3316

Delaware

Ben W. Barker
Director
Division of Vocational Rehab.
Dept. of Labor
State Office Bldg., 7th Floor
820 N. French Street
Wilmington, Delaware 19801
(302) 571-2850

District of Columbia

Vernon Hawkins
Acting Administrator
Vocational Rehabilitation Services Administration
Commission of Social Service
Dept. of Human Services
122 C Street, N.W., Fl. R-81
Washington, D.C. 20001
(202) 727-3227

Florida

J. David Sellars
Program Staff Director
Office of Vocational Rehab.
Dept. of Health & Rehabilitative Services
1309 Winewood Boulevard
Tallahassee, Florida 32301
(904) 488-6210

Georgia

James G. Ledbetter
Director
Division of Vocational Rehab.
Dept. of Human Resources
629 State Office Bldg.
Atlanta, Georgia 30334
(404) 656-2621

Guam

Lourdes Camacho (Mrs.)
Chief
Dept. of Vocational Rehab.
P.O. Box 10-C
Agana, Guam 96910
472-8806 (Dial 011671 First)

Hawaii

Kuniji Sagara
Administrator
Vocational Rehabilitation and Services for the Blind
Dept. of Social Services
P.O. Box 339
Honolulu, Hawaii 96809
(808) 548-4769

Idaho

Ray W. Turner
Administrator
Division of Vocational Rehab.
State of Idaho
1501 McKinney
Boise, Idaho 83704
(208) 334-3390

Illinois

Director
Illinois Dept. of Rehab. Services
623 East Adams Street
Springfield, Illinois 62705
(217) 782-2093

Indiana

Kenneth W. Reber, Ph.D.
Director
Indiana Rehabilitation Services
P.O. Box 7070
Indianapolis, Indiana 46204
(317) 232-6503

Iowa

Jerry L. Starkweather
Associate Superintendent & Director
Rehabilitation Education & Services Branch
Dept. of Public Instruction
510 East 12th Street
Des Moines, Iowa 50316
(515) 281-4311

Kansas

Gabriel R. Saimon
Director
Division of Vocational Rehab.
Dept. of Social & Rehabilitative Services
2700 W. 6th, Biddle Bldg., Second Floor
Topeka, Kansas 66606
(913) 296-3911

Kentucky

Paris E. Hopkins
Assistant Superintendent for Rehabilitation
Dept. of Education
Bureau of Rehab. Services
Capital Plaza Office Tower
Frankfort, Kentucky 40601
(502) 564-4440

Louisiana

Melvin J. Meyers, Jr.
Assistant Secretary
Office of Health & Human Resources
P.O. Box 44371
Baton Rouge, Louisiana 708
(504) 389-2876

Maine

C. Owen Pollard
Director
Bureau of Rehabilitation Services
Dept. of Health & Welfare
32 Winthrop Street
Augusta, Maine 04330
(207) 289-2266

Maryland

Assistant State Superintendent
Division of Vocational Rehab.
State Dept. of Education
200 West Baltimore Street
Baltimore Maryland 21201
(301) 659-2255

Massachusetts

Elmer C. Bartels
Commissioner
Mass. Rehabilitation Commission
11th Floor Statler Office Bldg.
20 Providence Street
Boston, Massachusetts 02116
(617) 727-2172

Michigan

Peter Griswold
Director
Vocational Rehab. Services
Dept. of Education
P.O. Box 30010
Lansing, Michigan 48909
(517) 373-3390

Minnesota

Edward O. Opheim
Assistant Commissioner for Vocational Rehabilitation
Division of Vocational Rehab.
Dept. of Economic Security
Space Center, 3rd Floor
444 Lafayette Road
St. Paul, Minnesota 55101
(612) 296-1822

Mississippi

John H. Webb
Director
Vocational Rehab. Division
P.O. Box 1698
Jackson, Mississippi 39205
(601) 354-6825

Missouri

William H. Keith
Assistant Commissioner
State Dept. of Education
Division of Vocational Rehab.
2401 E. McCarty
Jefferson City, Missouri 65101
(314) 751-3251

Montana

W. R. Donaldson
Administrator
Social & Rehabilitation Services
Rehabilitative Services Division
P.O. Box 4210
Helena, Montana 59601
(406) 449-2590

Nebraska

Jason D. Andrew, Ph.D.
Assistant Commissioner & Director
Division of Rehabilitative Services
State Dept. of Education
301 Centennial Mall, 6th Floor
Lincoln, Nebraska 68509
(402) 471-2961

Nevada

Del Frost
Administrator
Rehabilitation Division
Dept. of Human Resources
Kinkead Building, 5th Floor
505 E, King Street
Carson City, Nevada 89710
(702) 885-4440

New Hampshire

Bruce A. Archambault
Chief
Division of Vocational Rehab.
State Dept. of Education
105 Loudon Road, Bldg. No. 3
Concord, New Hampshire 03301
(603) 271-3121

New Jersey

George R. Chizmadia
Director
Division of Vocational Rehab. Services
Labor & Industry Bldg., Rm. 1005
John Fitch Plaza
Trenton, New Jersey 08625
(609) 292-5987

New Mexico

Robert A. Swanson, Ph.D.
Assistant Superintendent for Vocational Rehab.
Dept. of Education
P.O. Box 1830
Santa Fe, New Mexico 87503
(505) 827-2267

New York

Basil Y. Scott, Ph.D.
Deputy Commissioner for Vocational Rehab.
The University of the State of New York
The State Education Department
Office of Vocational Rehab.
99 Washington Avenue
Albany, New York 12230
(518) 473-4595

North Carolina

Claude A. Myer
Director
Division of Vocational Rehab. Services
Dept. of Human Resources
State Office
P.O. Box 26053
Raleigh, North Carolina 27611
(919) 733-3364

North Dakota

James O. Fine
Executive Director
Division of Vocational Rehab.
P.O. Box 1037
Bismarck, North Dakota 58501
(701) 224-2907

Ohio

Cooper Sontag
Administrator
Ohio Rehabilitation Services Commission
4656 Heaton Road
Columbus, Ohio 43229
(614) 438-1210

Oklahoma

L. E. Rader
Director
Social & Rehabilitative Services
Division of Rehabilitative & Visual Services
Dept. of Institutions
P.O. Box 25352
Oklahoma City, Oklahoma 73127
(405) 521-3374

Oregon

Dale Reeves
Administrator
Division of Vocational Rehab.
Dept. of Human Resources
2045 Silverton Road, N.E.
Salem, Oregon 97310
(503) 378-3728

Pennsylvania

John A. Haga, Jr.
Director
Bureau of Vocational Rehab.
Labor & Industry Bldg.
7th and Forster Streets
Harrisburg, PA 17121
(717) 787-5244

Puerto Rico

Luis A. Bonilla
Assistant Secretary for Vocational Rehabilitation
Dept. of Social Services
P.O. Box 1118
Hato Rey. Puerto Rico 00919
(809) 725-1792

Rhode Island

Edward J. Carley
Administrator
Vocational Rehabilitation Services
Division of Community Service
40 Fountain Street
Providence, Rhode Island 02901
(401) 421-7005

South Carolina

Joseph S. Dusenbury
Commissioner
South Carolina Vocational Rehabilitation Dept.
P.O. Box 4945
Columbia, South Carolina 29240
(803) 758-3237

South Dakota

John E. Madigan
Secretary
Division of Rehabilitative Services
Dept. of Vocational Rehab.
State Office Bldg., Illinois Street
Pierre, South Dakota 57501
(605) 773-3195

Tennessee

O. E. Reece
Assistant Commissioner
Division of Vocational Rehab.
1808 W. End Bldg., Suite 1400
Nashville, Tennessee 37203
(615) 741-2521

Texas

W. K. Harvey, Jr.
Commissioner
Texas Rehabilitation Commission
118 East Riverside Drive
Austin, Texas 78704
(512) 447-0108

Utah

Harvey C. Hirschi, Ph.D.
Administrator
Division of Rehab. Services
Utah State Office of Education
250 East Fifth South
Salt Lake City, Utah 84111
(801) 533-5991

Vermont

Richard W. Hill
Director
Vocational Rehab. Division
Osgood Bldg., Waterbury Complex
103 South Main Street
Waterbury, Vermont 05676
(802) 241-2186

Virginia

Altamont Dickerson, Jr.
Commissioner
Dept. of Rehab. Services
Commonwealth of Virginia
4901 Fitzhugh Avenue
P.O. Box 11045
Richmond, Virginia 23230
(804) 257-0316

Virgin Islands

Leonarda Crowley (Mrs.)
Director
Division of Vocational Rehab.
Dept. of Social Welfare
P.O. Box 539
St. Thomas, Virgin Island 00810
(809) 774-0930

Washington

Leslie James
Director
Division of Vocational Rehab.
State Office Bldg., No. II
Dept. of Social & Health Services
P.O. Box 1788 (MS 31-C)
Olympia, Washington 98504
(206) 753-2544

West Virginia

Earl W. Wolfe
Director
Division of Vocational Rehab.
State Board of Vocational Education
State Capitol Complex
Charleston, West Virginia 25305
(304) 348-2375

Wisconsin

Patricia Kallsen
Administrator
Division of Vocational Rehab.
Dept. of Health & Social Services
131 West Wilson Street, 7th Floor
Madison, Wisconsin 53702
(608) 266-2168

Wyoming

Robert D. Dingwall
Administrator
Division of Vocational Rehab.
Dept. of Health and Social Services
Hathaway Building
Cheyenne, Wyoming 82002
(307) 328-9387

Trust Territory

Risong Matsutaro (Ms.)
Chief
Vocational Rehab. Division
Office of the High Commissioner
Dept. of Education
Trust Territory of the Pacific Islands
Saipan, Mariana Island 96950
9334 (Dial 160671 First)

Mannie Villagomez
Chief
Vocational Rehab. Division
Commonwealth of Northern Mariana Island
Saipan, Mariana Island 96950
6538 (Dial 160671 First)

American Samoa

Palauni Puiasosopo
Assistant to the Governor of American Samoa
Pago Pago, American Samoa 96799
633-0116

APPENDIX 11

State Vocational Rehabilitation Agencies Specifically For Blind Persons

The following list should be used to locate the office nearest you — Call or write for further information:

Connecticut

William E. Patton, ACSW
Director
Board of Education & Services for the Blind
170 Ridge Road
Wethersfield, Conn. 06109
(203) 566-5800

Delaware

Norman Balot
Director
Division for the Visually Impaired
Dept. of Health & Social Services
305 W. Eight Street
Wilmington, Delaware 19801
(302) 571-3570

Florida

Donald H. Wedewer
Director
Division of Blind Services
Dept. of Education
2571 Executive Center Circle, East
Howard Building
Tallahassee, Florida 32301
(904) 488-1330

Idaho

Howard H. Barton, Jr.
Administrator
Idaho Commission for the Blind
Statehouse
Boise, Idaho 83704
(208) 384-3220

Iowa

John N. Taylor
Director
Commission for the Blind
Fourth and Keosauqua
Des Moines, Iowa 50309
(515) 283-2601

Kansas

Richard A. Schutz, Ph.D.
Director
Services for the Blind & Visually Handicapped
State Dept. of Social & Rehab. Services
Biddle Building, 1st Floor
2700 West 6th Street
Topeka, Kansas 66606
(913) 296-4454

Kentucky

Charles W. McDowell
Director
Bureau of Blind Services
Education and Arts Cabinet
State Office Building, Annex
Frankfort, Kentucky 40601
(502) 564-4754

Louisiana

George Marzloff
Director
Dept. of Health & Human Resources
Office of Human Development
Blind Services Program
1755 Florida Street
Baton Rouge, Louisiana 70821
(504) 342-5284

Massachusetts

Marie A. Matava
Commissioner
Massachusetts Commission for the Blind
110 Tremont Street, 6th Floor
Boston, Mass. 02108
(617) 727-5508

Michigan

Philip E. Peterson
Director
Commission for the Blind
Dept. of Labor
309 N. Washington Avenue
Lansing, Michigan 48909
(517) 373-2062

Minnesota

C. Stanley Potter
Director
State Services for the Blind & Visually Handicapped
Division of Rehab. Services
Dept. of Minnesota Public Welfare
1745 University Avenue, 1st Floor
St. Paul, Minnesota 55104
(612) 296-6034

Mississippi

James L. Carballo
Director
Vocational Rehab. for the Blind
P.O. Box 4872
Jackson, Mississippi 39215
(601) 354-6412

Missouri

Charles T. Stevens
Deputy Director
Bureau for the Blind
Division of Family Services
619 East Capitol
Jefferson City, Missouri 65101
(314) 751-4249

Montana

Joseph A. Baumgardner
Administrator
Visual Services Division
Dept. of Social & Rehab. Services
P.O. Box 4210
Helena, Montana 59601
(406) 449-3434

Nebraska

James S. Nyman, Ph.D.
Director
Services for the Visually Impaired
Dept. of Public Institutions
1047 South Street
Lincoln, Nebraska 68502
(402) 471-2891

New Jersey

Norma Farrar Krzjczar (Mrs.)
Executive Director
Commission for the Blind & Visually Impaired
1100 Raymond Boulevard
Newark, New Jersey 07102
(201) 648-2324

New York

Martin N. O'Connell
Director
State Dept. of Social Services
Commission for the Visually Handicapped
40 North Pearl Street
Albany, New York 12243
(518) 474-6739

North Carolina

L. Earl Jennings
Director
Division of Services for the Blind
N.C. Dept. of Human Resources
P.O. Box 2658
Raleigh, North Carolina
(919) 733-4231

Oregon

Charles Young
Administrator
Commission for the Blind
535 S.E. 12th Avenue
Portland, Oregon 97214
(503) 238-8380

Pennsylvania

Ralph E. Beistline
Commissioner
Office of the Visually Handicapped
Dept. of Public Welfare
Capital Association Bldg., Room 300
P.O. Box 2675
Harrisburg, Pennsylvania
(717) 786-6176

Rhode Island

E. Lyman D'Andrea
Administrator
Dept. of Social & Rehab. Services
Services for the Blind & Visually Impaired
46 Aborn Street
Providence, Rhode Island 02003
(401) 277-2300

South Carolina

Maxine R. Bowles (Ms.)
Commissioner
Commission for the Blind
1430 Confederate Avenue
Columbia, South Carolina 29201
(803) 758-2595

Tennessee

Pinkney C. Seale
Director
Division of Services for the Blind
Dept. of Human Services
303-304 State Office Bldg.
Nashville, Tennessee 37219
(615) 741-2919

Texas

Evans N. Wentz
Executive Director
State Commission for the Blind
P.O. Box 12866, Capital Station
Austin, Texas 78711
(512) 475-6810

Utah

Donald W. Perry
Administrator
Services for the Visually Handicapped
Utah State Office of Education
309 East First South
Salt Lake City, Utah 84111
(801) 533-9393

Vermont

Richard W. Hill
Acting Director
Division for the Blind & Visually Handicapped
Osgood Bldg., Waterbury Complex
103 South Main Street
Waterbury, Vermont 05676
(802) 241-2186

Virginia

William T. Coppage
Director
Virginia Commission for the Visually Handicapped
P.O. Box 7388
3003 Parkwood Avenue
Richmond, Virginia 23221
(804) 257-0591

Washington

Kenneth N. Hopkins
Director
State Commission for the Blind
3411 South Alaska Street
Seattle, Washington 98118
(206) 721-4447

APPENDIX 12

Request Form For Counseling From SBA

NOTE: This form is reproduced in its entirety for your information.

I request appropriate management or technical assistance from the Small Business Administration.

It is understood that such assistance will be provided to me free of charge and that I incur no obligation to reimburse SBA or its counselor(s) providing such assistance.

I authorize SBA to furnish information and data concerning me to the counselor(s) providing such assistance.

I understand that the counselor(s) providing assistance to me have agreed that they will not:

(1) recommend the purchase of goods or services from sources in which he has an interest. or represents, and

(2) accept fees or commissions from third parties who have supplied goods or services to me on their recommendations

This request may be withdrawn at any time upon written notice to SBA unless I am an SBA borrower.

In consideration of the furnishing of management and technical assistance to me, I waive all claims against SBA personnel or counselors arising in connection with this assistance.

Type of Service Requested (Check Appropriate Box)							
	SCORE-ACE		SBI		406		Prof. Assoc.

Complete Below and Sign		
Name of Company		Telephone
Address (Include ZIP Code)		
Referred to SBA By	Type of Business	
Signature and Title of Company Official		Date

SBA FORM 641 (6-75) PREVIOUS EDITIONS ARE OBSOLETE. PLEASE BE SURE TO COMPLETE REVERSE SIDE OF THIS FORM

Data To Be Completed By Applicant

For the assignment of a qualified counselor(s), please complete this questionnaire before returning to SBA. Any information given here or during counseling will be held in strictest confidence. (SBA personnel: insert address of your local office below)

As soon as you have completed this form and returned it to the address given above, a counselor will be assigned to you.

I request counseling regarding (check appropriate boxes):

☐ My present business   Year founded _____   ☐ Starting a new   ☐ Sole Proprietorship
☐ Purchasing a business No. of employees   business   ☐ Partnership
                         _____   ☐ Corporation

Kind of business and goods (or services) offered are as indicated below:

☐ Retail (Selling) _____   ☐ Wholesale (Selling) _____
☐ Service (Kind) _____   ☐ Other (Specify) _____
☐ Manufacturing (Product) _____   Years of experience in
                                            this kind of business _____

Can you furnish a recent balance sheet? ☐ Yes ☐ No   Have you ever applied for an SBA loan? ☐ Yes ☐ No
Can you furnish a recent profit-and-loss   Do you now have an SBA loan?   ☐ Yes ☐ No
statement?   ☐ Yes ☐ No

Check the problem areas for which you seek counseling

☐ 1. Sales promotion & advertising   ☐ 9. Office & Plant Management
☐ 2. Purchasing   ☐ 10. Government Procurement
☐ 3. Engineering and research   ☐ 11. Merchandising, inventory
☐ 4. Financial analysis   selection & control
☐ 5. Foreign trade   ☐ 12.
☐ 6. Records & Credit Collections   ☐ 13.
☐ 7. Market Research   ☐ 14.
☐ 8. Personnel   ☐ 15. Other

If the following information is available please complete, if not, leave blank.

Employer's ID # (IRS)	Social Security Number	Loan Number

Viet. Veteran ☐ Yes ☐ No	Veteran ☐ Yes ☐ No	Name of County

What in your opinion is the greatest problem in your business operation?

APPENDIX 13

How To Sell To The Government

Dated Sept. 1979

This is a reprint of a government publication — it contains valuable information for those interested in government contracts. Printed by the U.S. Department of Commerce, Industry and Trade Administration.

The Federal Government currently purchases approximately $110 billion worth of commodities, consumable goods, real estate, property and services.

Participation by the broadest range of American business in government procurement requirements is good for the economy and enhances the efficiency and effectiveness of government operations.

To assist American suppliers in selling their products and services to the government, a number of publications have been prepared, explaining how to find markets and the procurement process.

Information about government plans for the procurement of goods and services, as well as contract awards, is contained in *Commerce Business Daily*, published by the Department of Commerce five days a week. It contains information about procurements planned by the Department of Defense over $10,000, and by the civilian agencies over $5,000. Information regarding contract awards is also given to provide opportunities for subcontracting. The *Commerce Business Daily* subscription price is $105 per year by first class mail (priority) or $80 per year second class mail. A six month trial subscription can be entered at $60 (priority). To order, send remittance with full mailing address to the Superintendent of Documents, Government Printing Office, Washington, D.C. 20402, telephone (202) 783-3238. Purchase order must be accompanied by payment. Make checks payable to Superintendent of Documents. Allow approximately 6 weeks for delivery of first issue.

The *U.S. Government Purchasing And Sales Directory*, published by the Small Business Administration, contains: information on selling to the U.S. Government; listings of products and services bought by civilian and defense agencies indicating names and addresses of procurement offices which purchase them; directions on how to be placed on bidders lists and how to prepare bids and proposals; and other useful information. This 204-page book is available from the Superintendent of Documents, U.S. Government Printing Office, Washington, D.C. 20402, for $4 prepaid.

General Use Items

The General Services Administration (GSA) is the Federal Government's landlord with responsibility for contracting to build or lease, equip and maintain most Federal buildings. It is the primary purchasing agent for general use items, such as office equipment and space, transportation and janitorial services, computers and data sorting systems and numerous other items. GSA has recently issued a 45-page book entitled *Doing Business With The Federal Government.* The book includes discussions of a number of procurement subjects, including the following:

Principles and Procedures of Government Procurement

Consolidated Purchasing
Regulations Governing Procurement and Property Management
Product Classification
Procurement Methods
Responsible Bidders/Offerors
Specifications and Standards
Qualified Products List
Regular Supply Items
New or Improved Supply Items
Responsive Bids/Offers
Inspection of Government Purchases
General Contract Provisions
Termination of Contracts
Special Recommendations and Advice

Government Procurement Programs
Publicizing Business Opportunities
GSA Business Service Centers
Small Business Administration

Military Procurement Programs
Department of Defense
Department of the Army
Department of the Navy
Department of the Air Force
The Defense Logistics Agency

General Services Administration Procurement Program
Automated Data and Telecommunications Service
Public Buildings Service
Federal Supply Service

Business Services Directory

Doing Business With The Federal Government can be ordered nearest Business Service Center serving your area as identified in the following list:

Director or Manager	Mailing Address and Telephone	Area of Service
Robert J. Ireland Director of Public Services	General Services Administration 18th and F Streets, NW., Rm. 6008 Washington, DC 20405 (202) 566-1240	Nationwide
Frederick A. March Deputy Director, Business Service Centers Staff	General Services Administration 18th & F Streets, NW, Rm. 6008 Washington, DC 20405 (202) 566-1240	Nationwide
Joseph P. Lawless Regional Director of Business Affairs	Business Service Center General Services Administration John W. McCormack Post Office and Courthouse Boston, MA 02109 (617) 223-2868	Connecticut, Maine, Massachusetts, New Hampshire, Rhode Island, and Vermont
Warren E. Gardner Regional Director of Business Affairs	Business Service Center General Services Administration 26 Federal Plaza New York, NY 10007 (212) 264-1234	New Jersey, New York, Puerto Rico, and Virgin Islands
Richard F. Maloney Regional Director of Business Affairs	Business Service Center General Services Administration 7th and D Streets, SW., Rm. 1050 Washington, DC 20407 (202) 472-1804	District of Columbia, Maryland, Virginia, and West Virginia

Director or Manager	Mailing Address and Telephone	Area of Service
Walter Szpanka Manager	Mid-Atlantic Business Service Center General Services Administration 600 Arch Street Philadelphia, PA 19106 (215) 597-9613	Delaware and Pennsylvania
W. Quincy Culpepper Regional Director of Business Affairs	Business Service Center General Services Administration 1776 Peachtree Street, NW Atlanta, GA 30309 (404) 221-3032	Alabama, Florida, Georgia, Kentucky, Mississippi, North Carolina, South Carolina, and Tennessee
Benjamin M. Copenhaver Regional Director of Business Affairs	Business Service Center General Services Administration 230 South Dearborn Street Chicago, IL 60604 (312) 353-4401	Illinois, Indiana, Ohio, Michigan, Minnesota, and Wisconsin
F. Howard Whiteley Regional Director of Business Affairs	Business Service Center General Services Administration 1500 East Bannister Road Kansas City, MO 64131 (816) 926-7203	Iowa, Kansas, Missouri, and Nebraska
R. Tom Ratliff Regional Director of Business Affairs	Business Service Center General Services Administration 819 Taylor Street Fort Worth, TX 76102 (817) 334-3284	Arkansas, Louisiana, New Mexico Oklahoma, and Texas
M. Tony Williams Manager	Gulf Coast Business Service Center General Services Administration Federal Office Building and Courthouse 515 Rusk Street Houston, TX 77002 (713) 226-5787	Gulf Coast from Brownsville, Texas, to New Orleans, Louisiana
John E. Holden Regional Director of Business Affairs	Business Service Center General Services Administration Building 41, Denver Federal Center Denver, CO 80225 (303) 234-2216	Colorado, Montana, North Dakota, South Dakota, Utah, and Wyoming
Martin Perlmutter Regional Director of Business Affairs	Business Service Center General Services Administration 525 Market Street San Francisco, CA 94105 (415) 556-0877	
Stanley Anderson Manager	Business Service Center General Services Administration 525 Market Street San Francisco, CA 94105 (415) 556-2122	California (northern), Hawaii, and Nevada (except Clark County)

Cecil L. Sanders
Manager

Business Service Center
General Services Administration
300 North Los Angeles Street
Los Angeles, CA 90012
(213) 688-3210

Arizona, California (southern),
and Nevada (Clark County
only)

Dennis Bracy
Regional Director of
Business Affairs

Business Service Center
General Services Administration
440 Federal Building
915 Second Avenue
Seattle, WA 98174
(206) 442-5556

Alaska, Idaho, Oregon, and
Washington

Procurement By Veterans Administration (VA)

The Veterans Administration Marketing Center was established to help provide supplies and equipment to the 171 VA hospitals, 215 outpatient clinics and many other governmet agencies that need supply support for medical items.

VA has six marketing divisions, each handling a common grouping of products such as:

Medical, dental and scientific supplies
Medical equipment
Administrative medical supplies and equipment
Subsistence
Drugs and chemicals
Radiological and nuclear equipment and supplies

For further information on what and how VA purchases, write to:

Director
Veterans Administration
Marketing Center
P.O. Box 76
Hines, Illinois 60141

Armed Forces Buying

There are four basic methods of procurement for the armed forces:

Departmental programs
Consolidated purchasing programs (interdepartmental)
Procurement by other government agencies (principally GSA)
Local sources of supply

Specific information about these programs can be found in *Selling To The Military.* This publication, priced at $1.80, is available from the Superintendent of Documents, U.S. Government Printing Office, Washington, D.C. 20402.

It lists purchasing/procurement offices by location, gives telephone numbers, and matches buying offices, research centers and training activities with the products and services they buy. It also includes a guide for submitting proposals to the Department of Defense (DOD).

Commissaries and Post Exchanges

A wide range of consumer products, of the kind found in drug stores, supermarkets and discount houses, are purchased by the government for resale through commissary stores and military post exchanges (PX's). This important market, the military resale market, can be approached through the headquarters listed below or through individual commissary stores.

Headquarters for the PX System

Army & Air Force Exchange Service
3911 Walton Walker Blvd.
Dallas, Texas 75236
Phone: (214) 330-3721

Marine Corps Exchange Svc. Div.
Headquarters, U.S. Marine Corps
Bldg. No. 3074
MCB Quantico, Virginia 22134
Phone: (703) 640-2917

Navy Resale System Office
Third Avenue & 28th Street
P.O. Box Drawer 12
Brooklyn, New York 11232
Phone: (212) 965-5000

Navy Resale System Office
West Coast, Bldg. No. 310
Naval Supply Center
Oakland, California 94625
Phone: (415) 466-5733

Military Commissary Stores

The majority of resale products purchased by commissary stores are from brand-name contracts issued by Headquarters, Defense Personnel Support Center, Defense Supply Agency, 2800 South 20th Street, Philadelphia, Pennsylvania 19101. Purchases made against brand-name contracts are not restricted in monetary value.

In addition, officers in charge of commissary stores are authorized to make direct purchases of resale merchandise, supplies, services and minor equipment within established dollar levels. Requirements exceeding the purchase authority of the officer in charge and which are not available from brand-name contracts, are submitted to the nearest field or base purchasing activity to be filled.

For further information, vendors may contact the Defense Personnel Support Center, Philadelphia, Pennsylvania, or the commissary stores located at various military installations.

Vendors interested in selling equipment to Navy Commissary Store should contact the Navy Resale System Office, 29th Street and Third Avenue, Brooklyn, New York 11232.

Defense Supplies

The Defense Logistics Agency (DLA), which was formerly the Defense Supply Agency, manages approximately 1.8 million general supply items for the military services. Some typical items DLA buys are food, clothing, textiles, medical and dental equipment, industrial and chemical equipment, electrical equipment and electronics, food preparation equipment, construction equipment, automotive equipment and fuel, and petroleum products and services.

The six DLA supply centers that buy and manage specific commodities are listed below:

Defense Construction Supply Center
3990 East Broad Street
Columbus, Ohio 43215
(614) 236-3541

Defense Electronics Supply Center
1507 Wilmington Pike
Dayton, Ohio 45444
(513) 296-5231

Defense Fuel Supply Center
Cameron Station, Building 8
5010 Duke Street
Alexandria, Virginia 22314
(202) 274-7428

Defense General Supply Center
Bellwood, Petersburg Pike
Richmond, Virginia 23297
(804) 275-3617 or 275-3287

Defense Industrial Supply Center
700 Robbins Avenue
Philadelphia, Pennsylvania 19111
(215) 697-2747

Defense Personnel Support Center
2800 South 20th Street
Philadelphia, Pennsylvania 19101
(215) 271-2321

Interested suppliers should contact the small business and economic utilization specialist of the appropriate supply center to obtain Standard Form 129, Bidder's Mailing List Application Form, and the appropriate commodity list. These forms should be completed and returned to the supply center so the company can be placed on the appropriate bidders mailing list.

Management and administration of most Defense contracts are consolidated under DLA through the Defense Contract Administration Services (DCAS) regional offices. Firms interested in subcontracting should contact the small business and economic utilization specialist at the nearest DCAS regional office listed below:

Defense Contract Administration
Services Region
805 Walker Street
Marietta, Georgia 30069
(404) 424-6000, Ext. 231

Defense Contract Administration
Services Region
666 Summer Street
Boston, Massachusetts 02210
(617) 542-6000, Ext. 886

Defense Contract Administration
Services Region
O'Hare International Airport
P.O. Box 66475
Chicago, Illinois 60666
(312) 694-6390

Defense Contract Administration
Services Region
Federal Office Building
Room 1821
1240 E. Ninth Street
Cleveland, Ohio 44199
(216) 522-5122 or 522-5150

Defense Contract Administration
Services Region
500 South Ervay Street
Dallas, Texas 75201
(214) 744-4581, Ext. 205

Defense Contract Administration
Services Region
11099 South La Cienega Blvd.
Los Angeles, California 90045
(213) 643-0620 or 643-0621

Defense Contract Administration
Services Region
60 Hudson Street
New York, New York 10013
(212) 264-9090 or 264-9091

Defense Contract Administration
Services Region
2800 South 20th Street
P.O. Box 7478
Philadelphia, Pennsylvania 19101
(215) 271-4006

Defense Contract Administration
Services Region
1136 Washington Avenue
St. Louis, Missouri 63101
(314) 268-6223

DLA, through the Defense Property Disposal Service (DPDS), has worldwide responsibility for disposal of military surplus personal property. DPDS maintains a centralized bidders mailing list at Battle Creek, Michigan. To be placed on this list, individuals and firms should write to Defense Property Disposal Service, P.O. Box 1370, Battle Creek, Michigan 49016.

Additional information concerning DLA procurement is contained in the booklets *How To Do Business With DLA*, *An Introduction To DLA*, and *An Identification Of Commodities Purchased By The DLA*. Copies of these publications are available from the Public Affairs Office or the Office of the Small Business and Economic Utilization Advisor, DLA, Cameron Station, 5010 Duke Street, Alexandria, Virginia 22314, (202) 274-6242.

Procurement of Special Services

Special procurement rules apply to the procurement of special services such as special mailings, surveys, studies, etc., where the dollar value of the purchase is small. The following guidelines generally apply:

1. Purchases under $10,000 are handled by the Small Purchase Section of the Procurement Office of the individual agency in question.

2. Purchase decisions involving $500 or less can be made by the office in the agency seeking the service and do not require quotations and need not go through the Procurement Office.

3. Purchases over $500 require three (3) quotations and are negotiated through the Procurement Office.

4. Purchases over $5,000 are the same as #3 but must also be advertised in *Commerce Business Daily.* (A government publication).

Just because you have followed the proper procedures and submitted a bid, does not guarantee that you will receive a government contract any more than it would result in automatically obtaining a company order. Perseverance, legwork and communications play an important part in the process even though they are not as important as quality and price. These factors are especially meaningful if you are offering a service rather than a product. Products are usually repetitively purchased by the same agency, procurement office or individual. The need for services such as a survey, a study or a particular consulting requirement may develop in almost any area. Even though the agency's procurement office negotiates the transaction, the qualified vendor familiar with the agency's mission, organization and problems stands a better chance of zeroing in on the solution and needs when outside help is sought, than a group totally unfamiliar with the situation which is forced to submit a "cold" bid.

If, as you develop plans to sell to the government, questions arise and you need additional help or guidance in implementing your program it is suggested that you seek assistance from the nearest Department of Commerce field office or from:

Office of the Ombudsman
U.S. Department of Commerce
Washington, D.C. 20230
Telephone: (202) 377-3176

Additional Situation Reports on Small Business

Title	Date Issue
Bulletin 1. Getting Paid Promptly on Government Contracts	Sept. 1977
Bulletin 2. Marketing Industrial Products on a Low Budget	Sept. 1978
Bulletin 3. Developing a Successful Loan Application Package	May 1978
Bulletin 4. Small Business Investment Company Financing	May 1978
Bulletin 5. Selling to Large Corporations	Jan. 1979
Bulletin 6. Locating Business Statistics	Feb. 1979

Epilogue

To go into business for myself or not, THAT IS THE QUESTION? Thousands of people from every walk of life wrestle with this dilemma each day. There are probably as many good reasons not to start a business as there are to start one. In the 1820s, three out of four workers owned their own businesses. By the 1970s, for the first time in over 100 years only one out of twelve persons were self-employed. During the late 1970s however, the number of self-employed rose significantly with about 1,200 new businesses being formed every day. All evidence indicates that this trend is continuing in the decade of the '80s. WHY? The answers are many, but each individual must arrive at his or her own reasons for wanting to be an independent businessperson. Perhaps there are some clues to understanding this exciting trend.

Daniel Yankelovich, a foremost analyst of social trends and attitudes stated, "In these hard economic times, if people are not to jeopardize their future, they must exercise caution. But the impulse to take risks as part of the search for a new pattern of commitment is, I believe, the epochal experience of our time."

303

If you are seriously thinking of MAKING IT ON YOUR OWN we hope that you will examine yourself and your motivation for starting a business venture. Review carefully the steps needed to make the most of your entrance to the world of business before you take the plunge. Keep up to date on what you need to know in your type of business. As we have pointed out in the book, there is no substitute for good planning and the facts necessary to make a wise decision.

We wish you every success as you prepare for what may well be the most important career step that you take in your lifetime. Your choice will make the big difference in your life style. The limits as to how far you go is up to you.

Daniel Yankelovich, "Are You Taking Risks With Your Life?" Parade Publications, Inc., New York, NY, May 24, 1981.

Index

A

B

K

L

M

N

ACROPOLIS BOOKS LTD., 2400 17th St. N.W., Washington, D.C. 20009

Suggested Reading
Available at bookstores everywhere

If unavailable through your bookseller, you may order
directly for the the publisher, Acropolis Books Ltd.

The Retirement Money Book
New Ways To Have More Income When You Retire

by Ferd Nauheim

Whether you are planning for retirement, or already
there, it is practically impossible to read this clear and
practical book without discovering a variety of ways to
have more income throughout your retirement years.

THE RETIREMENT MONEY BOOK will show
you . . .

- how to calculate how much capital you'll need during
  your retirement,
- how to plan a retirement career that insures your
  financial stability — and success
- how to live out your life in your own home — with
  somebody else paying off the mortgage

. . . how to maintain your standard of living despite
inflation, taxes and high interest rates.

THE RETIREMENT MONEY BOOK avoids banking,
Wall Street and legalistic jargon, as well as long columns
of figures. It is a book full of down-to-earth, practical, but
richly rewarding ways to make your retirement years free
of financial fears and sacrifices.

Ferd Nauheim

Ferd Nauheim is a nationally known pioneer in
modern financial planning. He was the first Chairman of
the Board of Regents of the College of Financial Planning
and has been a partner of a New York Stock Exchange
firm, author, lecturer, teacher for twenty-two years.

ISBN 87491-437-X/$10.95 hardcover
250 pages, 8 x 9, index

Working Wardrobe
Affordable Clothes that Work for You!

by Janet Wallach

" . . . what to wear where . . . how-to for career women." —**New York Post**

Working Wardrobe addresses the fifty percent of all adult American women who work full time. All of them want to dress to reflect their own self-image—and the image they wish to create—but they frequently lack the time to build an exciting wardrobe.

Now in Working Wardrobe noted designer and fashion director, Janet Wallach, explains her "Capsule Concept," an easy affordable way to build a wardrobe that works for you.

The Capsule Concept is based on two-color "capsules," or groups of basic clothing pieces—all in the same two colors. A color capsule can be black/white, plum/cream, navy/wine—or any two-color combination a woman chooses. But the clothes in that capsule should be limited to two chosen colors so that everything will go together. Twelve basic clothing elements—2 jackets, 3 skirts, 4 blouses, 2 sweaters, and 1 dress—become forty different outfits.

To demonstrate how the Capsule Concept works in the real world, Janet Wallach has interviewed women who are successful, not only in their careers, but in the way they put their wardrobes together. All of these notable women, including Nancy Kissinger, Carla Hill, and Lenore Benson, relate the way they dress to the kind of work they do. Their revelations are an education for all women who want to succeed.

The possibilities of the Capsule Concept are endless. A young woman may begin with one color capsule and then add others, as her budget and position demand. But through the Capsule Concept, she can quickly develop a personal style, dress with comfort and ease, and most importantly, get a good return on her clothing investment. A woman can look today like what she aspires to!

Janet Wallach

Janet Wallach was a Seventh Avenue clothing designer when she conceived of her "Capsule Concept" collection for store buyers around the country. She has been Fashion Director for Garfinckel's, a famous Washington, D.C. department store, and has now turned her talents to writing. She has made frequent television talk show appearances and is often quoted by newspaper fashion editors.

ISBN 87491-072-2/$14.95 hardcover
212 pages, 8 x 9, illustrated, color

ACROPOLIS BOOKS LTD.,

Suggested Reading
Available at bookstores everywhere

If unavailable through your bookseller, you may order
directly for the the publisher, Acropolis Books Ltd.

Spell It Fast!
The Quick Way to Spell
Using 60 Stimulating Word Lists

by Robert C. Gilboy

Most dictionaries are no help: if you can't spell it, you can't find it. And today, more than ever, people in all walks of life—from students to top executives—need spelling help.

Now in *Spell It Fast!* Robert Gilboy makes spelling easy. He has grouped more than 20,000 hard-to-spell words into sixty sensible (and quite fascinating) subject categories from "Animals" to "Violence." The lists under each subject category are actually fun to read and can be a jog to your memory. For instance, when you can't remember the name of that river in Germany that starts with an "R", turn to "Rivers" and you'll find it faster than with your atlas.

Few people realize that Noah Webster's speller, published in 1783, outsold his dictionary! Now there is *Spell It Fast*—a unique way to cope with the difficulties of the English language.

ISBN 87491-071-4/$5.95 quality paper
300 pages, 6 x 9, 5,000 word "Spelling Demons" appendix

Dictating Effectively
A Time-Saving Manual

by Jefferson D. Bates

Dictating Effectively is more than a manual on how to dictate all your correspondence, reports, even books. It's a complete guide to efficient management of your office workload or your creative outpourings.

Not just for business people, but for anyone who does much writing and has little time to do it, chapters include . . .

• How to Beat the Time Trap: Dictate
• Overcoming Dictaphobia
• Handling Correspondence
• Organizing for Dictation
• Audience Analysis
• The Mechanics of Dictating
• How to Dictate Speeches, Reports, Books
• Dictating without a Secretary
and much, much more.

Dictating Effectively can help you double or even triple your output!

ISBN 87491-411-6/$12.50 hardcover
ISBN 87491-414-0/$6.95 quality paper
150 pages, 6 x 9, index, illustrated

Writing with Precision
How to Write So That You
Cannot Possibly Be
Misunderstood

by Jefferson D. Bates

With 30,000 copies in print,
Writing with Precision" . . . picks up
where Strunk & White leaves off,"
says Writer's Digest.

This step-by-step guide to good
writing begins with ten principles of
editing, then moves on to seven
axioms of writing. Editing and
writing instructions are accompanied
by a wealth of vivid and often
humorous examples from author Jefferson Bates' 25 years as a professional writer for both government
and industry. Each chapter ends with
reinforcing exercises.

Writing with Precision is used as a
writing text by government agencies
and companies like Coca Cola Food
Division and by universities like
Harvard and Georgetown.
• Continued author workshops and
seminars nationwide
• A selection of Writers Digest,
Preferred Choice, and McGraw-Hill
book clubs

ISBN 87491-184-2/$12.50 hardcover
ISBN 87491-185-0/$6.95 quality paper
232 pages, 6 x 9, Handbook of Grammar,
index

Practical Law
for the Layman

by Foster Furcolo, L.L.B.

*"***I**f you buy a book for its content
. . . this book will be a bargain for
you . . . the information which tells
you your rights and the law's side of
a dispute, is the handiest book you
could have around in times like
these."
—*West Coast Review of Books*

Practical Law for the Layman is the
complete, easy-to-use legal reference
for the average person who wants
general knowledge about the law and
how to handle specific problems—like divorce, auto accidents,
unmarried living arrangements, and
more—which do not require the expertise and expense of a lawyer.

In *Practical Law for the Layman,* Foster
Furcolo takes the Latin out of the law
and enables everyone to avail
themelves of their legal rights for less
than $10.00!

ISBN 87491-612-7/$6.95 quality paper
225 pages, 6 x 9, index

ACROPOLIS BOOKS LTD.,

Suggested Reading
Available at bookstores everywhere

If unavailable through your bookseller, you may order
directly for the the publisher, Acropolis Books Ltd.

Job Power
The Young People's
Job-Finding Guide

by Bernard Haldane

"The book's usefulness to millions of teenagers cannot be overstated," said Jeffrey Newman, Executive Director of the National Child Labor Committee. Revised and expanded, this comprehensive job-finding manual is especially geared to the needs of everyone entering the job market for the first time. Learn the famous Haldane "System to Identify Motivated Skills," how to manufacture contacts, how to beat the "no experience" syndrome, how to develop a "Career Journal," and how to get assurance of a pay increase. "A highly resourceful book," praised Jerome M. Rosow, President, Work in America Institute.

•Excerpted in Reader's Digests Working Worlds

The Humane Society of the United States Guide to

Careers Working With Animals

Now in its third printing, this much praised resource book contains detailed "Career Profiles" for 23 animal-related occupations with duties, salaries, and employment outlook, and descriptions of 75 others.

" . . . the most comprehensive manual on job opportunities in the animal field . . . an absolute must for anyone who wants to work with animals," praised Zoogoer.

"Absolutely everything you want or need to know about occupational opportunities in animal protection, conservation and allied professions," sang National Wildlife Magazine.

ISBN 87491-608-9/$9.95 hardcover
ISBN 87491-609-7/$4.95 quality paper
182 pages, 6 x 9, "Where the Jobs Are"
index

ISBN 87491-259-8/$7.95 quality paper
152 pages, 8 1/2 x 11, Career Profiles,
index
Third printing

How to Help Your Child Plan a Career

by Dean Hummel and Carl McDaniels

This comprehensive book has games, activities and questionnaires for working with children in the important quest for future career success.

Includes suggestions on how to develop children's interests and self-esteem, how to understand and use aptitude tests and how to use reference sources. Occupational outlooks for 300 careers!

"People can pick the right job without trial and error if they get proper advice when young".

—*U.S. News & World Report*

ISBN 87491-227-X/$12.50 hardcover
ISBN 87491-228-8/$6.95 quality paper
196 pages, 6 x 9, complete Career Sort family game, bibliography, index

200 WAYS TO SAVE ON PROBATE, INFLATION, TAXES

By Art Linkletter and Ferd Nauheim. A super successful entertainer/entrepreneur/investor and a partner in a New York Stock Exchange firm tell you—in layman's language—about annuities, variable life insurance, real estate investment, trusts, tax hedges, and much, much more.
ISBN 87491-199-0/$4.95 quality paper

200 WAYS TO SAVE ON ENERGY IN THE HOME

By George Roscoe. This invaluable guide tells you and your family how to save hundreds, even thousands, of dollars on energy bills—all year 'round. Whether you own or rent your home or apartment, you should not be without this guide to a total energy system that saves! New chapters on tax credits you can earn by installing energy-saving devices now.
ISBN 87491-216-4/$3.95 quality paper

EDUCATION FOR EMPLOYMENT

By the Task Force on Education and Employment, Clark Kerr, Chairman. This provocative study tackles the weighty question of how well our educational institutions are preparing young people for careers of the future and offers significant recommendations on what schools and universities, government agencies and unions can do to help make the working life meaningful for more of us.
ISBN 87491-243-1/$14.95 hardcover

PROFESSIONAL'S INVESTMENT GUIDE, THE

How to Multiply the Profits from your Practice. By Martin (Bud) Schulman. Any investor without much time for study should read this book. Clear advice backed up by easy-to-read charts makes this guide a must for anyone, especially the professional, who wishes to make intelligent investment decisions in real estate, the stock market, insurance.
ISBN 87491-024-2/$28.50 deluxe edition

FREE!

ABSOLUTELY FREE!

Just for asking for one, we will send you our catalog of hundreds of books you will enjoy.   You will find dozens of books on a variety of subjects... something for everyone.

Just drop us a note and ask for our most recent catalog of current and upcoming books.

Acropolis Books
2400 17th Street, N.W.,
Washington, D.C. 20009